Arabic Script

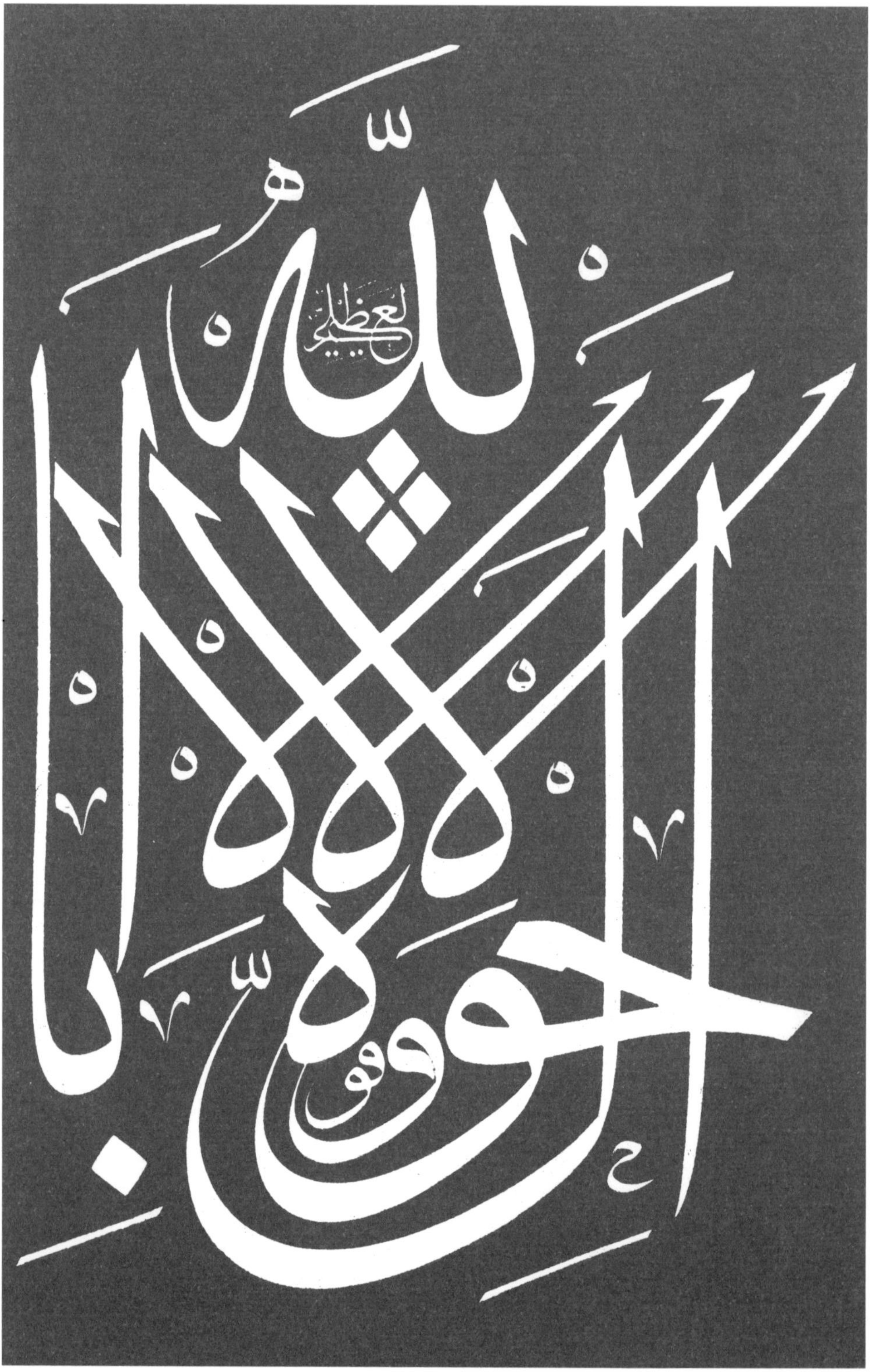

GABRIEL MANDEL KHAN

Arabic Script

STYLES, VARIANTS, AND CALLIGRAPHIC ADAPTATIONS

Translated from the Italian by
ROSANNA M. GIAMMANCO FRONGIA, Ph.D.

ABBEVILLE PRESS PUBLISHERS
New York • London

English Language Edition
Translator: Rosanna M. Giammanco Frongia, Ph.D.
Editor: Susan Costello
Cover Designer: Julietta Cheung
Copyeditor: Mary Christian
Production Editor: Ashley Benning
Production Director: Louise Kurtz

First published in the United States of America in 2001 by Abbeville Press, 137 Varick Street, New York, NY 10013.

Printed and bound in Spain by
Artes Gráficas Toledo, S.A.U.
D.L.TO:303-2001

First paperback edition
10 9 8 7 6 5 4 3 2
ISBN 978-0-7892-0879-8

Front cover: The Archangel Michael from the Ajaib al-Makhlukat of al-Kazwini. Iraq, late fourteenth century. Courtesy of the Freer Gallery of Art, Smithsonian Institution, Washington, D.C. (54.52v)
Back cover: Calligraphy in the form of a lion, by an unknown Sufi *alide*. Iran, sixteenth century

Note: The illustrations without legend are calligraphic examples excerpted from Hakkāzāde Mustafa Hilmi Efendi, *Mizānü'l Hat* (1849).

Page 2: *thuluth jalī* calligraphy by Mustafa Raqim, 1797, Topkapi Sarayë Museum, Istanbul

All the illustrations in this book were graciously made available by the author.

The drawings on pages 22–23 are the work of Alessandro Nastasio.

Library of Congress Cataloging-in-Publication Data
Mandel Kâhn, Gabriel.
[Alfaberto arabo.English]
Arabic script: styles, variants, and calligraphic Adaptions / Gabriel Mandel Kahn; translated from the Italian by Rosanna M.Giacommanco Frongia—1st English ed.
p. cm.
Includes index.
1. Calligraphy, Arabic. I. Title.
NK3633.A2M3613 2001
745.6' 19927—dc21
00-052588

For Bulk and premium sales and for text adoption procedures, write to Customer Service Manager, Abbeville Press, 137 Varick Street, New York, NY 10013 or call 1-800-ARTBOOK.

Visit Abbeville Press online at www.abbeville.com.

TRANSLATOR'S NOTE

For transliteration of Arabic words and names, I followed primarily the rules of the Middle Eastern Studies Association of America, as published in the *International Journal of Middle Eastern Studies* (Cambridge, Mass.) and the *Chicago Manual of Style*. I also consulted the *ALA-LC Romanization Tables* published by the Library of Congress (1991). For the transliteration of most proper names, I consulted the "Index of Proper Names" of *The Encyclopaedia of Islam,* new edition, E. van Donzel, B. Lewis, and C. Pellat, eds. (Leiden: E. J. Brill, 1978). When in doubt, I followed the *Chicago Manual of Style's* recommendation to simplify. For pronunciation, I consulted J. A. Haywood and H. M. Nahmad, *A New Arabic Grammar of the Written Language* (Cambridge: Harvard University Press, 1978).

For citations from the Qur'ān I used *The Noble Qur'ān: The First American Translation and Commentary,* by T. B. Irving (al-Hajj Ta'lim 'Ali) (Brattleboro, Vt.: Amana Books, 1992). For citations from Omar Khayyam, I used the translation of E. H. Whinfield in *The Sufistic Quatrains of Omar Khayyam,* intro. by Robert Arnot (New York: M. Walter Dunne, Aladdin Book Company, 1901) and *Quatrains from Omar Khayyam, done into English by F. York Powell.* (Oxford: Howard Wilford Bell, 1901).

Every effort has been made to reach rightful copyright owners. The publisher will gladly correct all omissions in future editions.

CONTENTS

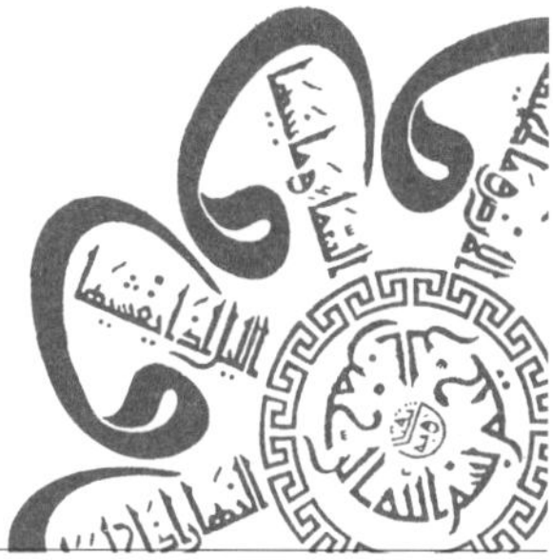

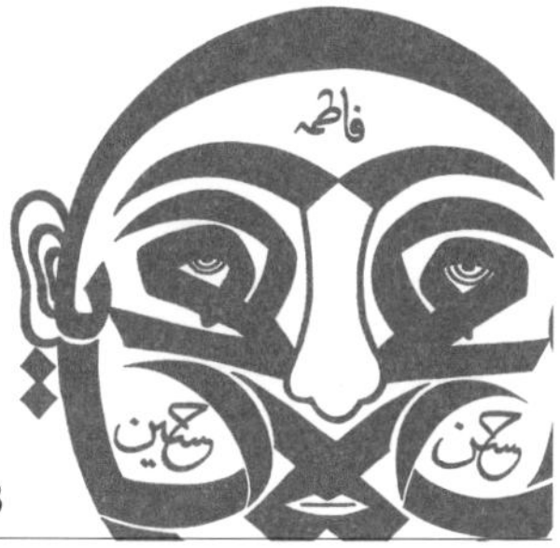

Letraset instant lettering®

1256

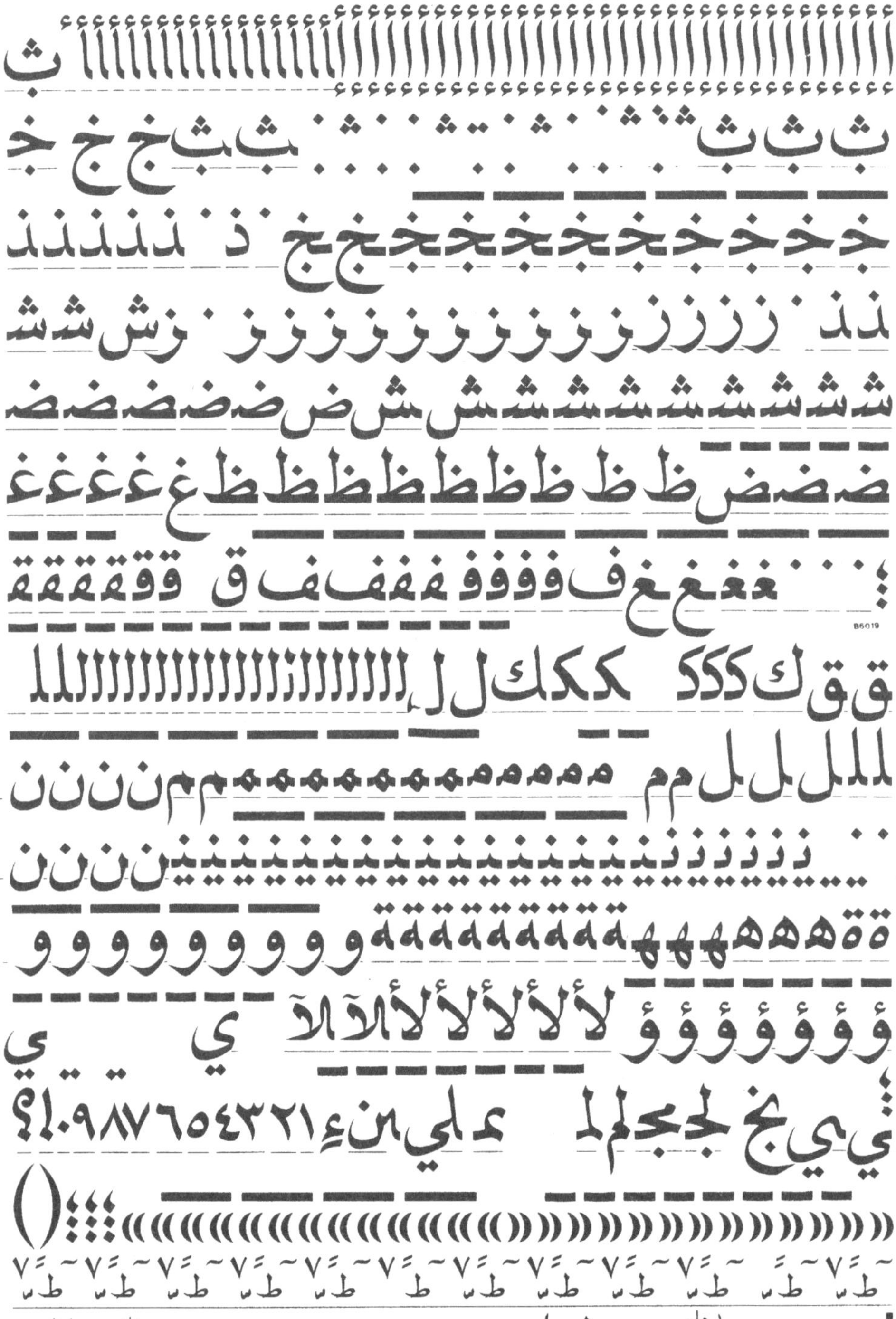

نسخي
Naskhi

برتولد
Berthold

لتراست

١ ملم
15.0mm

1256

INTRODUCTION

As the Prophet's sufferings grew, he exclaimed: "Bring me writing tools, that I may set down in writing what will save you from error after me."

Al-Bukhari, *The Sayings of the Prophet* (Title 3, 39:4)

In the night between the twenty-sixth and twenty-seventh of the month of Ramadan, in the year A.D. 612 of the Gregorian calendar, the "Night of Destiny" that all Muslims hold sacred, the first verse of the Qur'ān descended upon the prophet Muhammad (sura *al-Alaq*, 96:1–5): "Read, in the name of the Lord who creates, creates man from a clot! Read, for your Lord is most generous; [it is He] who teaches by means of the pen."

Thus was exalted the divine origin of the calamus, the reed pen that still today is the proper tool for elegant Arabic script. This veneration of writing naturally extended to reading, which is the source of all knowledge and paths of ascent, both scientific and spiritual.

From this belief sprang a powerful culture of the book and a love of the written word that turned Islamic calligraphy into an elevated, noble art. Almost higher than painting, such art can only be fully appreciated if one approaches it as one does music: like music, it has its own rules of composition, rhythm, harmony, and counterpoint—elements that bring joy to the eye of the experienced beholder and to the lover of beauty and form.

From the earliest days of Islam, Arabic writing evolved from an imperfect, primitive form to compositions rich in "hands" (also called "styles" or "characters") and a wealth of tracings such as lines, spaces, types, and other graphic arrangements.

It is not our intent to retrace the history of the alphabet in this book. Undoubtedly, the concept of alphabet originated in the Fertile Crescent, the region that extends from Egypt to Mesopotamia, an area that throughout the millennia has been so profoundly and diversely religious. In all likelihood, the alphabet evolved from the collusion between sedentary tribes and the nomadic groups that periodically attacked them. For social, economic and political reasons, sedentary tribes developed a need to create pictograms, and nomadic peoples

Opposite page: A sheet displaying *naskhī* dry transfer characters.

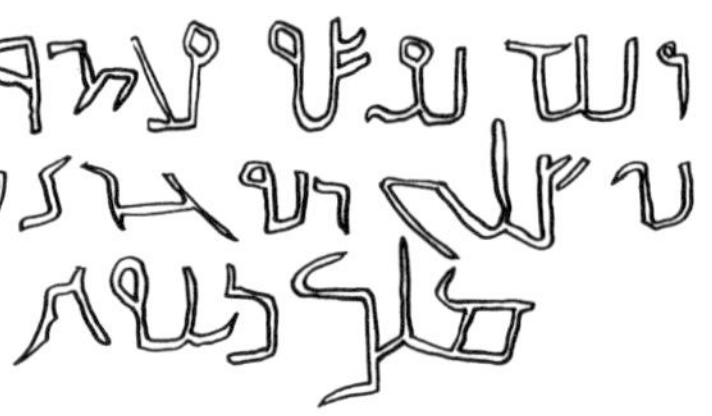

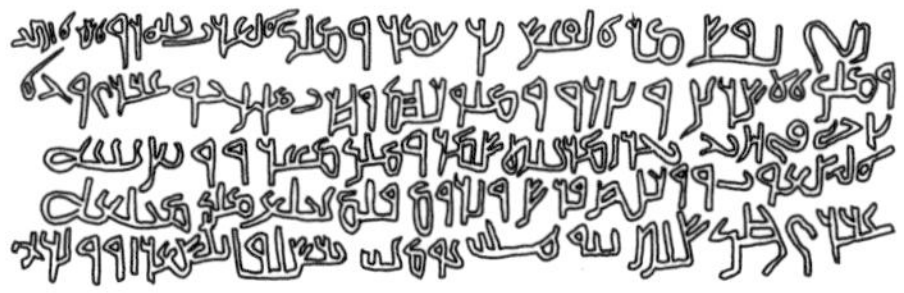

Above, left: Nabataean inscription from Umm al-Jimal, c. A.D. 250.

Above, right: Nabataean inscription from Namaran for the pre-Islamic bard Imru 'al-Qays, 328.

developed phonetic values from the pictographic meanings, thus arriving at the alphabet.

The first elaborate example of an alphabet dates from the fourteenth century B.C.: it is the alphabet from Ugarit, Syria, of Sinaitic derivation (seventeenth century B.C.). In all likelihood, the Arabic alphabet—a member of the Semitic alphabet group—is the result of that evolutionary endeavor. One precursor of the Arabic alphabet was undoubtedly Aramaic, possibly also Nabataean and Egyptian demotic script. Stylistically, however, the earliest version of Arabic script—which has squarish shapes—resembles, at least superficially, the earlier form of the Syriac alphabet known as Estrangelo.

In searching for the probable origins of the Arabic alphabet, it is useful to look at Nabataean inscriptions, such as that of Umm al-Jimal (c. A.D. 250); the epitaph found at Namaran on the tomb of the pre-Islamic bard Imru' al-Qays (328); the inscription from Zabad (512); and the bilingual epitaph from Harran in Greek and Arabic (518). Another Nabataean inscription from Umm al-Jimal, dated from the sixth century, closely resembles the formal fifth-century Arabic alphabet in use among the Hira and Anbar tribes in the north of the Arabian peninsula, and introduced to Mecca by Bishr ibn 'Abd al-Malik. This was the script used by the prophet Muhammad (c. 570–632) and his

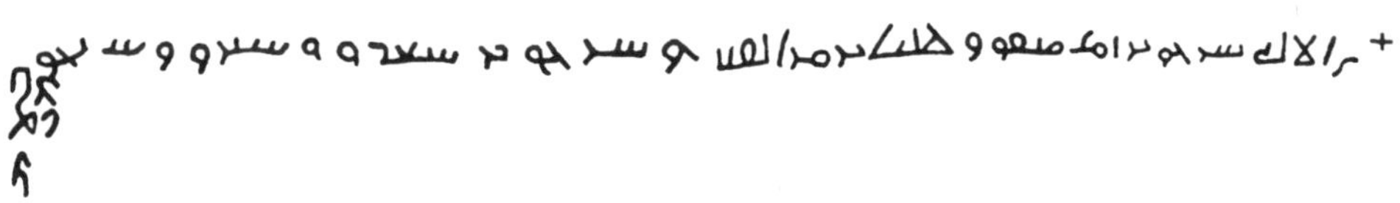

Below: Paleo-Arabic inscription from Zabad, 512. It begins with the *basmala*.

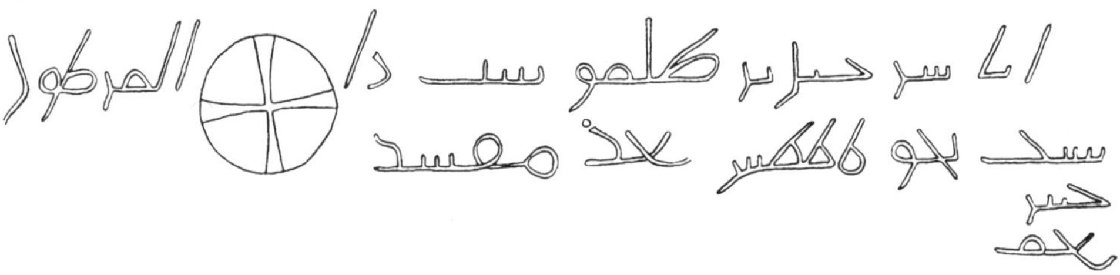

Bottom: Bilingual inscription from Harran, taken from a tomb. The paleo-Arabic text begins with the words *Ānā Sharḥīl* (I [am] Sharhil).

scribes, including Zayd ibn Thabit, who was to draw up one of the first complete Qur'āns at the time of the Uthman caliphate (644–656). This first type of alphabet, of north Arabian origin, is what was probably called at the time *jasm*.

But we shouldn't digress. The need to write the Qur'ān, to deliver the word of God intact and legibly, immediately brought many enhancements to the primitive *jasm* script that had been introduced to Mecca and Medina under the name of *ḥijāzī*. Local styles, which took their names from their place of origin and had no great distinctive characteristics, developed. Finally, a first, rough form of Kufic evolved, followed by the classic Kufic script that was adopted throughout the Arab world, from Spain to Iran.

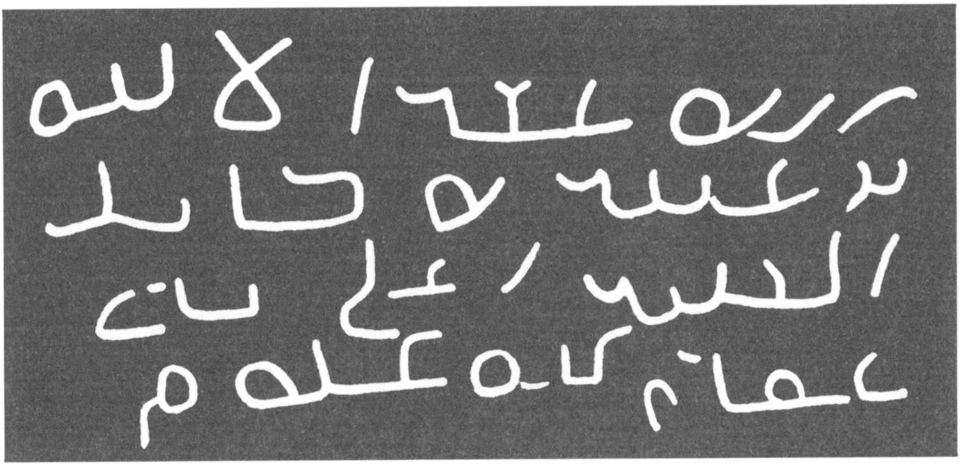

Another paleo-Arabic inscription from Umm al-Jimal, sixth century. It begins with the words *Āllāh ghafran* (God, forgive).

In Mecca and Medina, the rounded *mudawwar* and the triangular *muthallath* styles arose, as well as *etim*, a combination of those. These hands later gave way to *mā'il*, a slanted style, to *mashk*, an extended style, and to *naskh*, an inscriptional style. Thus, unlike the other Islamic arts that were still bent on imitating the classical forms of late antiquity, we can trace a history of Arabic calligraphy from the year 632. The earliest documents from this period may be found today in the library of the San'a mosque in Yemen.

From its inception, the Arabic alphabet was differentiated into two broad calligraphic currents: *muqawwar wa mudawwar*, characterized by curved and rounded styles, and *mabsūt wa mustaqīm,* having elongated and straight styles. Squarish, geometric hands such as *ma'il* and all types of Kufic lettering belong to the second current, while all cursive hands belong to the first. Early on, however, it was Kufic—

which, incidentally, originated in the city of Hira, not Kufa—that emerged as the most popular script, and the only one used to write the Qur'ān. It is remarkable to see how this script was adapted into the so-called Qarmatian or "eastern" Kufic, a beautiful, creative graphic lettering as fine as any accomplished Western abstract work of art.

As a result of the systematic revision of the Qur'ān imposed by Caliph Uthman, who died in 656, and the second systematic revision accomplished by Abd al-Malik the Umayyad (646–705), the short vowels were indicated with special marks in a process of vocalization (*tashkīl*) of the language. Accomplished primarily for religious reasons, this revision also met a real need for verbal clarity. At first, during the reign of Mu'awiya ibn Abi Sufyan (661–680), Abu al-Aswad al-Du'ali, the mythical founder of Arab grammar (d. 688), decreed that vowels should be indicated by dots of various colors. This method was

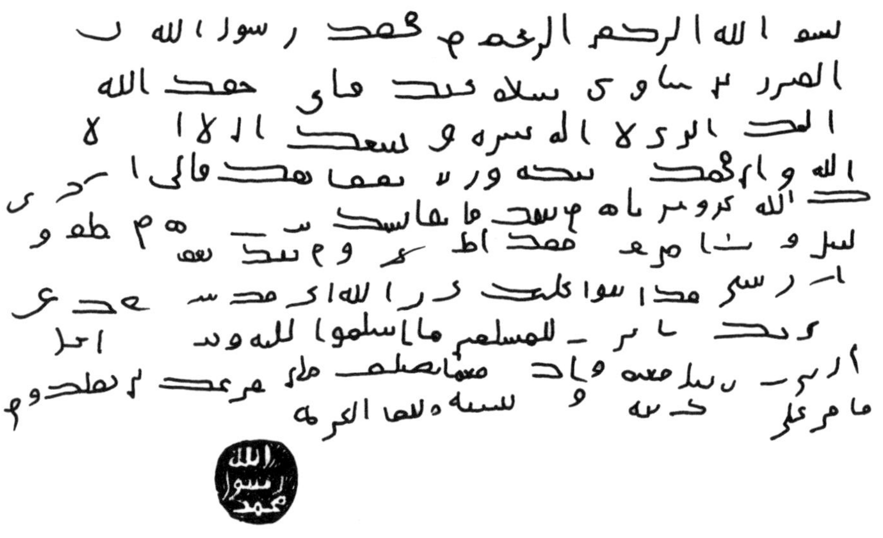

Letter sent by the prophet Muhammad to Mundhar ibn Saui, conqueror of al-Hasa. Baghdad, Museum of Iraqi Antiquities.

taught by the disciples of theologian Nasr ibn Ajini.

In a second phase, during the reign of Abd al-Malik ibn Marwan (685–705), diacritical marks to distinguish homographic letters were conceived by Nasr ibn 'Asim (d. 707) and Yahya ibn Ya'mur (d. 708), under the direction of Minister al-Hajjaj ibn Yusuf. One dot under the line was used for *b*, two dots above the line for *t*, and three dots above the line for *th*.

In a third phase, short vowels and other notations began to be expressed with specific marks or signs (see pages 90–91), as follows:

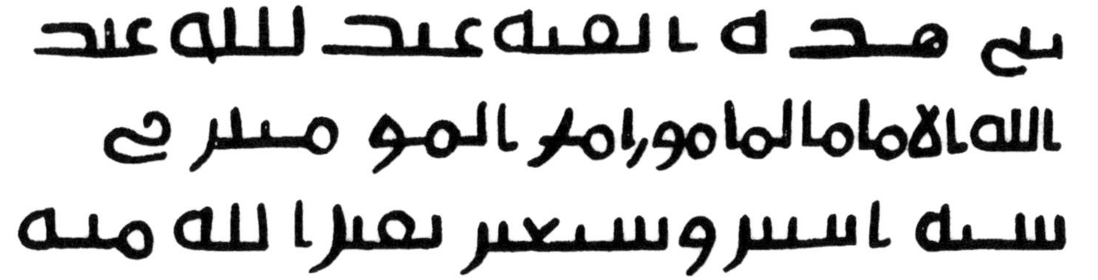

fatḥa for *a*; *kasra* for *i*, and *ḍamma* for *u*; *waṣla,* a ligature mark; *tashdīd*, a mark indicating a double consonant; *sukūn*, a mark indicating the absence of a short vowel after a marked consonant, and *tanwīn*, an ending after a final short vowel, which in Arabic is the ending that takes the place of the indeterminate article. For more details, refer to the glossary at the end of this book. All these improvements were the work of Khalil ibn-Ahmad al-Farahidi (d. 786), a lexicographer from Basra, who also perfected the first cursive form called *thuluth* (also known as *thülth* or *sülüs*), from which more than seventy secondary variations developed.

Above: An inscription placed in the Dome of the Rock mosque in Jerusalem in 692 by order of the Umayyad Abd al-Malik (646–705).

Arabic, of course, like Hebrew, is written from right to left, thus a book begins on what the Western reader would consider to be the last page. Two more characteristics unique to Arabic writing are the lack of capital letters and of word division at the end of a line. In Arabic, one carries the complete word to the following line using, if needed, aesthetic extensions of the last word to fill in the preceding line.

As a rule, in the past the language also lacked punctuation marks such as exclamation points, question marks, periods, and commas. In their place, literary formulas were used, such as beginning a phrase with *wa* (the conjunction "and"), signifying that the previous phrase ended in a period. Another formula was to use the verb *qāla*

Below: Inscription of the Caliph Mu'awiya (661–680), dated 677.

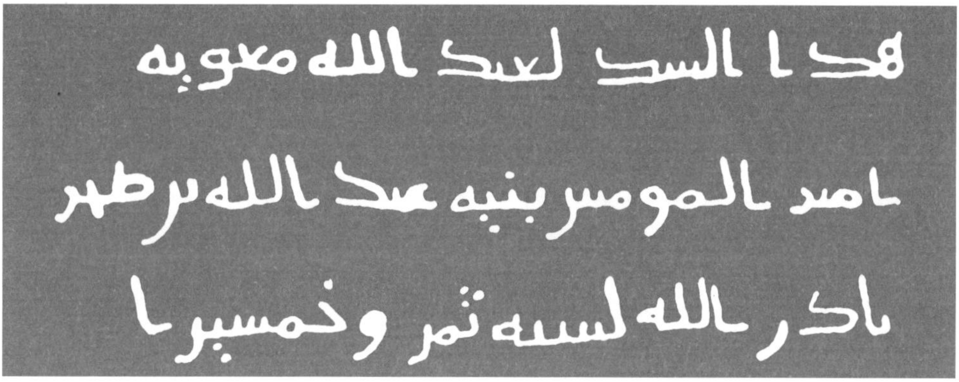

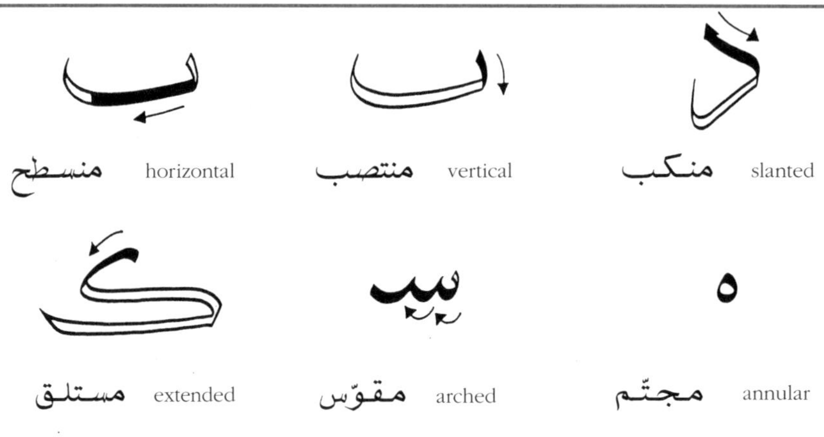

Above: The defining outlines of the letters in the Arabic alphabet.

(to say, to tell) in situations where we might use a colon or quotation marks.

Ali (656–661), the fourth "Righteous Caliph" and the Prophet's son-in-law, was a well-known calligrapher. During his lifetime, Arabic calligraphy developed two primary centers: the Mecca and Medina School, and the Kufa and Basra School. A third school was formed somewhat later, at Isfahan.

Thus, the history of the written language, like Islamic culture in general, retraced the parallel development of the other arts. The highly civilized populations conquered by the Arabs of the Arabian Peninsula—the Turks, the Iranians, the Afghans, the Indians, the North Africans, and the Spanish Andalusians—created all that we recognize today as being typical of Islamic civilization. For this reason, the history of Islamic calligraphy is far from linear, as it flourished in multiple and simultaneous cultural centers and experienced sudden parallel developments that coexisted for long stretches of time in the many countries that comprise the vast Islamic world.

In addition to the square, austere Kufic style, another type of writing had been in use since at least 643, especially for writing on papyrus and parchment. It was a neat, clear, easily legible, well-proportioned

Below: Three examples of stylistic variation in the diacritical points: archaic, *thuluth,* and *ta'līq.*

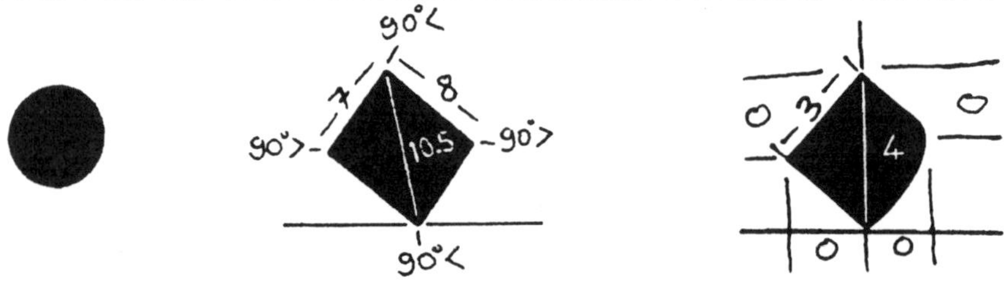

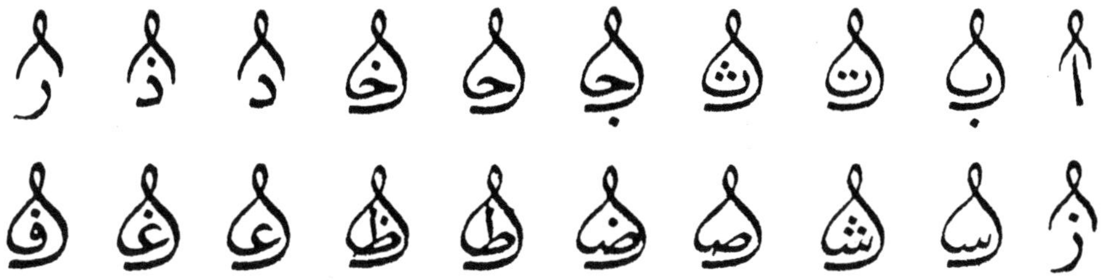

script that immediately became the favorite of koranic scribes and copyists of all kinds of theological, philosophical, and scientific treatises. Variants of this script evolved that also became popular. It became the Arabic script par excellence, and was the vehicle for disseminating knowledge to all corners of the Islamic world.

Thus, just as in the first two hundred years Islamic religion made vast inroads among the populations of Asia, Africa, and even Europe, over the centuries the use of the Arabic alphabet spread well beyond the confines of Arabic language. It replaced previous forms of writing and became the script of numerous other languages, including Turkish and all its dialects from Turkey to Chinese Turkestan, Farsi in Iran, Slavic in Bosnia, Andalusian Spanish (using the *jamia* style), Hindustani, a form of Hebrew, Berber, Swahili, Sudanese, and other lesser languages, especially in Indochina and Indonesia.

Thus, a multitude of new Islamic converts coming from diverse cultural, ethnic, and religious backgrounds brought to the Islamic language, culture, and religion a whole wealth of concepts and values that, beginning in the middle of the eighth century, were to contribute

Above: An example of the capital letters proposed in Egypt by Muhammad Mahfuz in 1930.

Below: Arabic letters with indications of the capital letters.

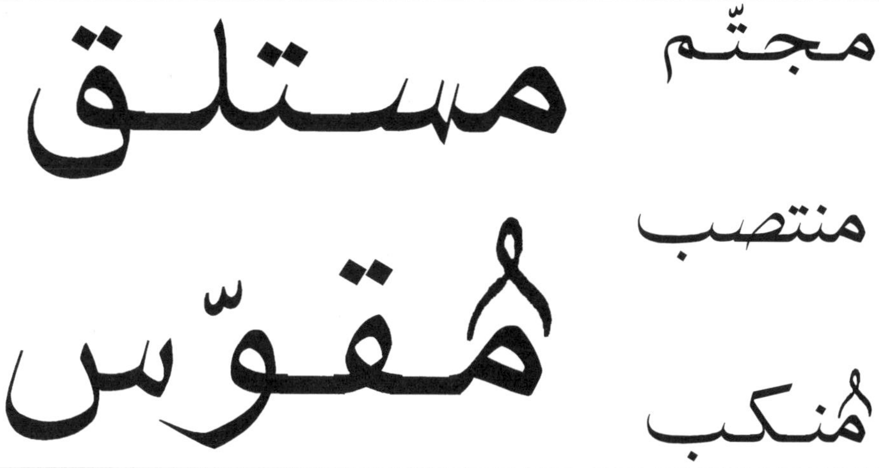

to make Islamic civilization among the richest ever, a fascinating world dense with themes, literatures, and page after page of artistic calligraphy.

Under the reign of the Umayyads (661–749) many skilled calligraphers copied large editions of the Qur'ān in Kufic script, although for bureaucratic texts, four cursive scripts became fashionable: *ṭūmār, jalīl, niṣf,* and *thuluth* (and its variant, *thuluthayn*). Khalid ibn Hajjaj, the official calligrapher of Caliph al-Walid (705–715), wrote both in *ṭūmār* and *jalīl*; furthermore, for everyday needs, the *niṣf* (one-half) script was created. Later, the calligrapher Qutba al-Mihrr (d. 771) created new stylistic variations on the four basic scripts: *āl-Jalīl āl-Kabīr* (the majestic), *āl-Tūmār āl-Kabīr* (the great sheet), *āl-Niṣf āl-Thaqīl* (the heavy one-half) and *āl-Thuluth āl-Kabīr* (the great one-third).

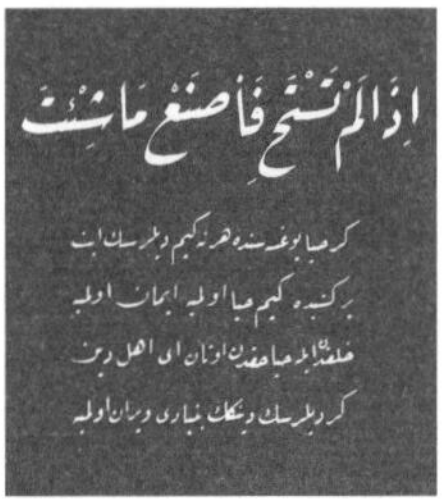

Examples of *riqā'* characters.

Above: A hadith (saying) of the prophet Muhammad drawn by Fethi Karamani. Istanbul, Suleymaniye Pestev Pasha, 608.

Below: A hadith of the prophet Muhammad drawn by Usuli. Istanbul, Suleymaniye Fatih Kutuphanesi, 5429.

During the first reign of the Abbasids (750–1055), the calligraphers Ibn Jilani and Ishaq ibn Hamad developed twelve different hands from the earliest classical scripts, later perfected by Vizier Abu Ali Muhammad ibn Muqla (886–940). This vizier created a vibrant, lively script, the earliest form of *naskh*, while in the Maghreb the scribe Ibn Ibrahim Timimi composed one of the first treatises on calligraphy, the *Toḥfat āl-Wāmiq*.

Vizier Ibn Muqla also created a proportional system of letters (*khaṭ mansūb*) by inscribing each letter within a circle and giving letters codified proportional dimensions using dot notations (*noqta*). He also set down and classified the traits of the most popular "six classical styles of writing" (*āqlām-i sitta*). These scripts are: *muḥaqqaq* (which means strongly expressed, tightly woven); *rīḥān* (the name of the basil plant); *thuluth* (one-third); *naskhī* (suppression, cancellation); *tawqī'*, a variant of *thuluth*; and *riqā'*, a smaller version of *tawqī'*. A good calligrapher was required to study, know, and write all of these styles. Thana al-Abdulat and Zaineb Shehede (known as Sitt al-Dar) are two women of this period who excelled in the art of beautiful writing.

We should mention, however, that this writing fervor that touched all of the Muslim world since the earliest days was also due to the wide diffusion of paper, which the Chinese had invented, along with printing, in the first century A.D. Introduced to Islamic countries, paper became widely used after the conquest of Samarkand by Ziyad ibn Salih in 751. Printing, however, though known and in use since the ninth century, was not as popular, as personalized handwritten books were much preferred.

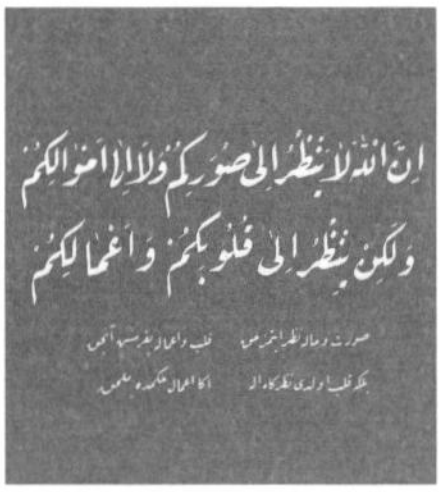

Besides, printing with movable types was (and still is) a laborious process (see pages 16–17, a typographer's case), and tabular engraving of a text in a cursive style was a lengthy and complex endeavor. Because the copyists (*warrāqīn*) were organized into an efficient capillary network of corporations, the difference in cost and time between copying a manuscript and printing a book was minor, so that there was little incentive to promote the craft of typography. In the tenth century, the copy shop of Abd Allah Abu Sa'id al-Mullah in Baghdad had so many copyists that it could produce in one day twelve copies of a 164-page handwritten and bound volume.

A monumental and lapidary style, Kufic continued to be the favorite script for copying the Qur'ān, while *thuluthayn* (two-thirds) was the script for notations and *niṣf* that of government chancelleries. Four principal forms of Kufic developed: *muraqqa'*, flowery and foliated; *mukhamal*, written on a floral background; *muẓfar*, with plaited upward strokes; and *handasī*, with geometric lettering inspired by Chinese calligraphy and Iraqi-Iranian forms. The Qarmatian Kufic style is particularly beautiful, evocative of the values and interpretive freedoms of the best modern art. We note that the Qarmatians were open-minded Iranian dissidents who were hostile to the Arabs; in 899 they built a strong kingdom on the western bank of the Persian Gulf.

After Vizier Ibn Muqla, during the Abbasid era, two calligraphers, Ibn al-Bawwab and Yaqut al-Musta'simi, opened a celebrated art school. Abu al-Hasan ibn Hilal, known as Ibn al-Bawwab, from Baghdad (d. 1022 or 1031) created the *mansūb fā'ikh* style (elegant *mansūb*) from which the Iranian calligraphic school was derived. Among his pupils was Muhammad ibn Khazin from Dinawar, who created the *riqā'* and the *tawqīt* styles, and Khoja Abu Ali, who invented *ta'līq*, a cursive, nervous, concise style. Jamal al-Din Yaqut al-Musta'simi (1242–1298), who created the *yāqūt* style, a variant of *thuluth*, is also known for modifying the nib of the calamus by clipping it at an angle. The Turkish calligraphic school grew from the use of this nib.

In the twelfth century, besides the Ayyubid *naskhī*, other styles became popular or were perfected further. They were: *muḥaqqaq*, characterized by broad, curving, downward strokes; a wider, rhythmic, steady *thuluth*; and a classic *rīḥān*. From these, more typical, regional scripts developed, such as the Iranian *nasta'līq*, ideal for the calligraphy of poetry and covered in detail later in this book; North Africa's *maghribī*, consisting of the *qayrawānī*, *fāsī*, and *sudani* styles; Spain's Andalusian; and India's *biḥārī* style.

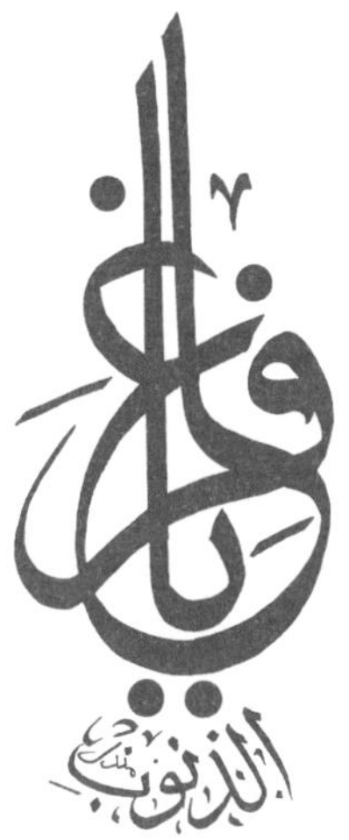

Thuluth jalī calligraphy by Abd Allah Sayrafi.

The *basmala* in five Kufic styles, from reliefs of the ninth, tenth, and twelfth centuries.

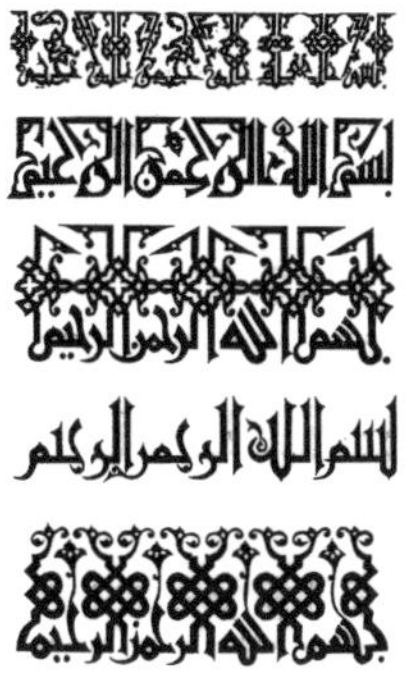

From their very inception, these styles became part of the classic tradition. Calligraphers studied them on *mufradāt*, which are catalogs or models that illustrated the proportions and size of each style. As mentioned, the most popular classic proportional system was that of Ibn al-Bawwad, which reported the dimensions and thickness of the letters by using squared dots (*noqta*).

1	3	4	5	6	7	8	9	10	11	12	13	14	15	
16	19	20	21	22	23	24	25	26	27	28	29	30	31	
32	33	36	37	38	39	40	41	42	43	44	52	54	55	
56	60	62	63	64	65	66	68	69	70	71	72	73	74	
76	77	78	79	80	81	82	84	85	86	88	89	90	91	
92	94	95	97	98	99	100	101	105	108	109	111	112	114	
115	116	117	119	120	121	122	123	124	125	126	127	128	129	
130	131	132	133	134	135	136	137	138	140	142	145	149	150	
151	152	153	154	155	156	157	158	160	161	162	163	167	168	
169	172	173	174	175	176	178	179	180	181	183	184	185	187	
188	189	191	192	193	195	196	200	201	202	204	205	207	208	
211	214	215	216	219	221	222	223	225	226	228	229	230	231	
233	234	235	236	237	241	242	243	244	245	246	247	252	257	
258	265	266	268	270	271	275	277	280	282	283	284	287	289	
290	291	292	293	294	295	296	297	298	299	300	301	302	303	

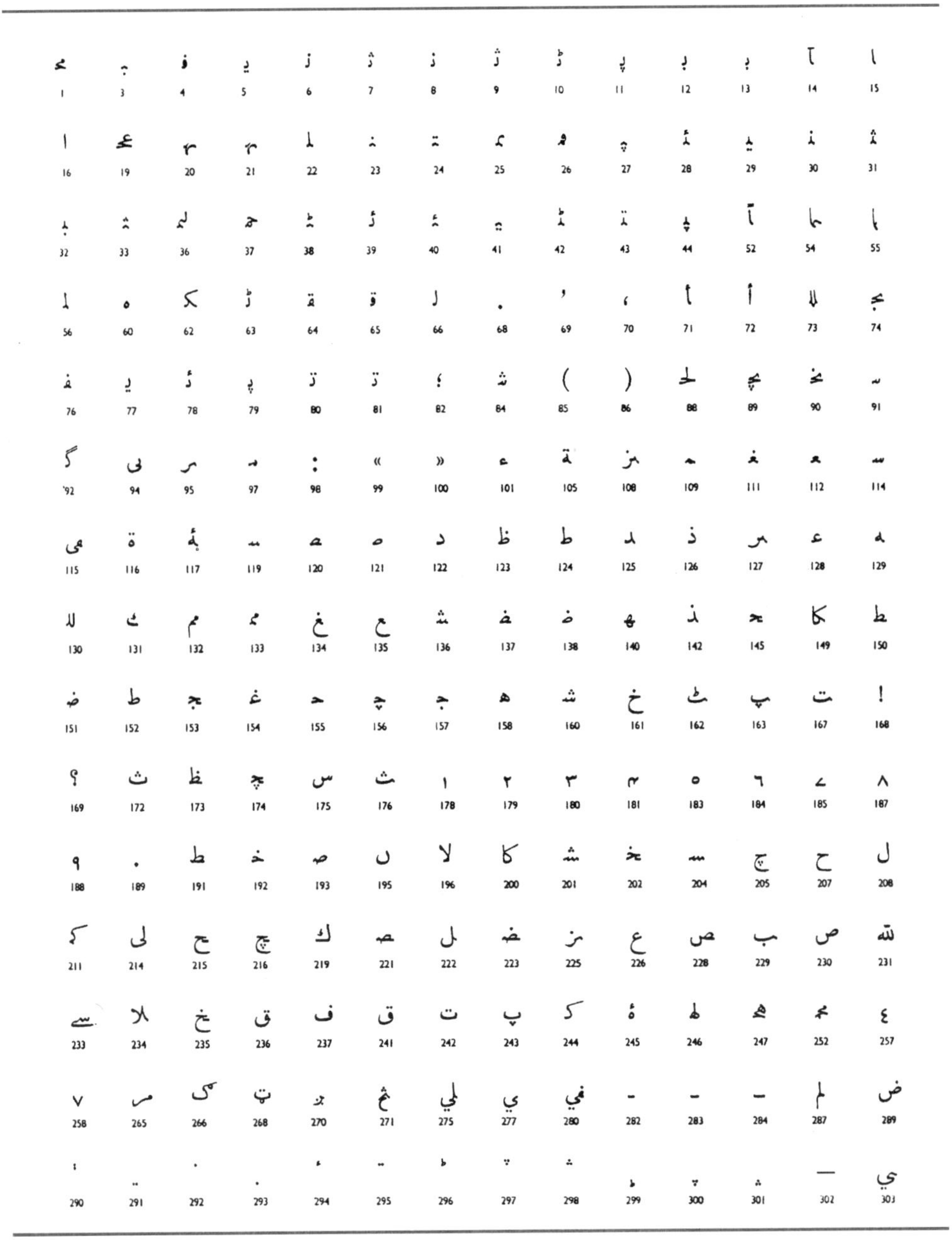

The long travail that brought Arabic writing from its origins to its full maturity and its highest calligraphic achievements in the thirteenth century had a period of arrested development when Genghis Khan's Mongols conquered a large part of the Islamic world, founding the vastest empire known to man. This interruption lasted until the Ilkhanids—the Mongol viceroys who ruled central Asia—converted to

The case of an Arab typographer with its movable type characters.

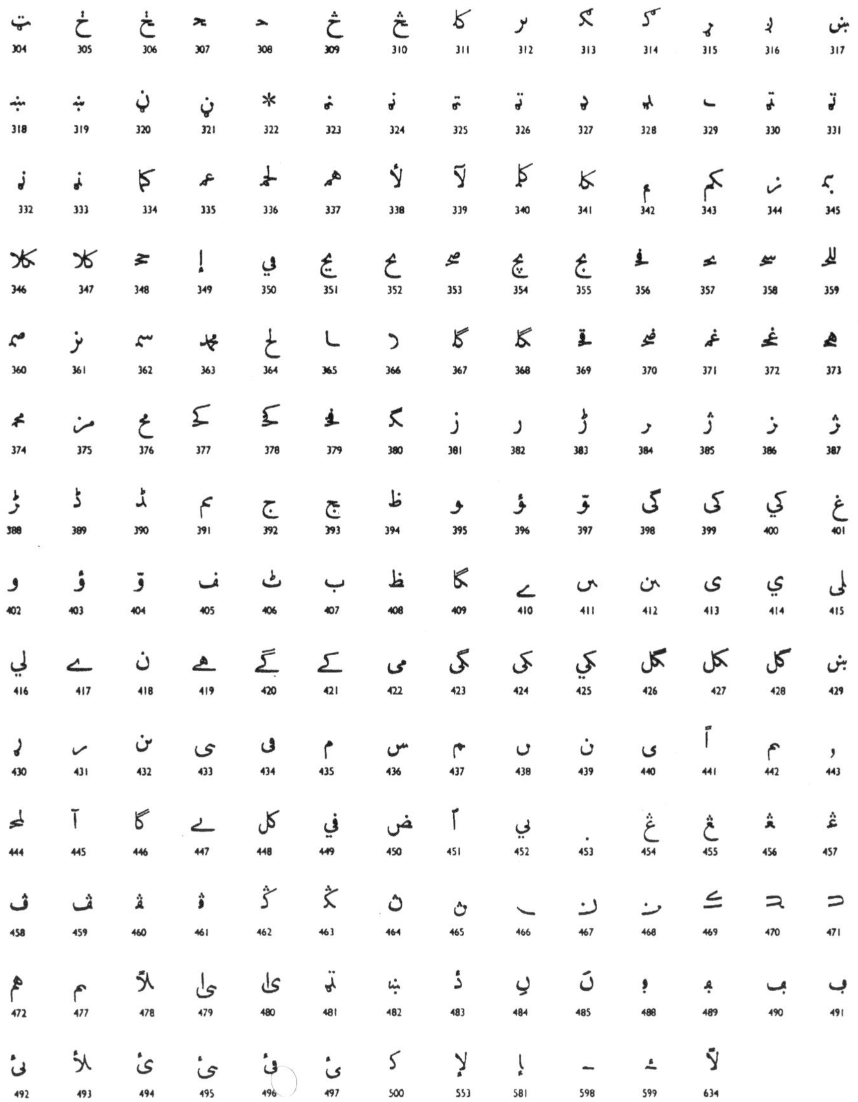

Islam and became enlightened patrons of the arts. At the beginning of the fourteenth century one of the foremost Ilkhanid calligraphers was Abd Allah Hamadani. Together with Ahmad Surahwardi, he founded two central Asian schools, whose preeminent teachers were Mubaraqq Shah al-Qubt (d. 1311), Sayyid Haydar (d. 1325), and Mubarak Shah Suyufi (d. 1334). They were all Sufi masters (the Sufis are Islamic mystics, organized in well-ordered brotherhoods) who succeeded in combining the mystical sentiment that inspired them with feelings of art and aesthetic perfection.

In the Mediterranean basin, the Mamluks, a Turkish dynasty that ruled Egypt from 1250 to 1517, were also enlightened patrons of the calligraphic art. The founders of this dynasty had repelled the Mongol invasion to the West, effectively saving Europe. One preeminent Mamluk was Abd al-Rahman ibn al-Sayigh, who founded an important school and in 1397 composed a large, six-foot-high Qur'ān in *muḥaqqaq* script, in competition with similar Ottoman and Uzbek works.

Thus, the art of calligraphy (*khaṭṭ*) knew a long series of traditionalist masters, including the great Ahmad Qarahisari (d. 1556), Sheikh Hamdullah (1436–1520), and Hafiz Osman (1642–1698), as well as innovative masters who fall into two leading schools, the Iranian and the Turkish. With the rise of these two schools, unusual stylistic forms, rather than becoming established as new hands, were seen as being stylistic variations on the look of the classic types. Among these new hands were large, monumental formats such as *jalīl* and, especially, *thulūth jalī,* in which the Iranians Abd Allah Sayrafi, Baysonghor, Ali Rida Abbasi-i Tabrizi, and Muhammad Rida Imami-i Isfahani were especially active. Other hands were *musalsal* (strung together), which required great skill; *siyāqat* and *tarassul,* used in government documents; and *syakat,* a style adopted in Turkey by Janissaries.

Early on in Iran, a local hand was used, the *pīrāmūz* (spelled *kīrāmīz* in Arabic*)*, which still survives in a few rare works. It evolved into two major schools: that of Khurasan, founded in Herat by Ja'far ibn Ali (d. c. 1456), and the southeastern school typified by Abd al-Rahim al-Khwarezmi. The most popular styles at the time were the *ta'līq,* founded by Abd al-Hajj from Astarabad, and a more elegant style, the *nasta'līq* (a variant on *naskh* and *ta'līq*), which means "like birds in flight." It was created by Mir Ali ibn Hasan from Tabriz, who adapted the cut of the calamus nib to create it. Also used, though not as extensively, was the *riyāsī,* perfected by Imad al-Din al-Husayni.

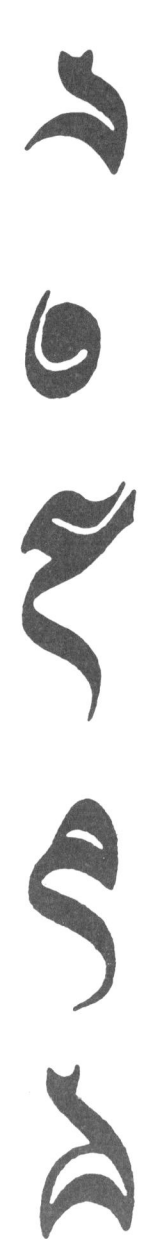

Later, among the better-known followers of Qhoja Abu Ali were Sayyid Mir Imad (d. 1615), who excelled in the *ta‘līq* script, and Abd al-Mejid Taliqani, who was unsurpassed in a new form of writing, the *shikasteh*. In Iran, the *nasta‘līq* became especially popular, and even a Safavid ruler, Hassan Khan Shamlu (d. 1688), excelled at calligraphy in this style.

In particular, the Iranian school generated the Indian school, which developed a typically strong, robust local *naskh* style and a *behari* style evocative of baroque rhythms. The Indian school had many excellent teachers, especially under the Moguls, the dynasty of Afghan Turks who claimed to be descended from the Mongol emperors and who ruled India from 1526 to 1857. Among this line of calligraphers we recall especially Shihab al-Din in the twelfth century, Ashraf Khan (d. 1572), and Ja‘far Khan. On the other hand, the Chinese Muslims who were in direct contact with Afghanistan, Uzbekistan, and India adapted Arabic writing into a fluttering, discontinuous style called *sini*, used especially on artifacts destined for the Ottoman market.

The Turkish school had two great initial masters: Uthman ibn Ali, known as Hafiz Osman, whose teachings are still followed today, and Hamd Allah Amasi (1436–1520), a Sufi shaykh who penned important treatises and even counted the Ottoman emperor Bayazid II among his students. Calligraphy among the Turks reached such a splendid artistic level that a saying was born: "The holy Qur'ān was revealed in Mecca, recited in Egypt, and written in Istanbul."

Many schools branched out from these two teachers, each with its own great artists, so numerous that we can recall here only the most prominent. One typical Turkish hand was the *dīwānī*, developed by Ibrahim Munif, which was an official, chancery style suited for many decorative variations (see pages 118–119). Other, traditional calligraphies—for example, the *shikasteh, shikasteh āmīz*, and *jalī* styles—were rejuvenated. The *dīwānī jālī* variant is also known as *humāyīnī*. Over time, the *sumbulī* hand evolved from the *dīwānī* as well.

In addition to these variants, the Ottomans also devised special styles, such as the *zulf-i ‘arūs* (curly); the *siyāqat*, a very functional style; the *gulzār* mode, which consists of filling the empty spaces between the letters with floral or figured motifs; the *muthannā* (or *mutannāzar*) style—also known as *aynali* or *ma‘kūs* (reflected) or *khatt-i muthannā* (self-facing calligraphy)—which repeats a phrase in mirror fashion (pages 132–133); the *tuğra*, a complex, fluttering type of signature (pages 128–129); and in particular, words or phrases

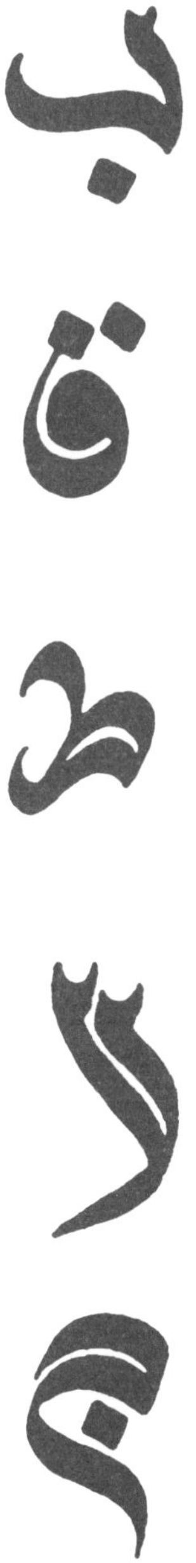

Monogram letters in *sunbulī*, a non-traditional style.

arranged so as to form figured compositions, especially of animals—faces, horses, birds, or lions (pages 152–157).

Besides these scripts, we should also mention a folkloric, rather than artistic, style called *ghubār* or *ghubārī* (dust, dusty), an almost microscopic hand invented in Turkey. Using this script, all the text of the Qur'ān, consisting of 77,934 words, was written on one single ostrich eggshell by Isma'il Abd Allah, also known as Ibn al-Zamakjala (d. 1386). Qasim Ghubari (d. 1624) did the same on a sheet measuring only eighteen by twenty-two inches (45 × 55 cm), while Mehmet Shefik Bey (1819–1879) wrote the Qur'ān on ninety-nine rosary beads. Known as *ghulān*, this script is still alive today, thanks to such contemporary artists as Nasib Makarim from Lebanon and Dawud al-Husayni from Afghanistan.

Arabic script is written on an ideal horizontal line, from which various curls and peaks rise above or fall below it. These calligraphic directions are said to symbolize the union of the values of the exterior, material, visual world (*ẓāhir*) with those of the interior, intimate, spiritual realm (*bāṭin*). For this reason, the art of calligraphy flourished in particular among the Sufi brotherhoods, becoming their preferred representational form. Furthermore, it was readily adapted to the three leading tongues of the Islamic world: Arabic, the language that universalized religious and scientific thought; Iranian, the language that expressed in the highest possible form the values of art and poetry; and Turkish, the language that institutionalized earthly laws and social organizations.

Thus, there was a time in Iran for the sinuous *ta'līq*, sensitive to poetry, and in Turkey for the imperial *dīwānī* and the clerical *riqā'*. The *ta'līq* style (suspension) was a result of combining *tawqī'*, *riqā'*, and *naskh*, and in it still survives an echo of the Pehlevi and Avestan scripts. The *riqā'*, a hand that includes a simple form and a larger one (*jalī*), was given precise rules by the Turkish Mumtaz Bag, councillor to Sultan Abdulmecid I (1823–1861). Several Ottoman sultans tried their hand at the *dīwānī* style, undoubtedly the richest in movement and in unique traits. Another Turkish form is the broad *shikasteh* (also known as *shikasta ta'līq*, or broken *ta'līq*), which has a rich sense of rhythm.

Of course, both tradition and renewal, the evolving of taste and refinement through the centuries, and the changing environments all contributed to inspire ever new variants and individual expressions in the art of calligraphy. The Great Tradition is still alive and fertile today,

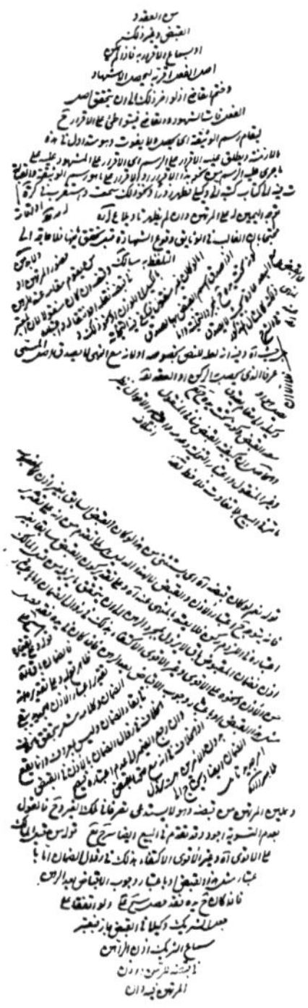

Above: Notes written in *ta'līq*, found in the margins of a treatise on the value of terms copied by Diya' al-Din Gumushkhanevi in 1843.

Below: Notes found in the margins of a treatise on cosmogony copied in 1812.

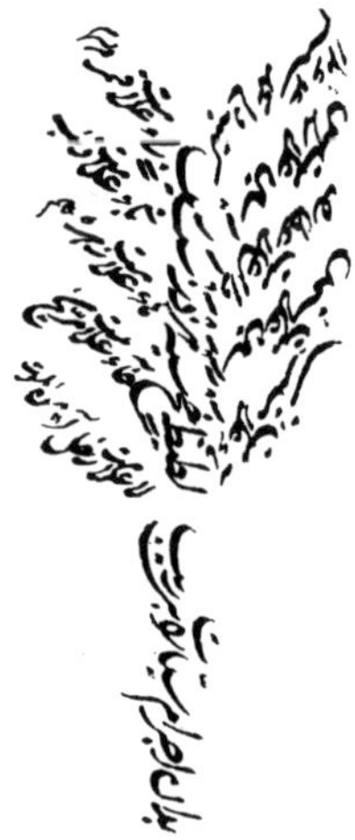

just as the Arabic script is still being renewed under the calami of new artists, including those in the West. Both classic and individual hands have multiplied throughout the centuries.

All these forms can be variously admired on the great expanses of mosque walls and in the almost microscopic minuteness of miniature art. Stone, metal, wood, faience, fabric, paper—every possible medium—has given a variety of themes and solutions to Arabic calligraphy from the very beginning, and the adventure continues to this day as Muslim calligraphers create new works, look for original solutions, and study modern styles. In 1930 Muhammad Mahfuz endowed Arabic with capital letters, called *ḥurūf āl-Taj.* In Istanbul every year, the cultural organization IRCICA organizes an international competition of traditional calligraphy and miniature painting; many modern artists include calligraphy in their works in highly sensitive and innovative iconographic adaptations. The work of artists such as Hassan Massoudi and his followers is proof that Arabic calligraphy is a living art capable of continuously renewing itself.

Painters also are experimenting with the versatility and potential for adaptation of Arabic writing. Among these—and this list is admittedly incomplete—we should mention Mohamed Melehi and Cherkaoui and Mustafa Rajaoui from Morocco, Yussef Saidah and Saad Kamel from Egypt, Nasser Assar from Lebanon, Ahmed Chibrine from Sudan, Hossein Zenderoudi from Iran, Majib Belkodja from Tunisia, Rachid Koraichi, Shakir Hassan, and Kamal-Boullata. Especially distinguished are the many Turkish masters, including my own teacher, Fevzi Gunuc, professor of calligraphy at the Seljuk University of Konya, and Mehmet Buyukcanga, Faruk Atabek, Filiz Kaya, Asuman Comezoglu, Bekir Pekten, and Sami Oksuz.

All this iconographic richness—heritage of all of humanity, beyond ethnic or religious boundaries—gives manifold meanings to the saying that "writing is an expression of the invisible."

The revelation of the Qur'ān began by mentioning the calamus, and the sixty-eighth sura (chapter) opens with these words: "By the pen, and whatever they record." Again, the Qur'ān tells us: "If only the trees on earth were pens and the [inky] sea were later on replenished with seven other seas, God's words would never be exhausted." (31:27) Indeed, for the Muslim, writing is intimately linked to the identity of God and the gifts he has bestowed upon his earthly creatures. The vitality of Arabic writing throughout the centuries is an accomplished testimonial of this.

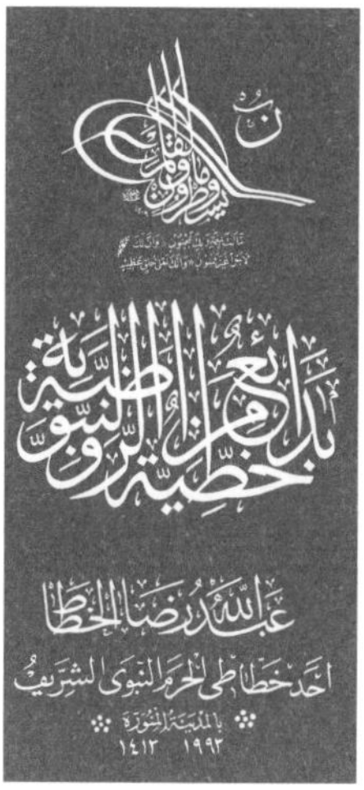

Above: The frontispiece of the work *Bedāiü'l-Hattiyye mina'r—Ravdati'n-Nebeviyye,* published in Istanbul in 1993 by Islam Tarih, Sanat ve Kultur Arashtirma Merkezi (IRCICA).

Below: The logo for the exhibition *The Art of the Mamluks* organized in 1981. Washington, D.C., Smithsonian Institution.

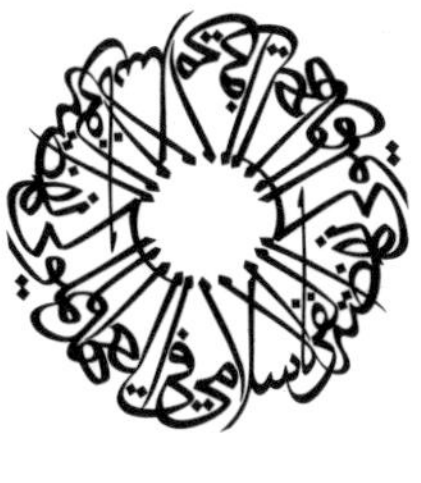

USING THE CALAMUS

The natural implement of Arabic writing, as that of Hebrew, is the calamus (*qalam*), a pen cut from a piece of reed. The reed used is the common giant reed or ditch reed—*Arundo donax* or *Phragmites communis*—which grow along watercourses (fig. 1). Calami can also be made using the thinner stems of roses or even some types of grass. Calami have different diameters, varying from a millimeter or two to three-quarters of an inch (2 cm). The wide-nib calami can also be made from thin strips of fruitwood.

After a section approximately ten inches (24 cm) in length is cut, the cane is dropped on a hard surface; the sound it makes will tell the craftsman whether it is free of holes or cracks, thus usable for a nib.

The nib is then cut using a straight, sharp, thin razor-like blade. The cut must be made from the body of the cane toward the tip, with a slight concave curve (fig. 2). The tip is then flattened on all sides until it resembles a bird's beak; at this point, the nib is cut at a slant by

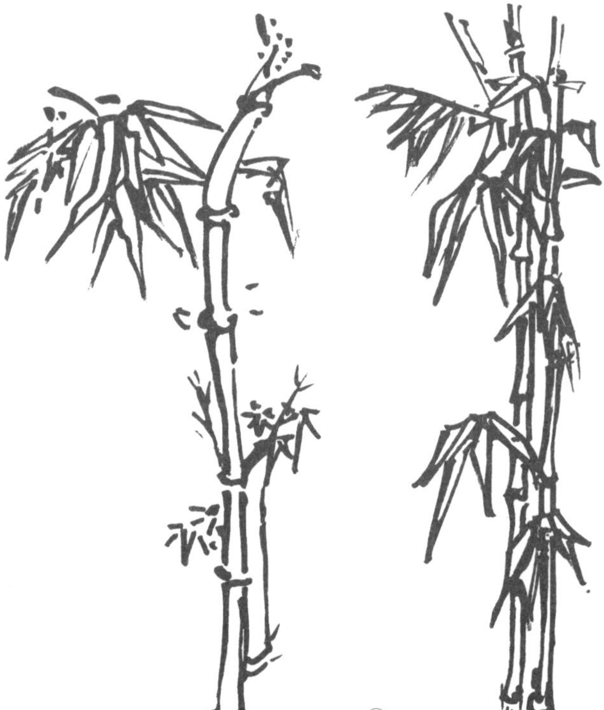

①

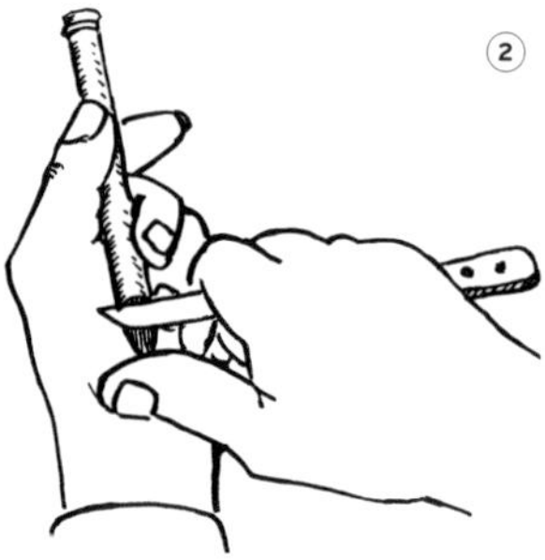

②

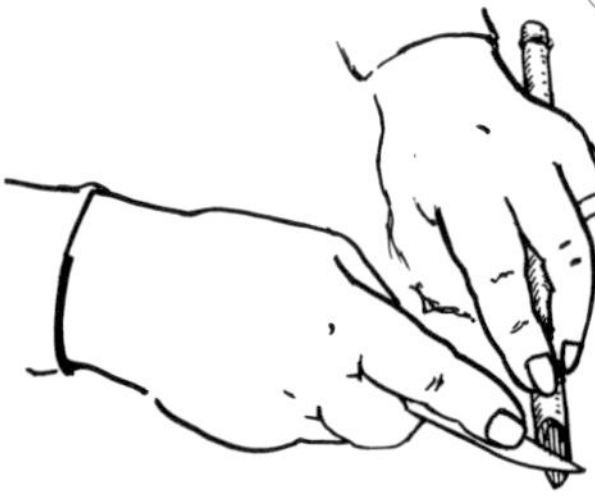

③

placing the cane on a special surface (fig. 3). Finally, the nib is cut vertically, in a position suitable to specific proportions (down to midway of the nib, or two-thirds, etc.); the various ways of cutting the nib make the calamus suitable for writing different calligraphic styles. We could even say that each character has its own slant (fig. 4).

The calamus is filled with silk waste, a woolen wad, or even a small sponge, so that when dipped into the inkwell it will absorb a certain amount of ink, and prevent the nib from becoming damaged if it hits the bottom of the inkwell.

The term *qalam* (plural, *āqlām*) is derived from the radical *q-l-m*, which yields a first-form verb, *qalama* (to cut, to prune). It is also the familiar name of the ninety-sixth sura of the Qur'ān (*al-Alaq*: "The Clot"), as the fourth verse says: *Ālladhī 'allama, bīl-Qalam* (He who teaches by means of the pen).

4

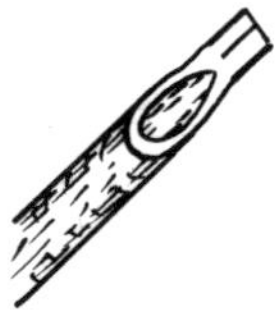

Nib used for the *naskh, thuluth, thuluth jalī, ijāza,* and *dīwānī* scripts.

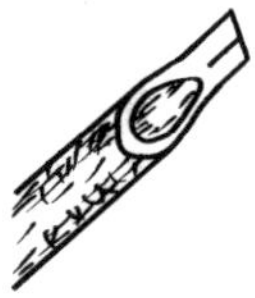

Nib used for the Kufic, *riqā'*, and Farsi scripts.

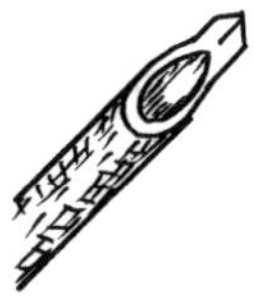

Nib used for the *maghribī* (North African) scripts.

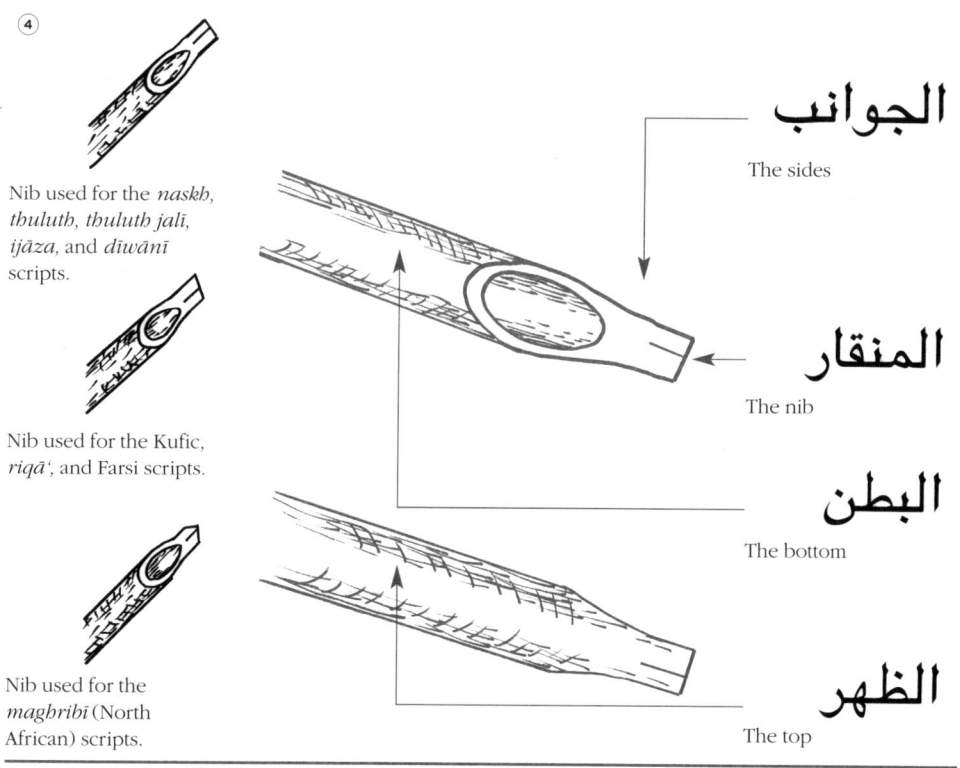

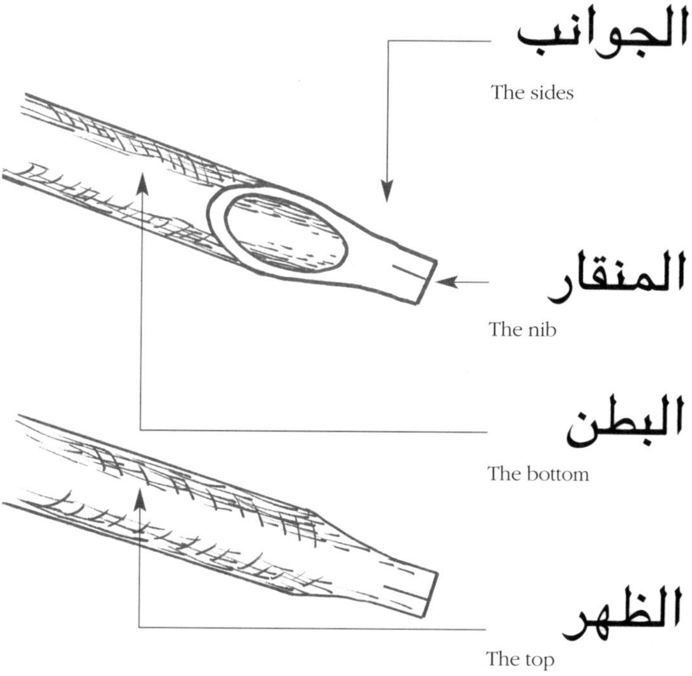

Alphabet sequence (from left to right):

ا	ب	ت	ث	ج	ح	خ
alif	ba	ta	sa	jim	ha	kha
د	ذ	ر	ز	س	ش	ص
dal	zal	ra	za	sin	shin	sad
ض	ط	ظ	ع	غ	ف	ق
dad	ta (ṭ)	za (ẓ)	'ayn	ghain	fa	qaf
ك	ل	م	ن	ه	و	ي
kaf	lam	mim	nun	ha	waw	ya

In North Africa the following sequence is used:
alif - ba - ta - sa - jim - ha - kha - dal - zal - ra - za - ta - kaf - lam - mim - nun - sad - dad - 'ayn - ghain - fa - qaf - sin - shin - ha - waw - lam-alif - ya

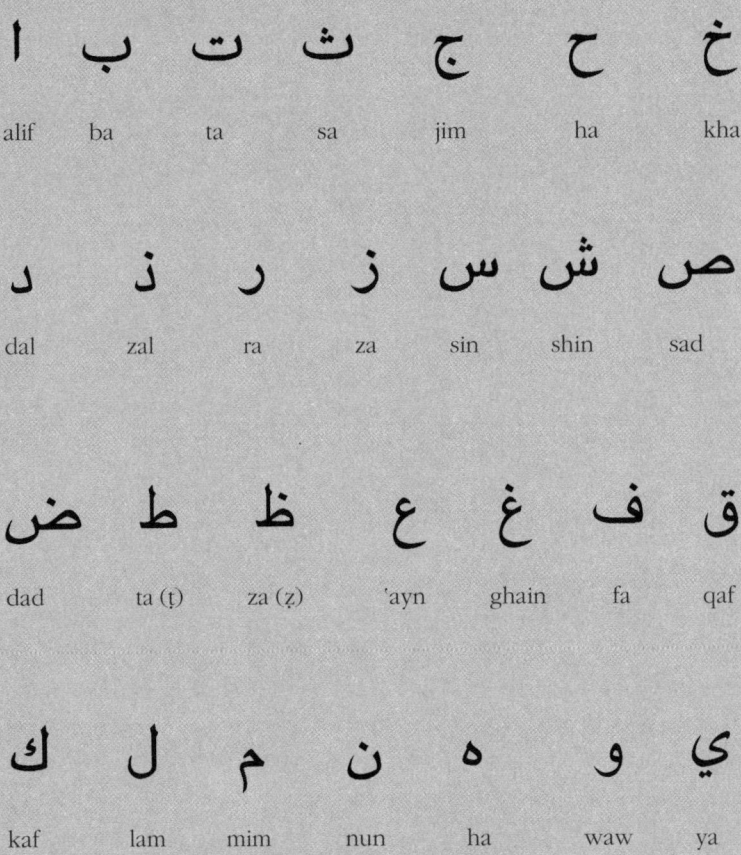

THE LETTERS OF THE ALPHABET

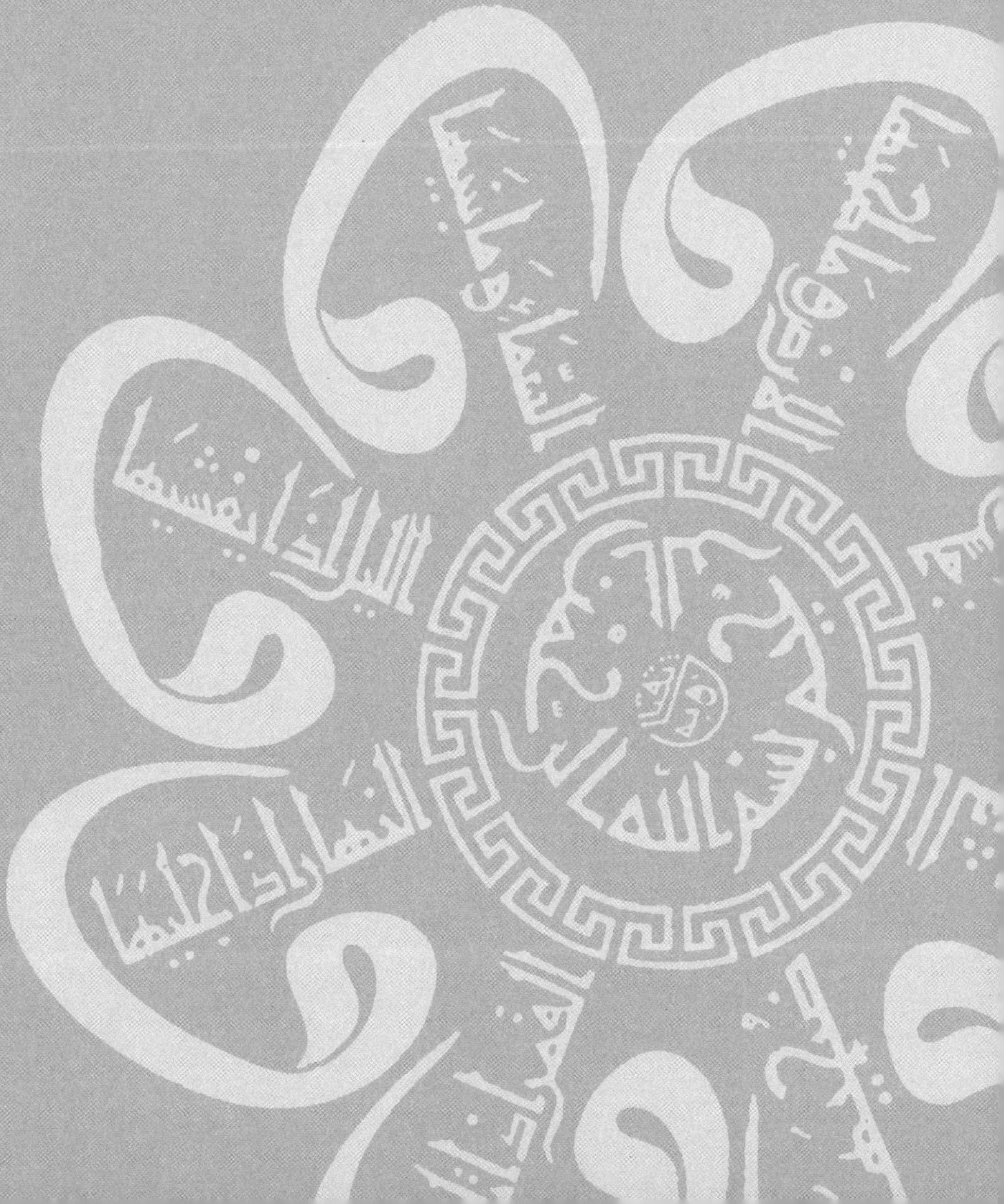

ALIF

Name: **alif**.

Transliteration: the sign ’ or **ā**.

Pronunciation: long **a**, as in f**ai**r (for special signs, see pages 90–91).

ـا Final	Medial	Initial	ا Isolated

ا	Alarz	ا	Diwani	ا	Nastaliq
ا	Al-Waleed	ا	Fairuz	ا	Omar
ا	Al-Qahira	ا	Firdawsi n.	ا	Rabee
ا	Al-Ruha	ا	Hadith	ا	Rouqai
ا	Amin	ا	Hijaz	ا	Shuweifat
ا	Annees	ا	Jarash	ا	Sidon
ا	Baalback	ا	Jiddah	ا	Silwan
ا	Baghdad	ا	Kufic	ا	Sirius
ا	Beirut	ا	Najaf	ا	Suraya
ا	Byblos	ا	Naskh	ا	Tadmur
ا	Dimashk	ا	Naskh cont.	ا	Thuluth

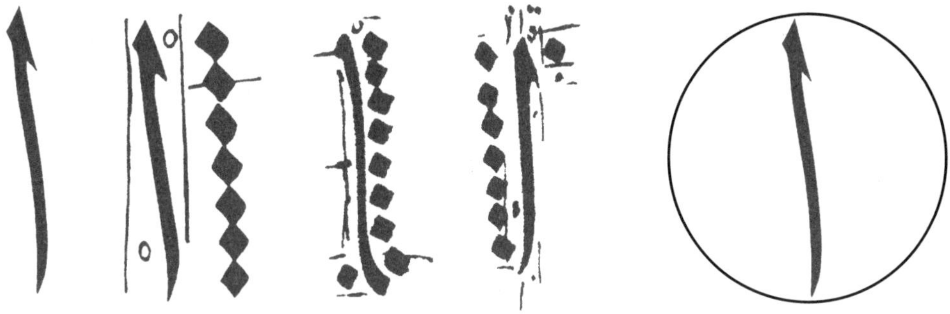

The first letter of the Arabic alphabet is the sign ' (*alif*); it has a guttural sound.

In the art of reciting the Qur'ān (*tajwīd*), it has the characteristics of sonority, tonicity, and softening, and the antonymies of lowering and opening.

This letter is the module of the whole calligraphic system. Calligraphers vary its length, measuring it in square points, or dots (*noqta*), as for other letters. The width of the *alif* is one point, and its length can vary from three to twelve points; for example, in the *naskhī* it has a height of five points, in *thuluth*, nine. From the length of the *alif* the diameter of a circle inside which all the other letters are written is also calculated. The characteristics of this letter are linearity (*qawam*), axiality (*mihwari*), balance (*mu'tadilan*), and a straight stroke (*muntasiban*).

Because the shape of the *alif* resembles the numeral 1, it symbolizes the selfness of God as well as his unity. Thus, this letter takes on the archetypal value of the whole alphabet, which it begins, and is thus also identified with Adam, the father of humankind (and thus any diacritical sign affirming this letter's value is identified with Eve).

The three main positions of Islamic prayer are: standing, like the *alif*; kneeling, like the *dal*; and prostrate, like the *mim*. These three letters also make up the name Ādm (Adam). According to the mystic Ibn Ata' Allah Abbas (d. 1309), "this name is derived from *ulfa* (good company), because it unites and agrees (*ta'līf*) with the other letters." For some sects, however, the *alif* represents Satan, because like him "it does not bow" to God (*ālīf mutaakhar al-Sujūd*).

Grammatically, *alif* is an interrogative particle (*ā Zaydun fy āl-Bayti?*: Is Zayd home?).

In the *Ḥurūf* system, *'ilm āl-Ḥurūf* is the science of the secrets of the letters of the alphabet, also known as *'ilm āl-Ābjad*, or *sīmiyā'*, from the Greek σημεια (letter magic, used in mystical speculation and magical practices); *alif* represents the number one, and belongs to the element of fire.

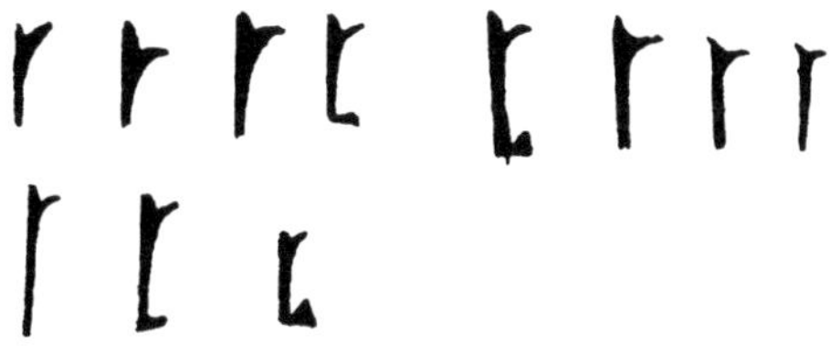

Examples of some of the oldest versions of the letter *alif* in lapidary Kufic.

COMPOSITIONS WITH THE *ALIF* LETTER

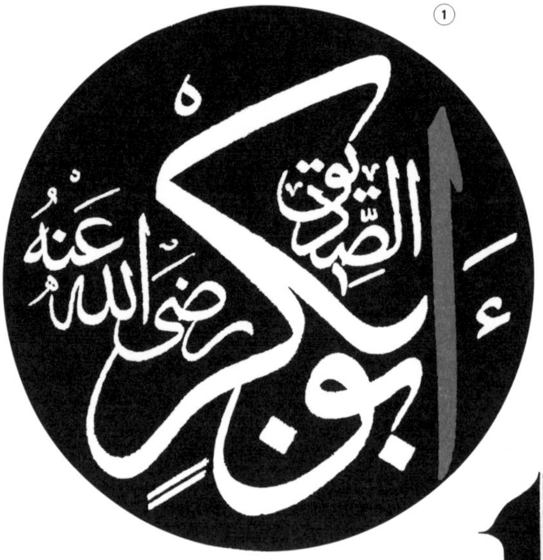

1. The name of Abu Bakr as drawn by Kazasker Mustafa Izzet (1801–1876) in a roundel in the Basilica of Saint Sophia, Istanbul.

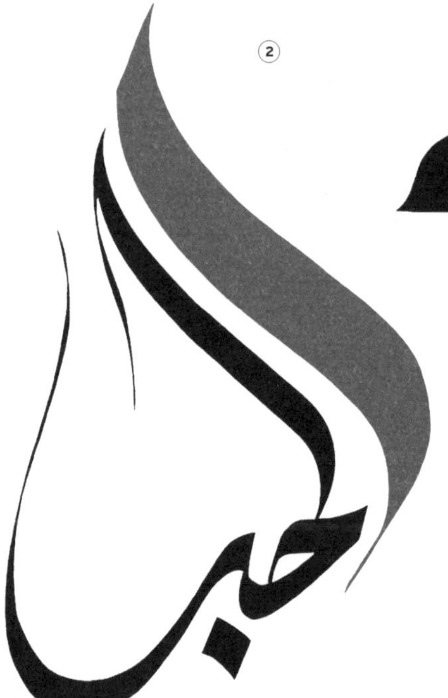

2. *Āl-Ḥubb* (love). Calligraphy, free from traditional canons, by contemporary artist Lassaad Métoui.

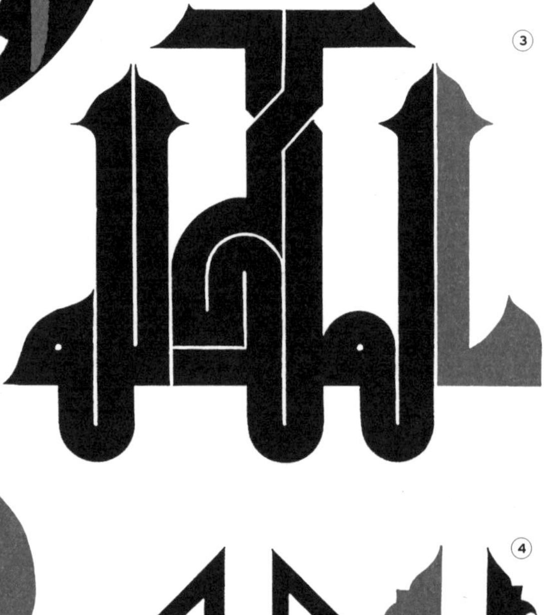

3. *Āl-Malaika Lillāhi* (the power is God's). From a Moroccan stucco.

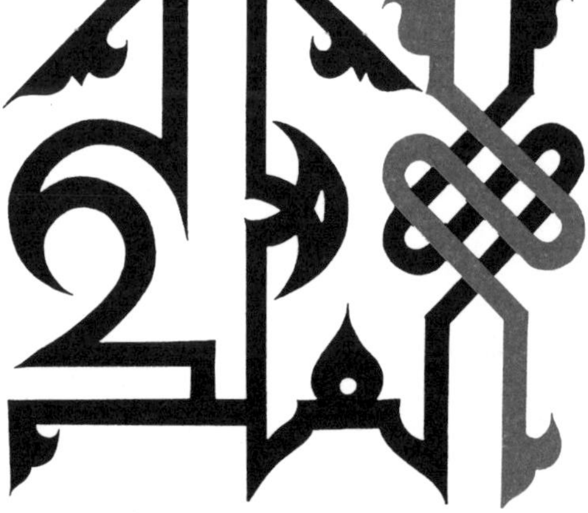

4. *Āl-Malik* (the king). Development of an Andalusian iconographic motif from the fourteenth century.

5

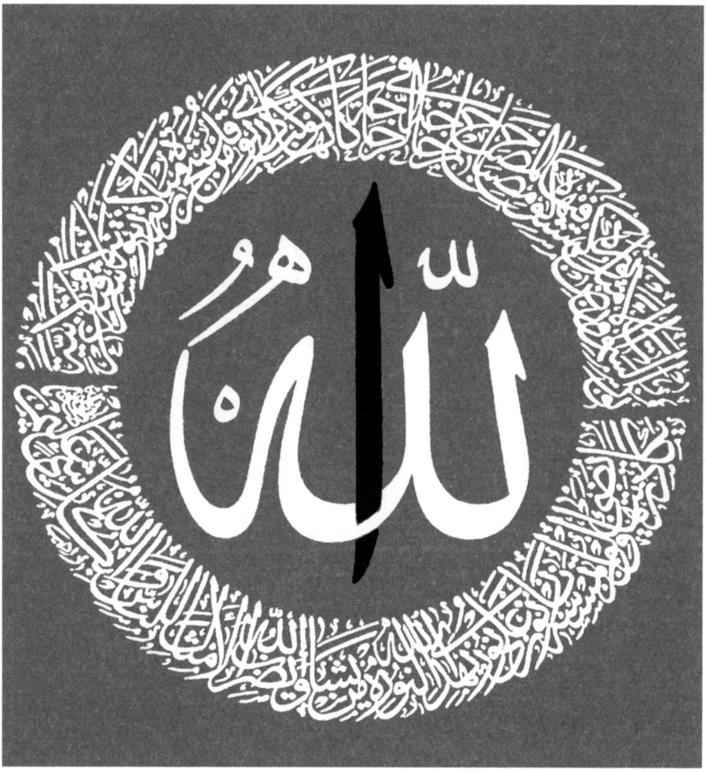

5. The *alif* of the word *Allah* in the center. It is surrounded by the "Light Verse" (Qur'ān, 24:35).

6. Kinetic effect produced by the lengthening of the letters *alif* and *lam* in Mamluk calligraphy with the name of Sultan Husayn ibn Shaban ibn Kalaun. Egypt, 1362.

7. A *basmala* drawn in *dīwānī jalī*, with aesthetic emphasis of the *alifs* and the *lams*, by Yahya Zakariyya 'Adawi, an artist born in Bethlehem in 1962.

6

7

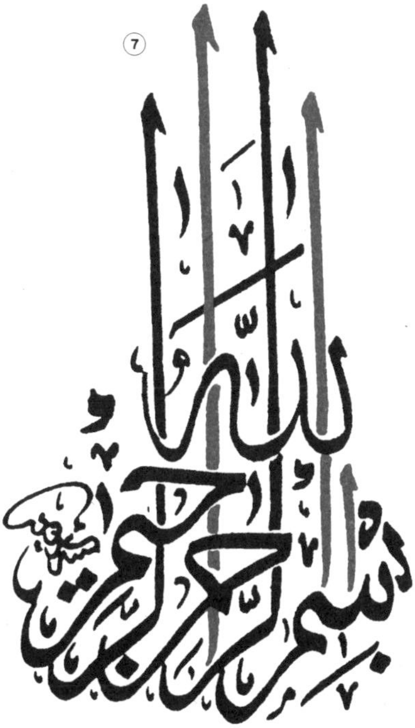

BA

Name: **ba**.
Transliteration: **b**.
Pronunciation: **b**, as in **b**ig.

ب

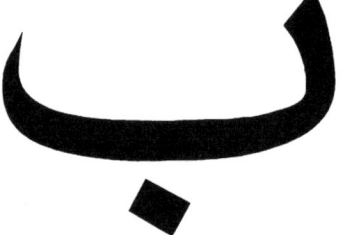

Final	Medial	Initial	Isolated
طب	طبو	بو	ب

Characters

ب	Alarz	ب	Diwani	ب	Nastaliq
ب	Al-Waleed	ب	Fairuz	ب	Omar
ب	Al-Qahira	ب	Firdawsi n.	ب	Rabee
ب	Al-Ruha	ب	Hadith	ب	Rouqai
ب	Amin	ب	Hijaz	ب	Shuweifat
ب	Annees	ب	Jarash	ب	Sidon
ب	Baalback	ب	Jiddah	ب	Silwan
ب	Baghdad	ب	Kufic	ب	Sirius
ب	Beirut	ب	Najaf	ب	Suraya
ب	Byblos	ب	Naskh	ب	Tadmur
ب	Dimashk	ب	Naskh cont.	ب	Thuluth

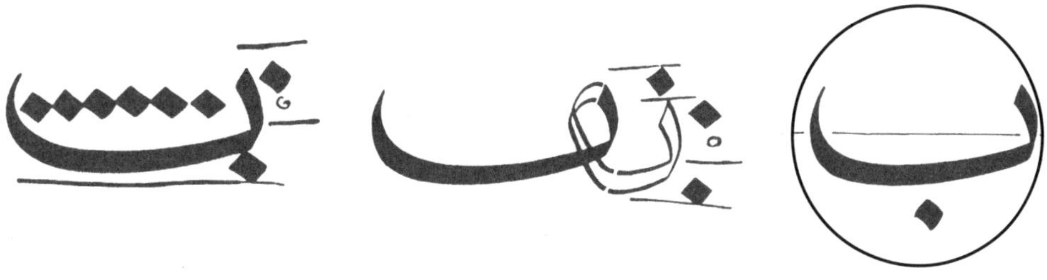

Ba is the second letter of the alphabet; it is labial.

In the art of reciting the Qur'ān (*tajwīd*) it has the characteristics of sonority and tonicity and the antonymies of vibration, lowering, opening, and volubility.

Just as *alif* is the first vertical letter, *ba* is the first horizontal letter and it is suitable for representing other letters such as *ta*, *tha*, and *nun*, according to the diacritical signs placed above or below the stroke. It is the initial letter par excellence, because it opens the *basmala* (*Bismi Āllāhi āl-Raḥmani āl-Raḥymi*: "In the name of God, the Mercy-giving, the Merciful"), the formula with which all the suras (chapters) of the Qur'ān, except for the ninth, begin. (We note, incidentally, that the Bible also begins with a *B*.)

The diacritical sign placed below the stroke represents, for scholars of Islamic esoteric lore, the origin, essence, and being of all things, in strict analogy with the *bindu* (.) of Tantrism and yoga. For this reason, some Muslims, though in disagreement with orthodox theology, believe that the content of all revealed Scripture is found in the Qur'ān; in turn, that the content of the Qur'ān is found all in the first sura, the Fātiḥa; that all the content of the Fātiḥa resides in the *basmala* and the whole content of *basmala* is enclosed inside *B*'s diacritical point. This exegesis was accepted by, among others, Abdullah ibn Mas'ud (seventh century) and Abd al-Karim al-Jili (d. 1494), according to whom the *B* of *Bismi* represents the resplendent beauty of God (*Bahā'*), the *S* his greatness (*Sanā'*), and the *L* his sovereignty (*Mamlaka*).

Grammatically, b^i (a, in, next to) gives a causative meaning to some verbs and gives to verbs of motion the meaning of "carrying, bringing, taking away."

Finally, this letter is a symbol of mediation, introduction, and presentation. In the "science of the secrets of letters" (*'ilm āl-Ḥurūf*), the letter *ba* represents the number two, and belongs to the element of air.

Examples of some of the oldest versions of the letter *ba* in lapidary Kufic.

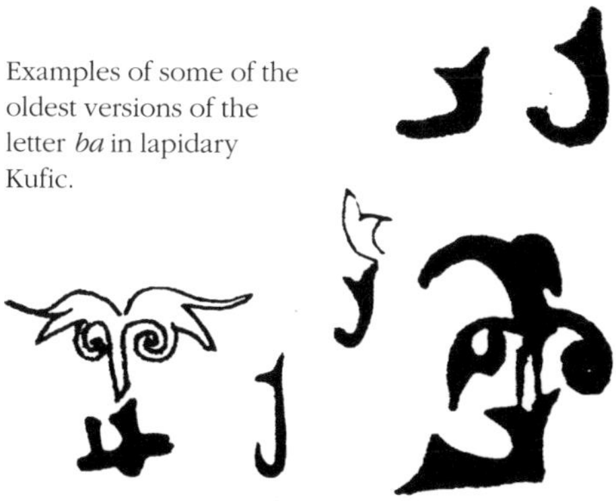

THE LETTER *BA* IN VARIOUS *BASMALAS*

1

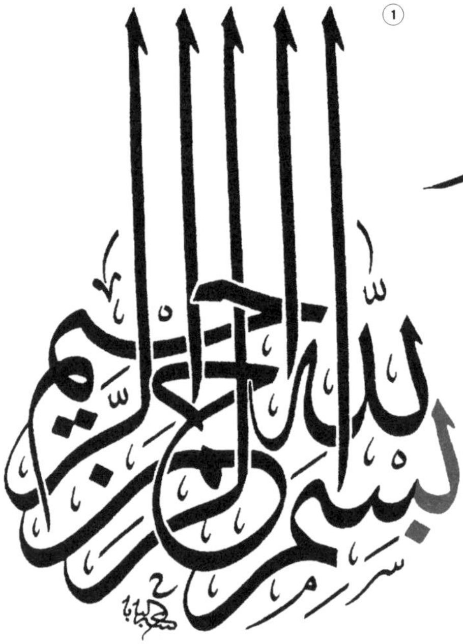

4

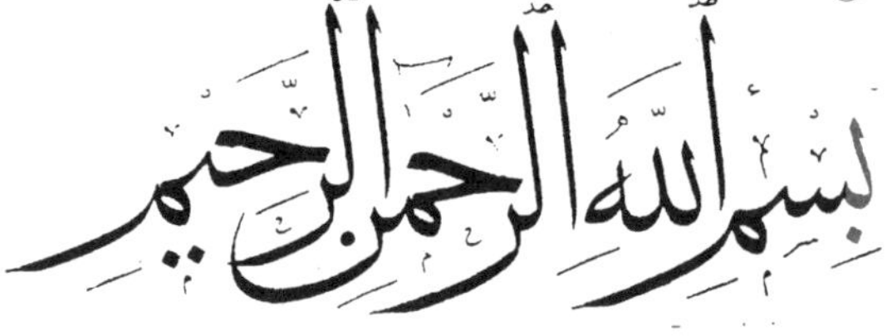

5

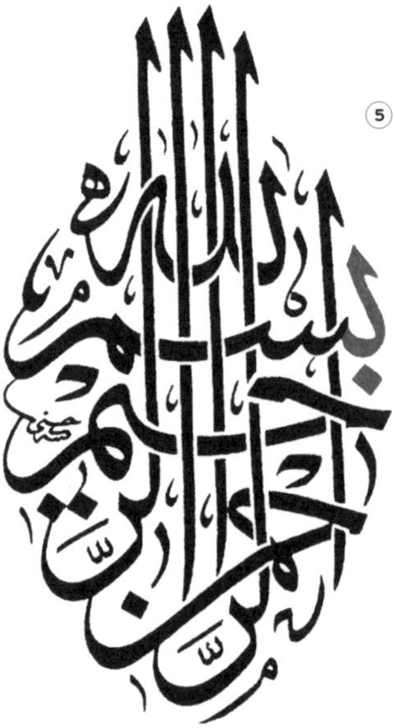

2

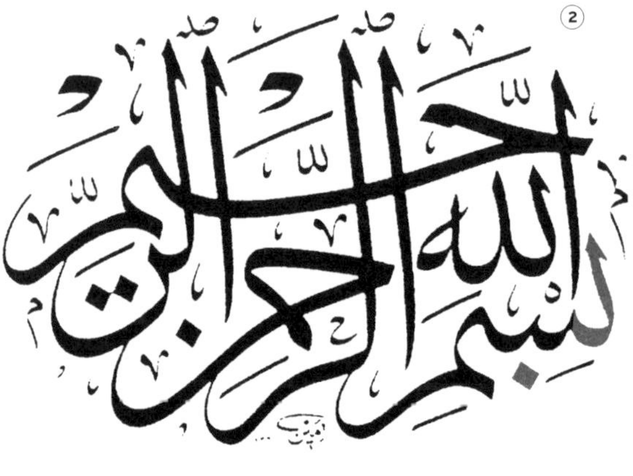

3

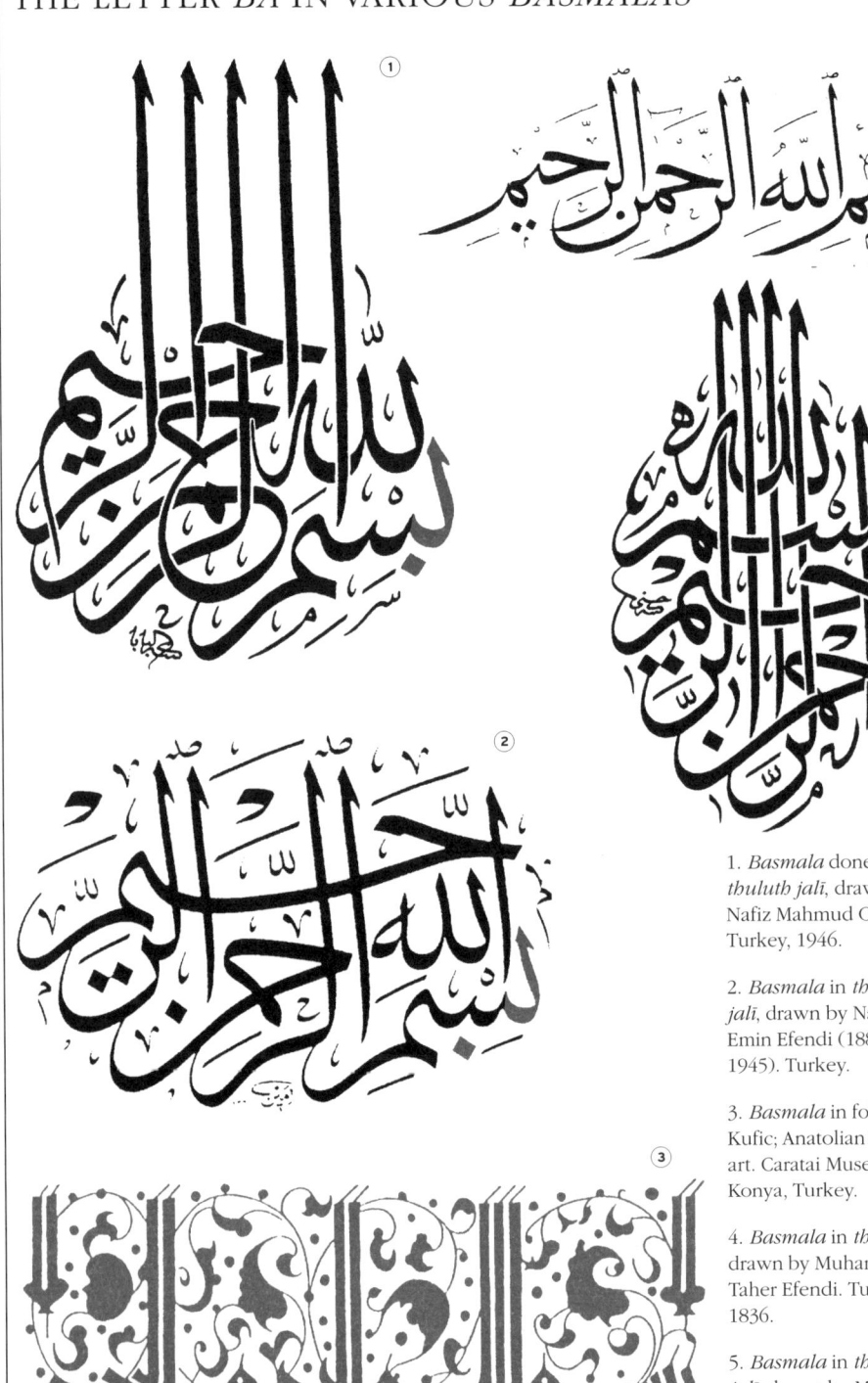

1. *Basmala* done in *thuluth jalī*, drawn by Nafiz Mahmud Oncu. Turkey, 1946.

2. *Basmala* in *thuluth jalī*, drawn by Nayzen Emin Efendi (1883–1945). Turkey.

3. *Basmala* in foliated Kufic; Anatolian Seljuk art. Caratai Museum, Konya, Turkey.

4. *Basmala* in *thuluth*, drawn by Muhammad Taher Efendi. Turkey, 1836.

5. *Basmala* in *thuluth jalī*, drawn by Mustafa Halim Ozyazici. Turkey, 1956.

(6)

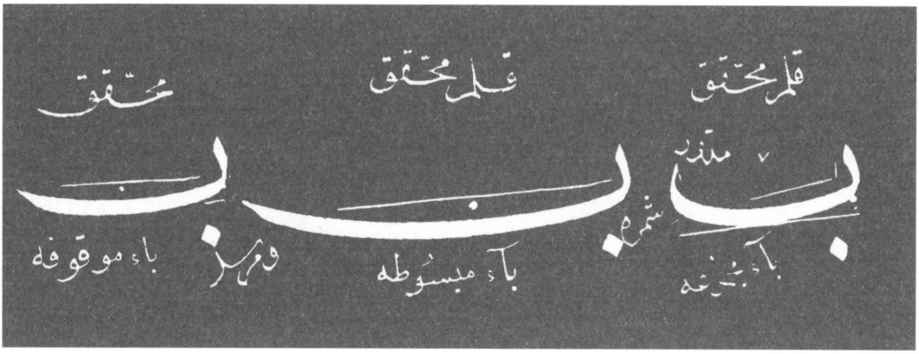

(7)

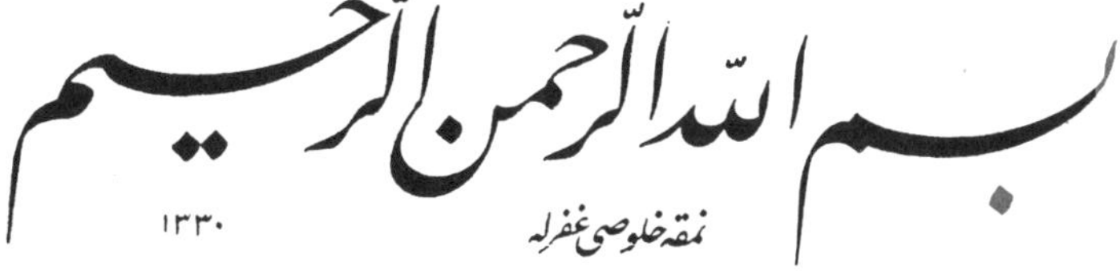

(8)

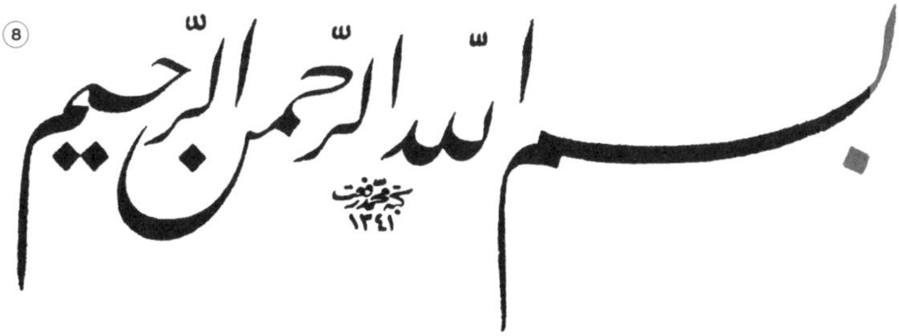

(9)

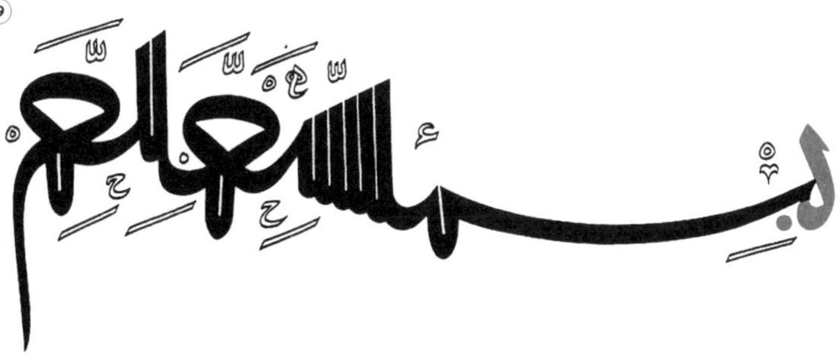

6. The letter *ba* as seen in examples by Hakkazade Mustafa Hilmi Efendi (d. 1852), in the calligraphy code *Mizanu'l Hatt,* 1849.

7. *Basmala* in *ta'līq*, drawn by Mir Malik Declami. Iran, seventeenth century.

8. *Basmala* in *ta'līq*, drawn by Hasan Celebi, 1937, in the Suleymaniye mosque of Istanbul.

9. A liberal interpretation of the *basmala* by Ahmed Karahisari (1468–1556). Istanbul, Suleymaniye Kutuphanesi.

TA

Name: **ta**.
Transliteration: **t**.
Pronunciation: **t**, as in **t**able.

ت

Final	Medial	Initial	Isolated
طت	طتو	تو	ت

ت	Alarz	ت	Diwani	ت	Nastaliq
ت	Al-Waleed	ت	Fairuz	ت	Omar
ت	Al-Qahira	ت	Firdawsi n.	ت	Rabee
ت	Al-Ruha	ت	Hadith	ت	Rouqai
ت	Amin	ت	Hijaz	ت	Shuweifat
ت	Annees	ت	Jarash	ت	Sidon
ت	Baalback	ت	Jiddah	ت	Silwan
ت	Baghdad	ت	Kufic	ت	Sirius
ت	Beirut	ت	Najaf	ت	Suraya
ت	Byblos	ت	Naskh	ت	Tadmur
ت	Dimashk	ت	Naskh cont.	ت	Thuluth

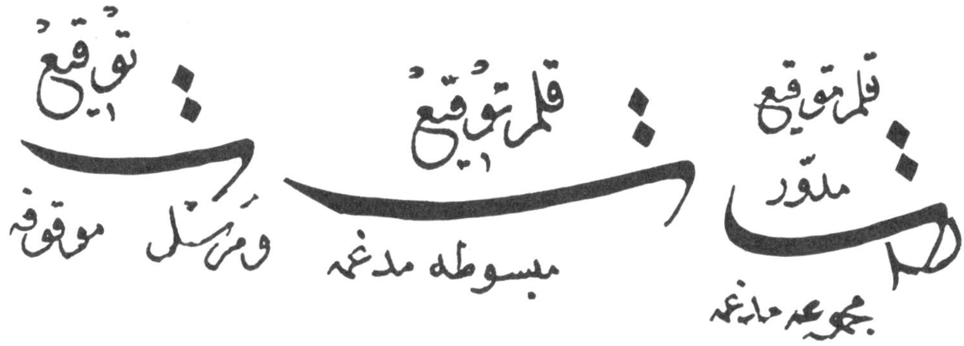

Ta is the third letter of the alphabet (the plural is *ta'at*); it is prepalatal.

In the art of reciting the Qur'ān (*tajwīd*) it has the characteristics of tonicity and softening and the antonymies of lowering, opening, and whispering.

This letter has great esoteric value, especially for Islam's mystics—the Sufis—because it is the first letter of the term *tawḥīd*, the science of professing God and his singleness (*waḥda*), and so it symbolizes monotheism, faith in the oneness of God.

It also symbolizes the state of ecstasy, the discovery of and return to God (*thawba*).

In this respect, the great Muslim mystic and Sufi martyr Hosein Mansur al-Hallaj (857–922) wrote a poem (*Muhatta'at* No. 49 with a *mim* rhyme and a *wāfir* meter), wherein he traces the word *tawḥīd* through enigmas: "Three letters without diacritical sign, two with signs and this is the whole speech. The first designates those who find it and the other serves for everyone to say 'yes.' As to the other letters, it is the mystery of the night, where it is no longer a question of traveling or stopping."

Explaining the above, we note that in Arabic the term *tawḥīd* is written with two letters, each of which has two diacritical signs, the *ta* and the *ya*, and three letters without signs: the *waw*, the *ha*, and the *dal*. Grammatically, *ta* is part of an oath, *ta-Āllāhi:* by God.

In the "science of the secrets of letters" (*'ilm āl-Ḥurūf*) this letter represents number four hundred and belongs to the element of air.

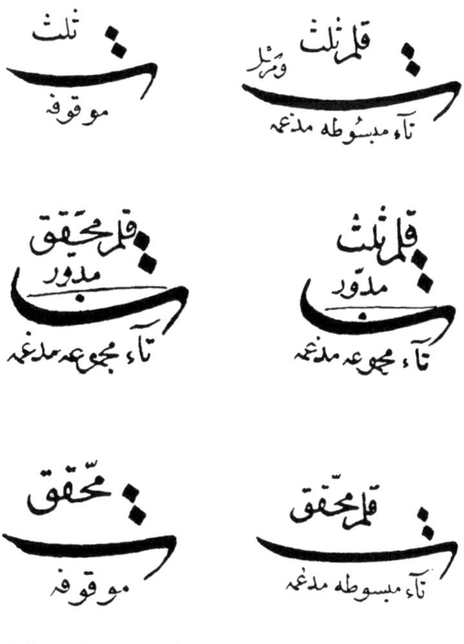

Calligraphic examples by Hakkazade Mustafa Hilmi Efendi, taken from the *Mizanü'l Hatt*.

THA

Name: **tha**.
Transliteration: **th**.
Pronunciation: emphatic **th**, as in **th**ink.

ث

Final	Medial	Initial	Isolated
طث	طثو	ثو	ث

ث	Alarz	ث	Diwani	ث	Nastaliq
ث	Al-Waleed	ث	Fairuz	ث	Omar
ث	Al-Qahira	ث	Firdawsi n.	ث	Rabee
ث	Al-Ruha	ث	Hadith	ث	Rouqai
ث	Amin	ث	Hijaz	ث	Shuweifat
ث	Annees	ث	Jarash	ث	Sidon
ث	Baalback	ث	Jiddah	ث	Silwan
ث	Baghdad	ث	Kufic	ث	Sirius
ث	Beirut	ث	Najaf	ث	Suraya
ث	Byblos	ث	Naskh	ث	Tadmur
ث	Dimashk	ث	Naskh cont.	ث	Thuluth

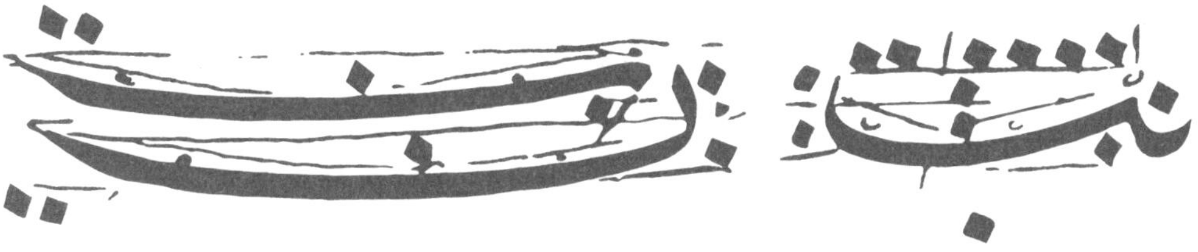

Tha is the fourth letter of the Arab alphabet; it is a palatal-gingival letter.

In the art of reciting the Qur'ān (*tajwīd*) it has the characteristic of softening; its antonymies are lowering, opening, atony, and whispering.

Tha is the abbreviation for *thānīt*, which means a second of a minute. Poems whose verses end with the letter *th* are called *thā'iyyt*.

This letter is a symbol of consolidation (*thubūt*). In the "science of the secrets of letters" (*'ilm āl-Ḥurūf*) it represents number five hundred and belongs to the element of water.

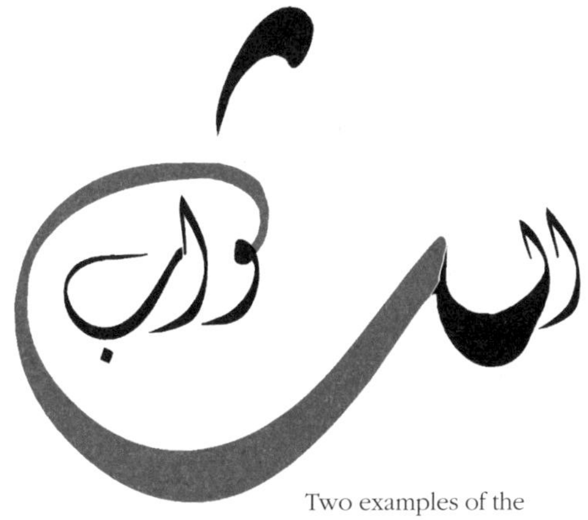

Two examples of the name *āl-Thawwāb* (the Remunerator), the eightieth name-attribute of God.

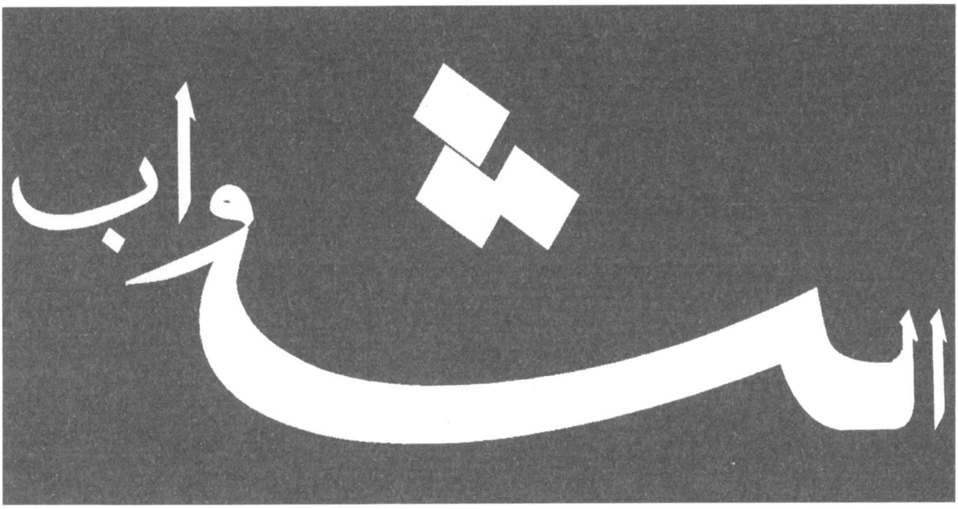

JIM

Name: **jim**.
Transliteration: **j**.
Pronunciation: **j**, as in **J**ohn.

ج

Final	Medial	Initial	Isolated
طج		جو	ج

ج	Alarz	ج	Diwani	ج	Nastaliq
ج	Al-Waleed	ج	Fairuz	ج	Omar
ج	Al-Qahira	ج	Firdawsi n.	ج	Rabee
ج	Al-Ruha	ج	Hadith	ج	Rouqai
ج	Amin	ج	Hijaz	ج	Shuweifat
ج	Annees	ج	Jarash	ج	Sidon
ج	Baalback	ج	Jiddah	ج	Silwan
ج	Baghdad	ج	Kufic	ج	Sirius
ج	Beirut	ج	Najaf	ج	Suraya
ج	Byblos	ج	Naskh	ج	Tadmur
ج	Dimashk	ج	Naskh cont.	ج	Thuluth

Jim is the fifth letter of the Arab alphabet, a subpalatal letter.

In the art of reciting the Qur'ān (*tajwīd*) it has the characteristics of sonority, tonicity, and softening and the antonymies of vibration, lowering, and opening.

In dictionaries, *j* is the abbreviation for *jam'* (plural).

In the "science of the secrets of letters" (*'ilm āl-Ḥurūf*) it represents number three and belongs to the element of water.

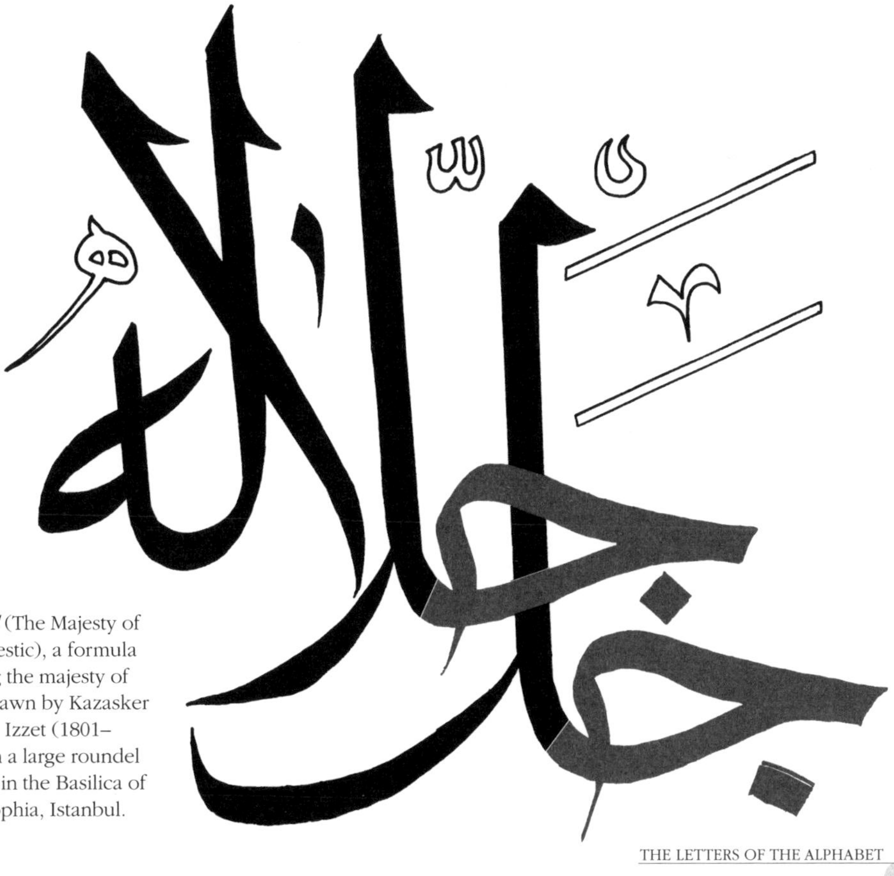

Jal jalāl (The Majesty of the Majestic), a formula exalting the majesty of God, drawn by Kazasker Mustafa Izzet (1801–1876) in a large roundel located in the Basilica of Saint Sophia, Istanbul.

HA

Name: **ha**.

Transliteration: **ḥ**.

Pronunciation: strongly aspired **h**, like the **h** in **h**otel and the Spanish **j** in **j**ota.

ح

Final	Medial	Initial	Isolated
طح	طحو	حو	ح

ح	Alarz	ح	Diwani	ح	Nastaliq
ح	Al-Waleed	ح	Fairuz	ح	Omar
ح	Al-Qahira	ح	Firdawsi n.	ح	Rabee
ح	Al-Ruha	ح	Hadith	ح	Rouqai
ح	Amin	ح	Hijaz	ح	Shuweifat
ح	Annees	ح	Jarash	ح	Sidon
ح	Baalback	ح	Jiddah	ح	Silwan
ح	Baghdad	ح	Kufic	ح	Sirius
ح	Beirut	ح	Najaf	ح	Suraya
ح	Byblos	ح	Naskh	ح	Tadmur
ح	Dimashk	ح	Naskh cont.	ح	Thuluth

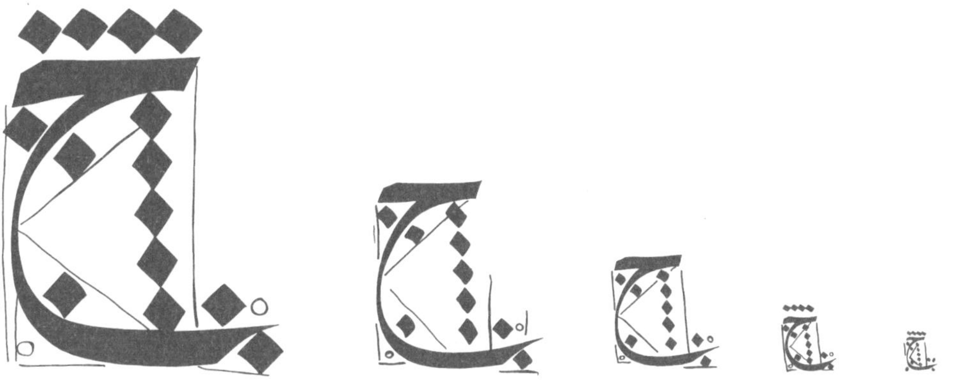

Ha is the sixth letter of the Arab alphabet; it is guttural. In the Arab system of pronunciation it is an unvoiced, pharyngeal, spirant consonant (*rikhwa mahmusa* or *awsaṭ āl-Ḥalq*).

In the art of reciting the Qur'ān (*tajwīd*) it has the characteristic of softening; its antonymies are whispering, lowering, atony, and opening.

This letter has an esoteric meaning for the Sufis because it is the first letter of the verb *ḥabba* (to love): *Īnna Āllāh jamyl yuḥibbu āl-Jamāl* (Truly God is beautiful and loves beauty). Thus also the saying: *ḥabba man ḥabba wakariha man kariha* (He loves whomsoever he chooses to and he hates whomsoever he wishes to).

This letter symbolizes human intuition. In the "science of the secrets of letters" (*'ilm āl-Ḥurūf*) it represents number eight and belongs to the element of earth.

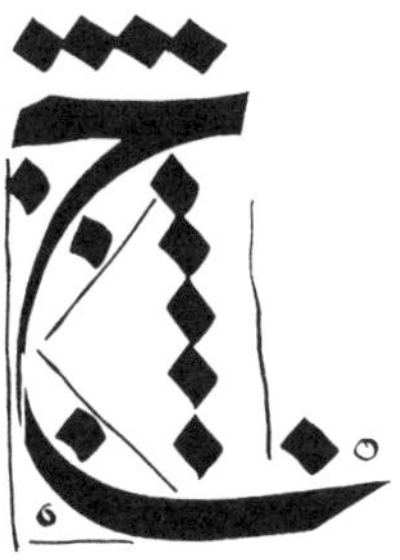

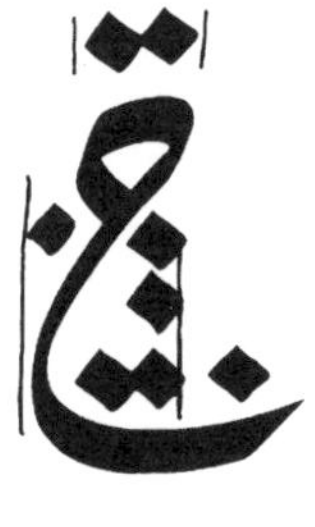

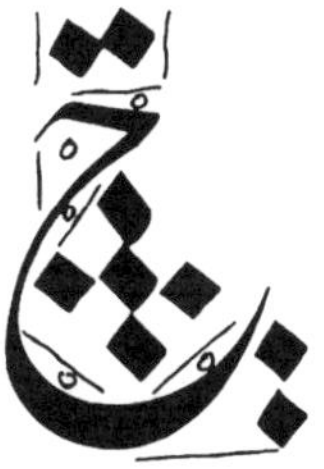

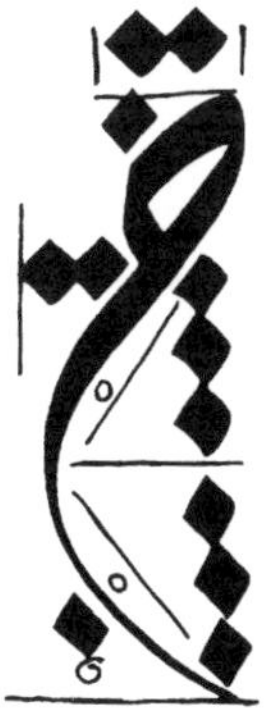

Below: Calligraphy by Mehmet Shefik Bey (1819–1879), in which the *ha* of Hassan (good) is repeated seven times and written as a final letter to underline its aesthetic rhythm.

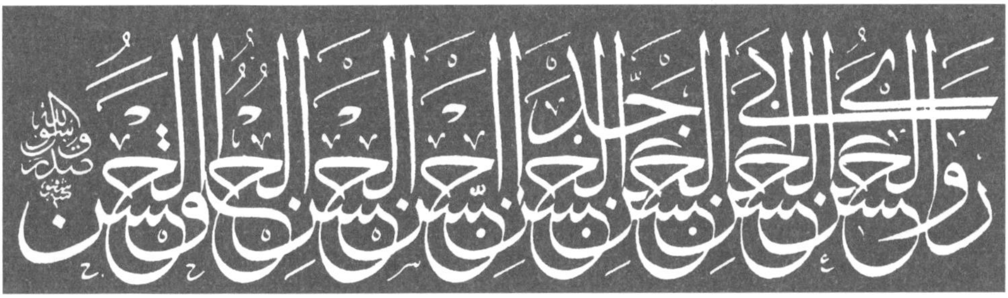

KHA

Name: **kha**.
Transliteration: **kh**.
Pronunciation: guttural **ch**, as in the Scottish lo**ch**.

خ

طخ	طخو	خو	خ
Final	Medial	Initial	Isolated

Characters

خ	Alarz	خ	Diwani	خ	Nastaliq
خ	Al-Waleed	خ	Fairuz	خ	Omar
خ	Al-Qahira	خ	Firdawsi n.	خ	Rabee
خ	Al-Ruha	خ	Hadith	خ	Rouqai
خ	Amin	خ	Hijaz	خ	Shuweifat
خ	Annees	خ	Jarash	خ	Sidon
خ	Baalback	خ	Jiddah	خ	Silwan
خ	Baghdad	خ	Kufic	خ	Sirius
خ	Beirut	خ	Najaf	خ	Suraya
خ	Byblos	خ	Naskh	خ	Tadmur
خ	Dimashk	خ	Naskh cont.	خ	Thuluth

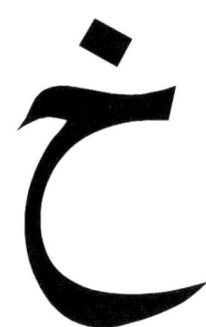

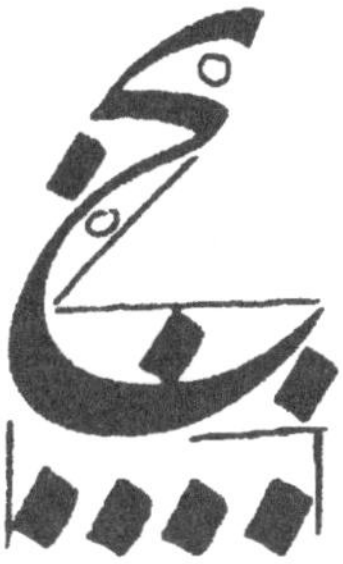

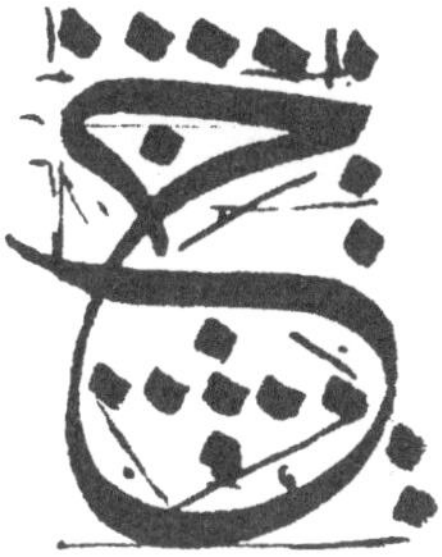

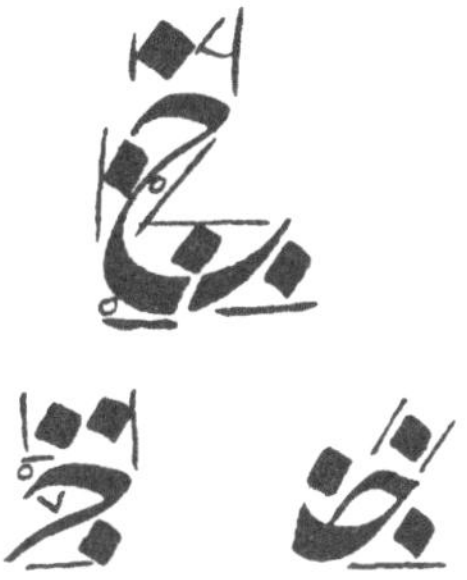

Kha is the seventh letter of the Arab alphabet; it is guttural. In the Arab system of pronunciation it is a fricative, post-velar, unvoiced consonant (*rikhwa mahmūsa musa'liya* or *min ādnā āl-Ḥalq*).

In the art of reciting the Qur'ān (*tajwīd*) it has the characteristics of elevation and softening and the antonymies of whispering, atony, and opening.

In the esoteric literature of the Sufi brotherhoods it symbolizes the eternal good (*khayr dā'im*).

In the "science of the secrets of letters" (*'ilm āl-Ḥurūf*) it represents number six hundred and belongs to the element earth.

Below: Calligraphy by Muhammad 'Abd al-Aziz al-Rifa'i. Egypt, 1928.

Right: Examples of some of the oldest versions of the letter *kha* in lapidary Kufic.

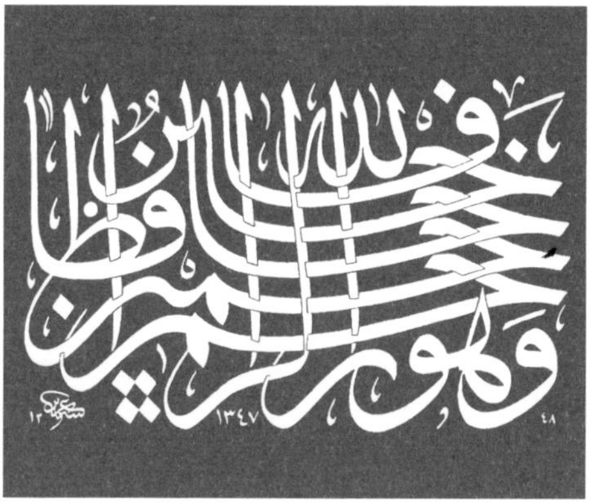

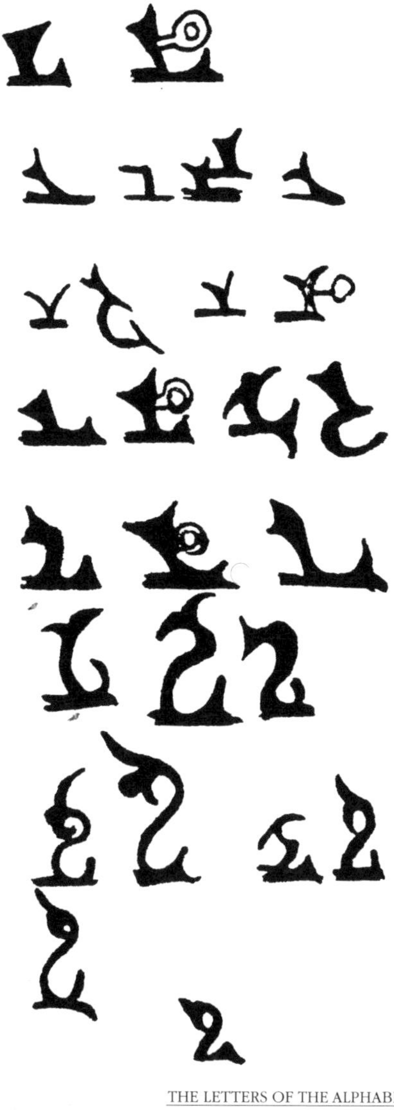

DAL

Name: **dal**.
Transliteration: **d**.
Pronunciation: **d**, as in **d**ead.

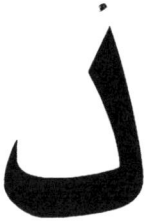

د

طد Final	Medial	Initial	د Isolated

د	Alarz	د	Diwani	د	Nastaliq
د	Al-Waleed	د	Fairuz	د	Omar
د	Al-Qahira	د	Firdawsi n.	د	Rabee
د	Al-Ruha	د	Hadith	د	Rouqai
د	Amin	د	Hijaz	د	Shuweifat
د	Annees	د	Jarash	د	Sidon
د	Baalback	د	Jiddah	د	Silwan
د	Baghdad	د	Kufic	د	Sirius
د	Beirut	د	Najaf	د	Suraya
د	Byblos	د	Naskh	د	Tadmur
د	Dimashk	د	Naskh cont.	د	Thuluth

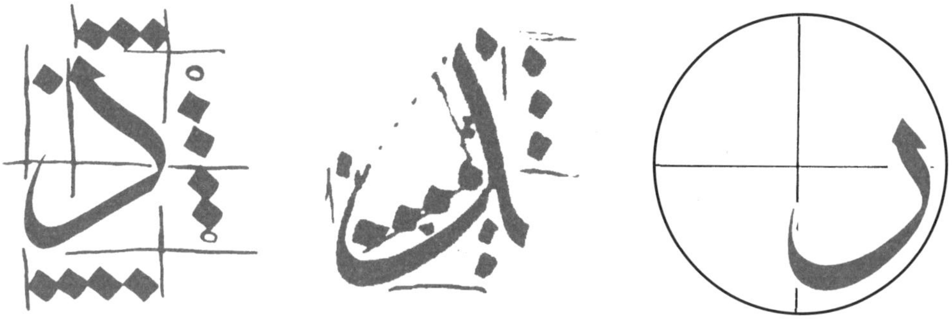

Dal is the eighth letter of the Arab alphabet; it is prepalatal.

In the art of reciting the Qur'ān (*tajwīd*) it has the characteristics of sonority, tonicity, and softening and the antonymies of vibration and lowering.

In Sufi esoteric literature and in the *Contemplations* of the Hurufi, a deviant sect, it symbolizes the equilibrium of all things created.

In the "science of the secrets of letters" (*'ilm āl-Ḥurūf*) it represents number four and belongs to the element of earth.

Because of this, and also because it is the initial letter of the verb *daāba fī āw 'alā* (to work, to labor, to be committed, to make an effort in something for someone; to work with commitment, to do something with effort; to labor unceasingly; to apply oneself, to dedicate oneself; to be constant; to become accustomed to), in the esoteric world this letter represents the earthly condition of human beings who are forced to labor in the realm of material things, but must also evolve spiritually and strive to behave in the best possible way among a multitude of challenges and temptations.

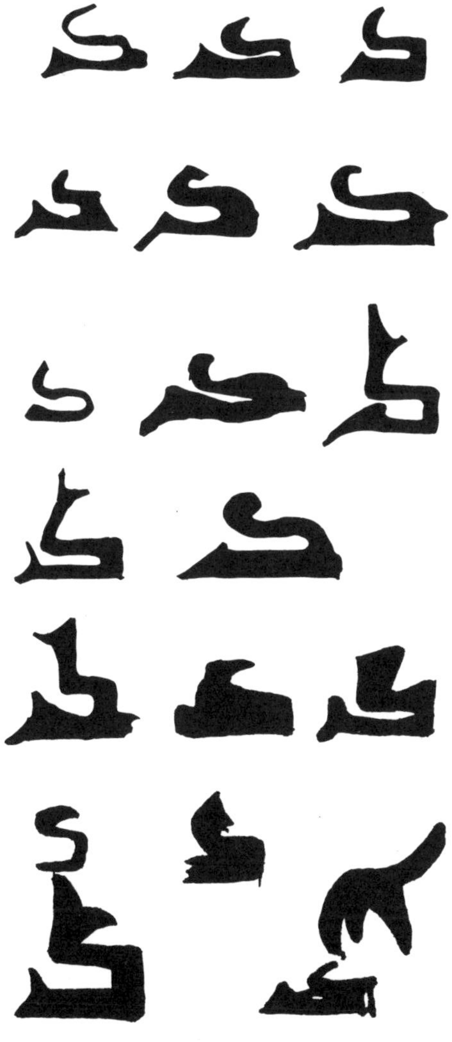

Examples of some of the oldest versions of the letter *dal* in lapidary Kufic.

DHAL

Name: **dhal**.
Transliteration: **dh**.
Pronunciation: **th**, as in **th**at or **th**is.

ذ

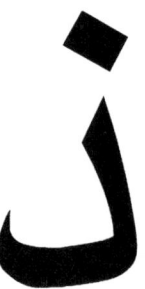

Final	Medial	Initial	Isolated
طذ			ذ

Characters

ذ	Alarz	ذ	Diwani	ذ	Nastaliq
ذ	Al-Waleed	ذ	Fairuz	ذ	Omar
ذ	Al-Qahira	ذ	Firdawsi n.	ذ	Rabee
ذ	Al-Ruha	ذ	Hadith	ذ	Rouqai
ذ	Amin	ذ	Hijaz	ذ	Shuweifat
ذ	Annees	ذ	Jarash	ذ	Sidon
ذ	Baalback	ذ	Jiddah	ذ	Silwan
ذ	Baghdad	ذ	Kufic	ذ	Sirius
ذ	Beirut	ذ	Najaf	ذ	Suraya
ذ	Byblos	ذ	Naskh	ذ	Tadmur
ذ	Dimashk	ذ	Naskh cont.	ذ	Thuluth

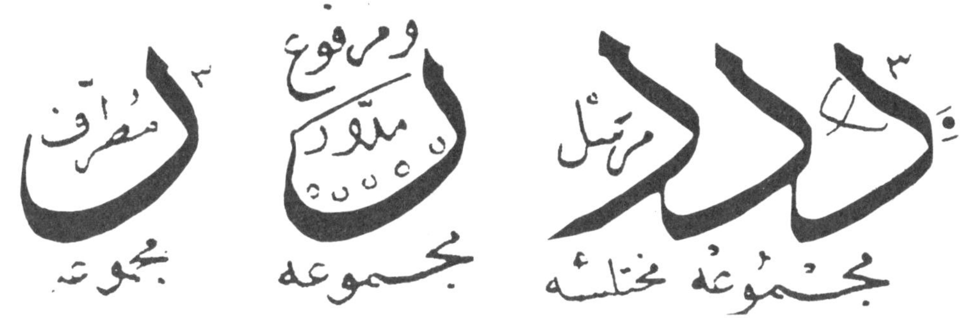

Dhal is the ninth letter of the Arab alphabet; it is gingival and vibrating.

In the art of reciting the Qur'ān (*tajwīd*) it has the characteristics of sonority and softening and the antonymies of lowering, opening, and atony.

In Sufi esoteric knowledge, it symbolizes the heart of an idea, the kernel of a thing.

In the "science of the secrets of letters" (*'ilm āl-Ḥurūf*) it represents number seven hundred and belongs to the element of fire.

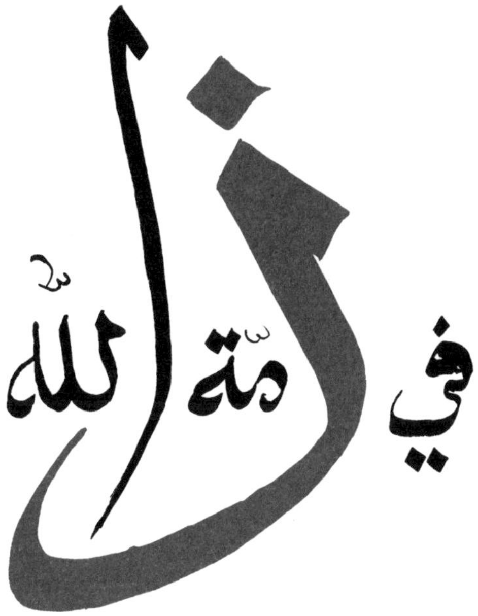

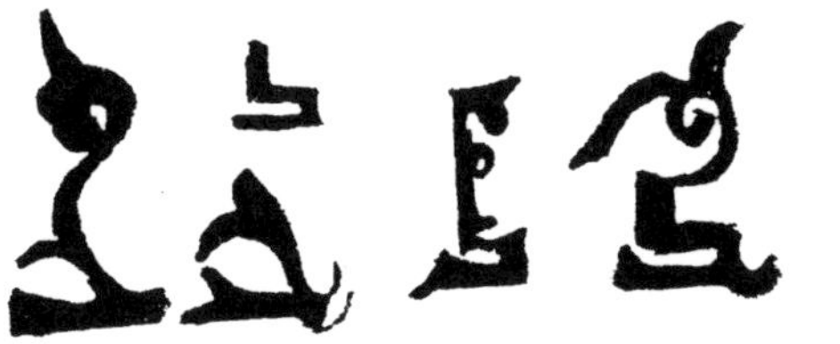

Above, left: Examples of some of the oldest versions of the letter *dhal* in lapidary Kufic.

Above, right: The formula *fi dhimmat Āllāh* (under the protection of God).

Below: The title of the fifty-first sura: *al-Dhāriyāt* (Winnowing).

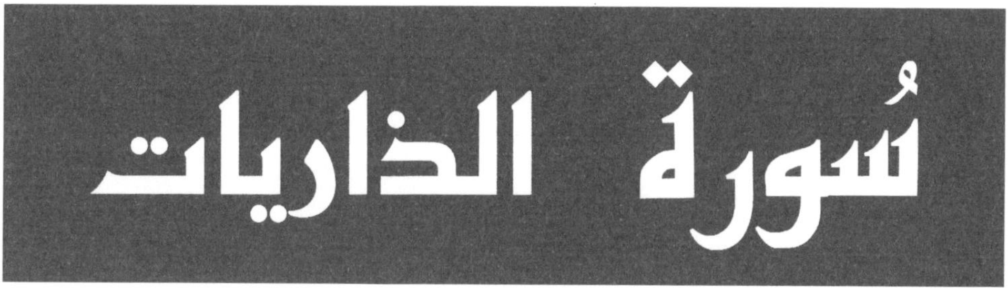

RA

Name: **ra**.

Transliteration: **r**.

Pronunciation: rolled **r**, as in **R**uth.

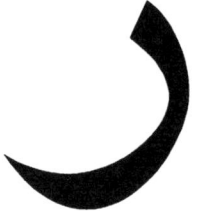

ر

Final	Medial	Initial	Isolated
طر			ر

ر	Alarz	ر	Diwani	ر	Nastaliq
ر	Al-Waleed	ر	Fairuz	ر	Omar
ر	Al-Qahira	ر	Firdawsi n.	ر	Rabee
ر	Al-Ruha	ر	Hadith	ر	Rouqai
ر	Amin	ر	Hijaz	ر	Shuweifat
ر	Annees	ر	Jarash	ر	Sidon
ر	Baalback	ر	Jiddah	ر	Silwan
ر	Baghdad	ر	Kufic	ر	Sirius
ر	Beirut	ر	Najaf	ر	Suraya
ر	Byblos	ر	Naskh	ر	Tadmur
ر	Dimashk	ر	Naskh cont.	ر	Thuluth

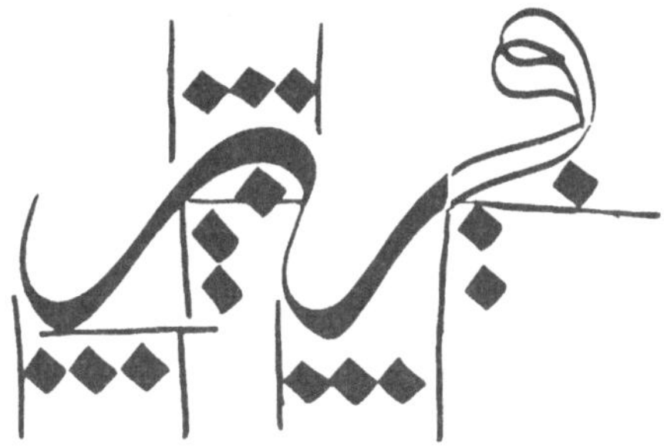

Ra is the tenth letter of Arab alphabet. It is vibrating, apical, alveolar, and voiced (*tafkhīm*).

In the art of reciting the Qur'ān (*tajwīd*) it has the characteristics of sonority and moderation and the antonymies of deflection, repetition, opening, lowering, and atony.

It symbolizes a part, a message, the sura. In the "science of the secrets of letters" (*'ilm āl-Ḥurūf*) it represents number two hundred and belongs to the element of earth.

Examples of some of the oldest versions of the letter *ra* in lapidary Kufic.

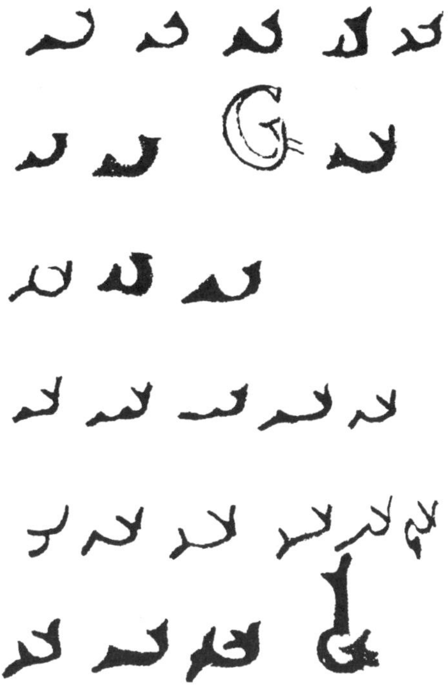

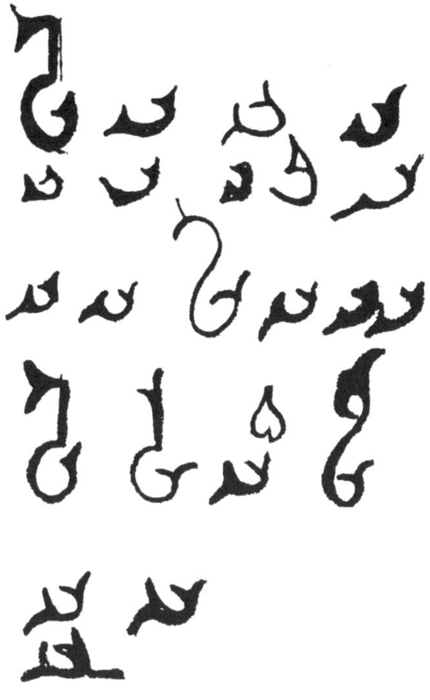

ZA

Name: **za**.

Transliteration: **z**.

Pronunciation: soft **z**, as in **z**ero.

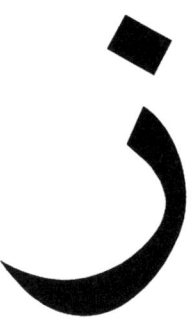

ز

Final		Medial	Initial	Isolated	
طز	Final	Medial	Initial	ز	Isolated

ز	Alarz	ز	Diwani	ز	Nastaliq
ز	Al-Waleed	ز	Fairuz	ز	Omar
ز	Al-Qahira	ز	Firdawsi n.	ز	Rabee
ز	Al-Ruha	ز	Hadith	ز	Rouqai
ز	Amin	ز	Hijaz	ز	Shuweifat
ز	Annees	ز	Jarash	ز	Sidon
ز	Baalback	ز	Jiddah	ز	Silwan
ز	Baghdad	ز	Kufic	ز	Sirius
ز	Beirut	ز	Najaf	ز	Suraya
ز	Byblos	ز	Naskh	ز	Tadmur
ز	Dimashk	ز	Naskh cont.	ز	Thuluth

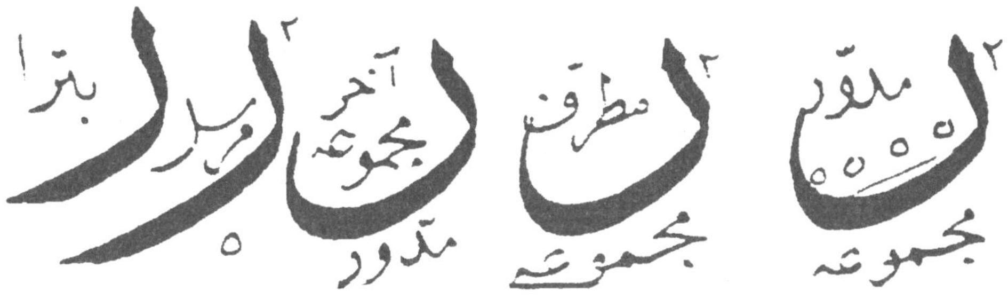

Za is the eleventh letter of the Arab alphabet and is lingual.

In the art of reciting the Qur'ān (*tajwīd*) it has the characteristics of sonority and softening and the antonymies of deflection, repetition, lowering, opening, and volubility.

It symbolizes achievement.

In esoteric alchemy, it represents the process of change, because it is the initial letter of the terms mercury (*zaybaq*), vitriol (*zāj*), and sulfuric acid (*zayb, zāgin*). *Zār* is also the exorcism practiced by women.

In the "science of the secrets of letters" (*'ilm āl-Ḥurūf*) it represents number seven and belongs to the element of water.

Below: The title of the forty-third sura, *āl-Zukhruf* (Luxury).

Bottom: The title of the thirty-ninth sura, *āl-Zumar* (Throngs).

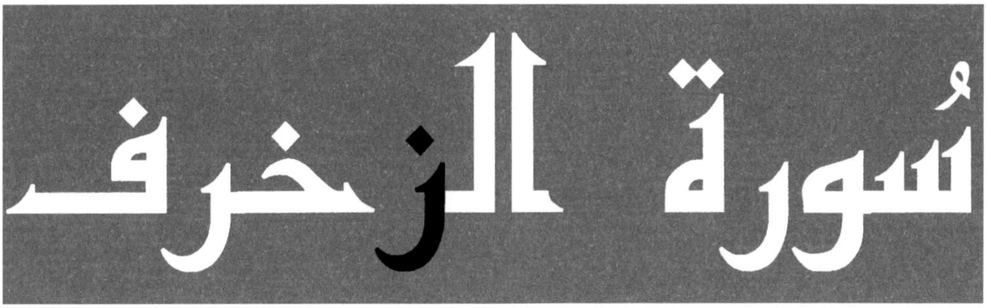

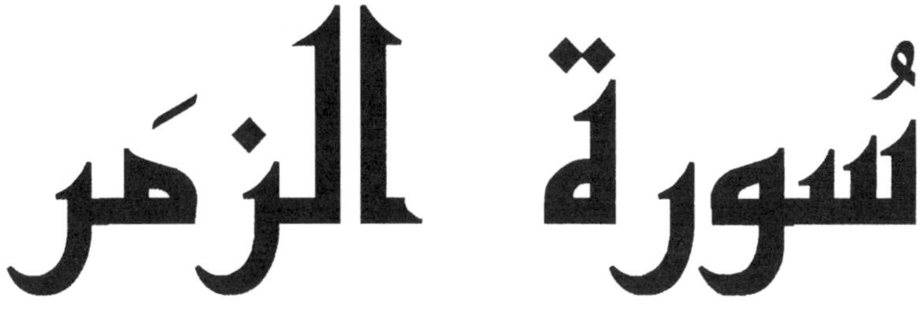

SIN

Name: **sin**.
Transliteration: **s**.
Pronunciation: **s**, as in **s**ew.

س

Final	Medial	Initial	Isolated
طس	طسو	سو	س

س	Alarz	س	Diwani	س	Nastaliq
س	Al-Waleed	س	Fairuz	س	Omar
س	Al-Qahira	س	Firdawsi n.	س	Rabee
س	Al-Ruha	س	Hadith	س	Rouqai
س	Amin	س	Hijaz	س	Shuweifat
س	Annees	س	Jarash	س	Sidon
س	Baalback	س	Jiddah	س	Silwan
س	Baghdad	س	Kufic	س	Sirius
س	Beirut	س	Najaf	س	Suraya
س	Byblos	س	Naskh	س	Tadmur
س	Dimashk	س	Naskh cont.	س	Thuluth

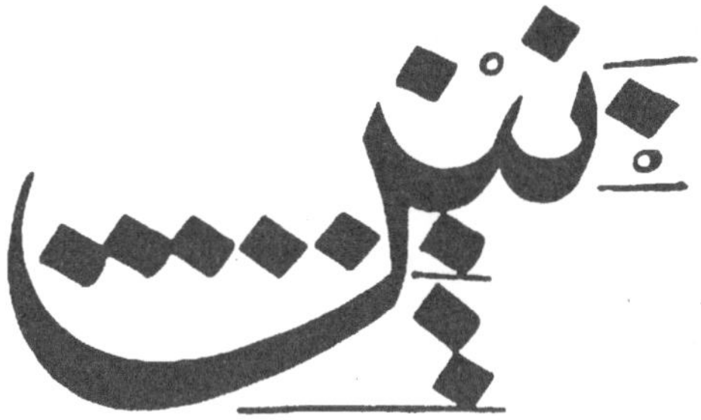

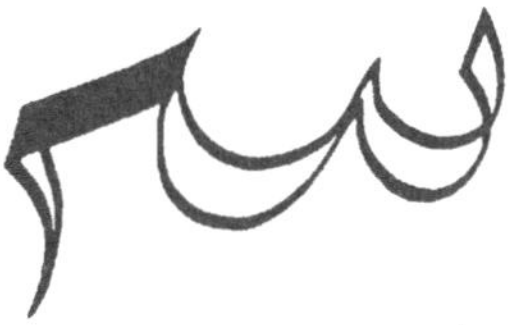

Sin is the twelfth letter of the Arab alphabet and is lingual.

In the art of reciting the Qur'ān (*tajwīd*) it has the characteristic of softening and the antonymies of whispering, lowering, opening, and atony.

S is the abbreviation of *sū'al* (question); *salaam* (peace, greetings); *sahm* (a surface unit of measurement); and *santimitr* (centimeter). In grammar, *sa* is the abbreviated form of *saūfa*, a prefix of the imperfect tense, to which it gives the meaning of future.

It symbolizes the glory of God.

In the "science of the secrets of letters" (*'ilm āl-Ḥurūf*) it represents number sixty and belongs to the element of water, though in North Africa it is believed to belong to the element of fire.

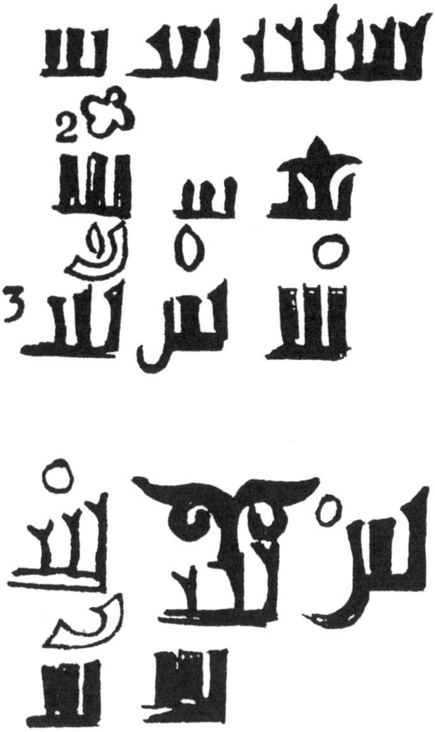

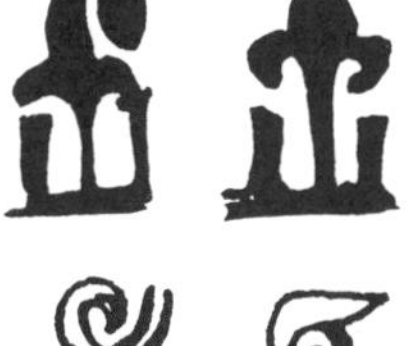

Examples of some of the oldest versions of the letter *sin* in lapidary Kufic.

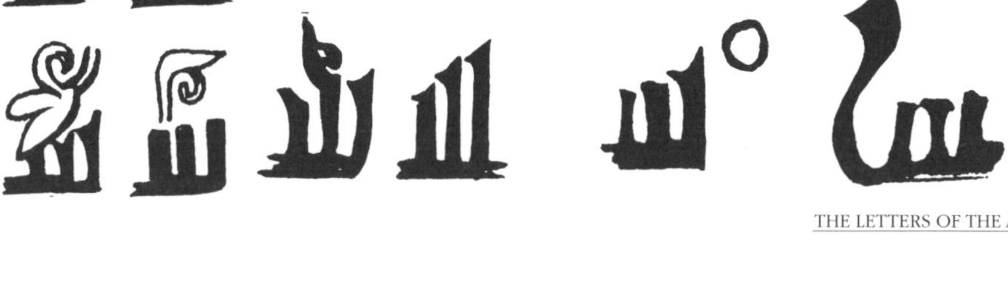

SHIN

Name: **shin**.
Transliteration: **sh**.
Pronunciation: **sh**, as in **sh**all.

ش

Final	Medial	Initial	Isolated
طش	طشو	شو	ش

ش	Alarz	ش	Diwani	ش	Nastaliq
ش	Al-Waleed	ش	Fairuz	ش	Omar
ش	Al-Qahira	ش	Firdawsi n.	ش	Rabee
ش	Al-Ruha	ش	Hadith	ش	Rouqai
ش	Amin	ش	Hijaz	ش	Shuweifat
ش	Annees	ش	Jarash	ش	Sidon
ش	Baalback	ش	Jiddah	ش	Silwan
ش	Baghdad	ش	Kufic	ش	Sirius
ش	Beirut	ش	Najaf	ش	Suraya
ش	Byblos	ش	Naskh	ش	Tadmur
ش	Dimashk	ش	Naskh cont.	ش	Thuluth

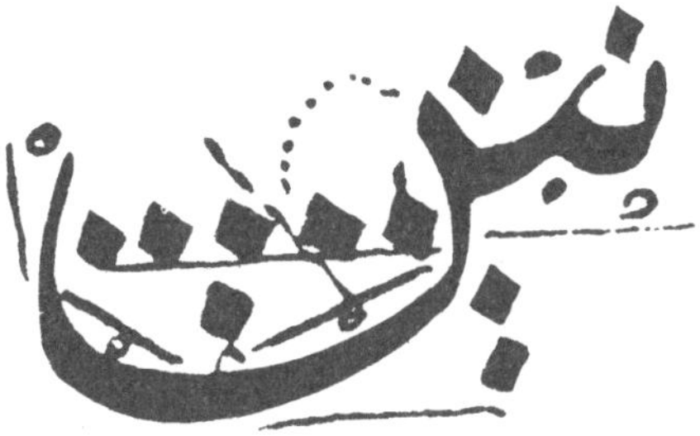

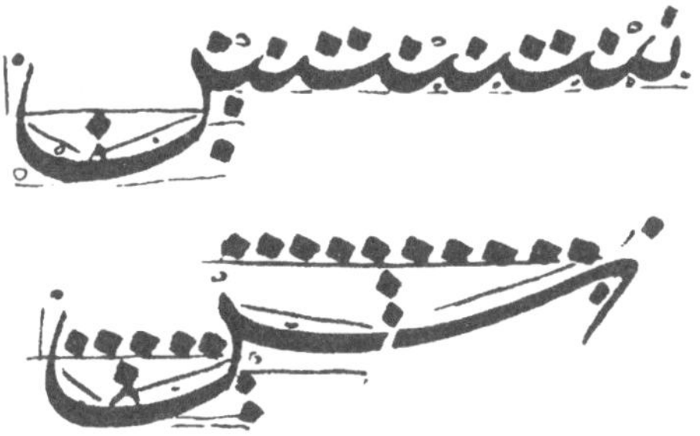

Shin is the thirteenth letter of the Arab alphabet and it is subpalatal.

In the art of reciting the Qur'ān (*tajwīd*) it has the characteristic of lowering and the antonymies of whispering, opening, diffusion, and softening.

It is the abbreviation of *shāri'a*: path, way.

In Sufi esoteric knowledge, this letter symbolizes personal destiny.

In the "science of the secrets of letters" (*'ilm āl-Ḥurūf*) it represents number three hundred and belongs to the element of fire, while in North Africa it is believed to belong to the element of earth.

Above: The letter *shin* from a *maghribī* Qur'ān in a monumental Kufic type from 1023.

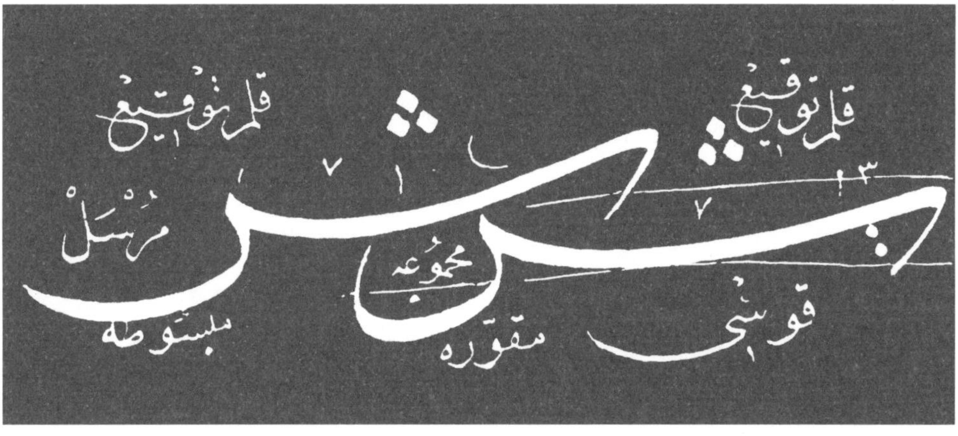

SAD

Name: **sad**.
Transliteration: **ṣ**
Pronunciation:
emphatic **s**, with tongue pressed against the edge of the upper teeth, then withdrawn forcefully.

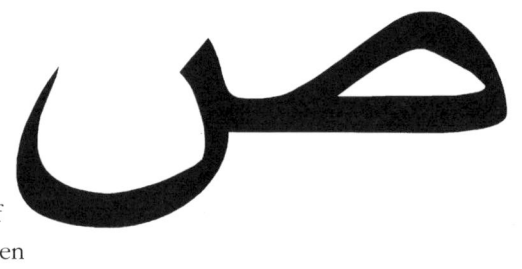

ص

طص	Final	طصو	Medial	صو	Initial	ص	Isolated

ص	Alarz	ص	Diwani	ص	Nastaliq
ص	Al-Waleed	ص	Fairuz	ص	Omar
ص	Al-Qahira	ص	Firdawsi n.	ص	Rabee
ص	Al-Ruha	ص	Hadith	ص	Rouqai
ص	Amin	ص	Hijaz	ص	Shuweifat
ص	Annees	ص	Jarash	ص	Sidon
ص	Baalback	ص	Jiddah	ص	Silwan
ص	Baghdad	ص	Kufic	ص	Sirius
ص	Beirut	ص	Najaf	ص	Suraya
ص	Byblos	ص	Naskh	ص	Tadmur
ص	Dimashk	ص	Naskh cont.	ص	Thuluth

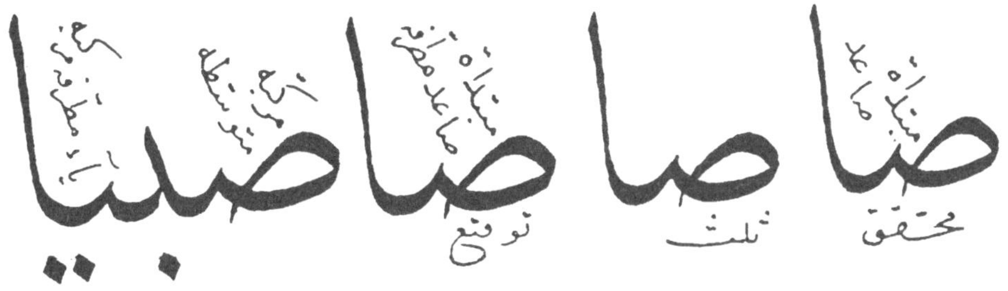

Sad is the fourteenth letter of the Arab alphabet and is lingual.

In the art of reciting the Qur'ān (*tajwīd*) it has the characteristics of sonority, elevation, occlusion, and softening and the antonymies of whistling, whispering, and atony.

It is the abbreviation of *ṣafḥat* (page) and *ṣafar*, the name of the second month in the Muslim lunar year.

It symbolizes sincerity and truth.

In Arabic, the term *ṣād* also means "copper."

In the "science of the secrets of letters" (*'ilm āl-Ḥurūf*) it represents number ninety and belongs to the element of water.

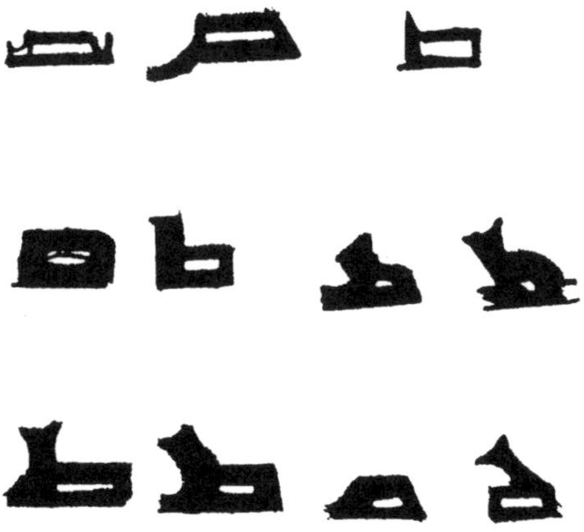

Above: Examples of some of the oldest versions of the letter *sad* in lapidary Kufic.

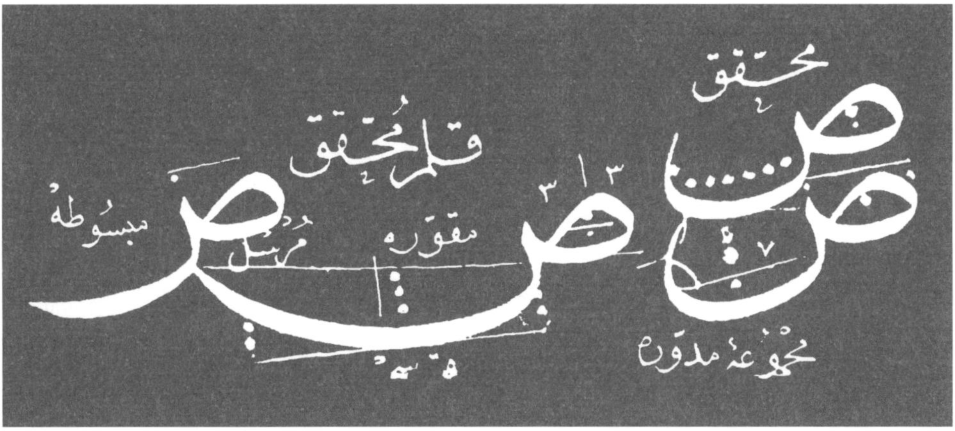

DAD

Name: **dad**.
Transliteration: **ḍ**.
Pronunciation:
emphatic **d**, similar
to that of **sad**.

ض

Final	Medial	Initial	Isolated
طض	طضو	ضو	ض

ض	Alarz	ض	Diwani	ض	Nastaliq
ض	Al-Waleed	ض	Fairuz	ض	Omar
ض	Al-Qahira	ض	Firdawsi n.	ض	Rabee
ض	Al-Ruha	ض	Hadith	ض	Rouqai
ض	Amin	ض	Hijaz	ض	Shuweifat
ض	Annees	ض	Jarash	ض	Sidon
ض	Baalback	ض	Jiddah	ض	Silwan
ض	Baghdad	ض	Kufic	ض	Sirius
ض	Beirut	ض	Najaf	ض	Suraya
ض	Byblos	ض	Naskh	ض	Tadmur
ض	Dimashk	ض	Naskh cont.	ض	Thuluth

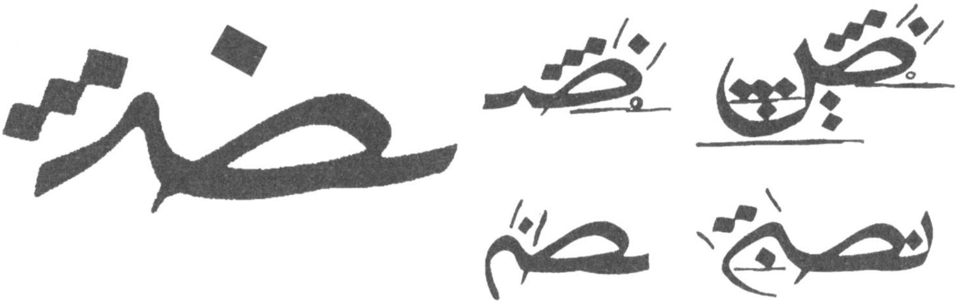

Dad is the fifteenth letter of the Arab alphabet and is subpalatal.

In the art of reciting the Qur'ān (*tajwīd*), the letter *dad* has the characteristics of sonority, elevation, occlusion, and softening and the antonymies of extension and atony.

It symbolizes "to disclose."

In the "science of the secrets of letters" (*'ilm āl-Ḥurūf*) it represents number eight hundred and belongs to the element of air.

Examples of some of the oldest versions of the letter *dad* in lapidary Kufic.

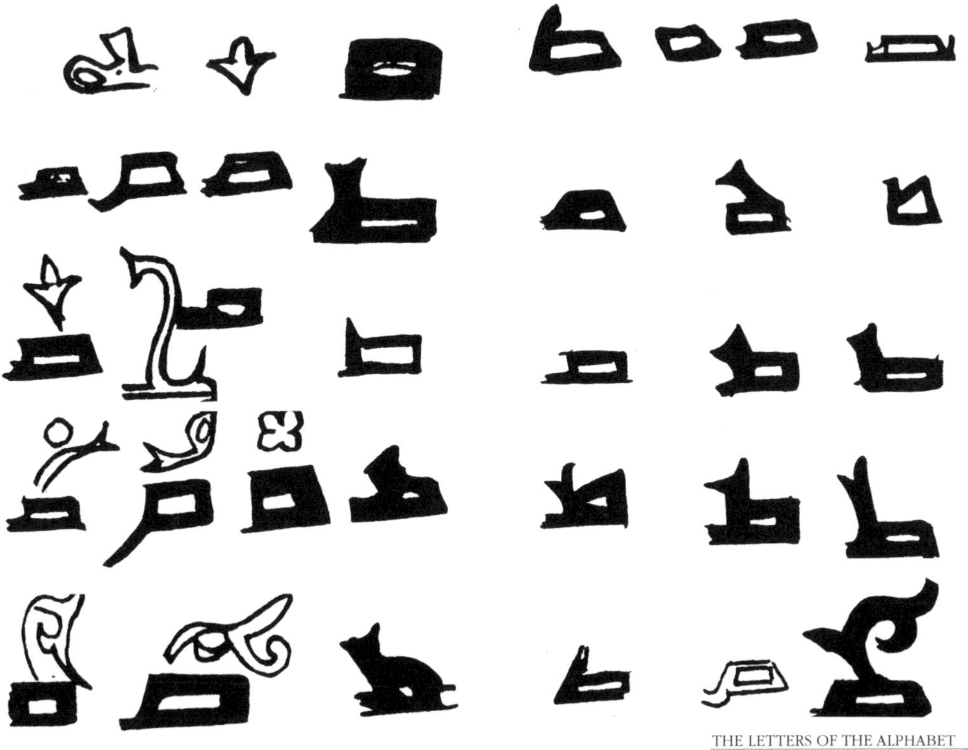

TA

ط

Name: **ta**.

Transliteration: **ṭ**.

Pronunciation: emphatic **t**, articulated like **sad** and **dad**.

Final	Medial	Initial	Isolated
بط	بطو	طو	ط

Characters

ط	Alarz	ط	Diwani	ط	Nastaliq
ط	Al-Waleed	ط	Fairuz	ط	Omar
ط	Al-Qahira	ط	Firdawsi n.	ط	Rabee
ط	Al-Ruha	ط	Hadith	ط	Rouqai
ط	Amin	ط	Hijaz	ط	Shuweifat
ط	Annees	ط	Jarash	ط	Sidon
ط	Baalback	ط	Jiddah	ط	Silwan
ط	Baghdad	ط	Kufic	ط	Sirius
ط	Beirut	ط	Najaf	ط	Suraya
ط	Byblos	ط	Naskh	ط	Tadmur
ط	Dimashk	ط	Naskh cont.	ط	Thuluth

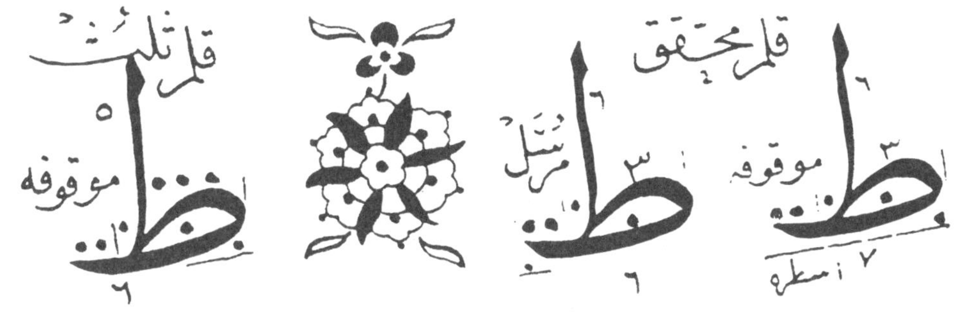

Ta is the sixteenth letter of the Arab alphabet and is prepalatal.

In the art of reciting the Qur'ān (*tajwīd*) it has the characteristics of sonority, elevation, occlusion, and softening and the antonymy of vibration.

It is the abbreviation of *qyrāṭ*, a unit of measurement.

In the esoteric texts of the Sufi masters this letter, taken in isolation, symbolizes divine holiness.

In the "science of the secrets of letters" (*'ilm āl-Ḥurūf*) it represents number nine and belongs to the element of fire.

Examples of some of the oldest versions of the letter *ta* in lapidary Kufic.

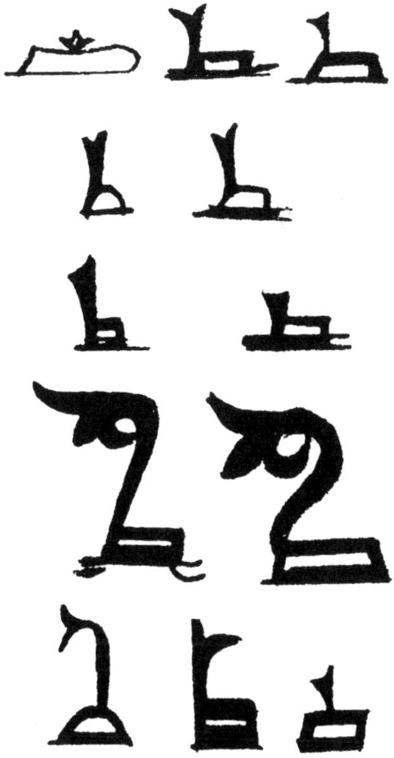

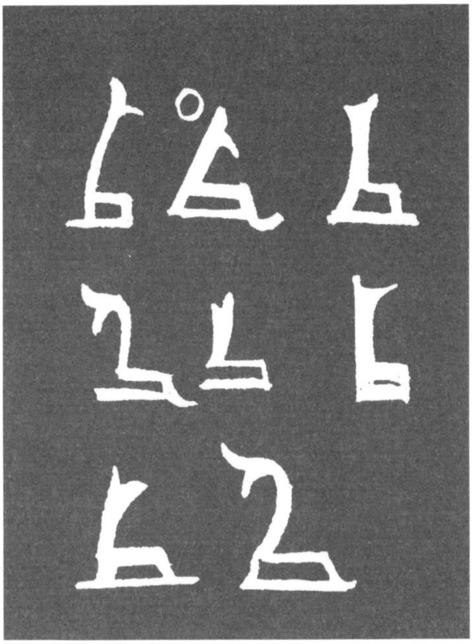

ZA

ظ

Name: **za**.
Transliteration: **ẓ**.
Pronunciation: emphatic **z**, articulated like **sad**, **dad** and **ta**.

بظ	Final	بظو	Medial	ظو	Initial	ظ	Isolated

Characters

ظ	Alarz	ظ	Diwani	ظ	Nastaliq
ظ	Al-Waleed	ظ	Fairuz	ظ	Omar
ظ	Al-Qahira	ظ	Firdawsi n.	ظ	Rabee
ظ	Al-Ruha	ظ	Hadith	ظ	Rouqai
ظ	Amin	ظ	Hijaz	ظ	Shuweifat
ظ	Annees	ظ	Jarash	ظ	Sidon
ظ	Baalback	ظ	Jiddah	ظ	Silwan
ظ	Baghdad	ظ	Kufic	ظ	Sirius
ظ	Beirut	ظ	Najaf	ظ	Suraya
ظ	Byblos	ظ	Naskh	ظ	Tadmur
ظ	Dimashk	ظ	Naskh cont.	ظ	Thuluth

Za is the seventeenth letter of the Arab alphabet and is gingival.

In the art of reciting the Qur'ān (*tajwīd)* it has the characteristics of sonority, elevation, occlusion, and softening and the antonymy of atony.

It symbolizes the epiphany or manifestation of God.

In the "science of the secrets of letters" (*'ilm āl-Ḥurūf*) it represents number nine hundred and belongs to the element of water, though in North Africa it is considered to belong to the element of air.

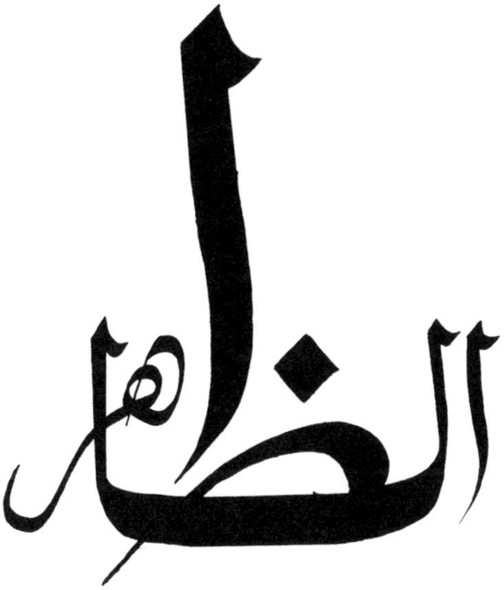

Above, right: The seventy-fifth name-attribute of God, *āl-Ẓāhir* (the Visible).

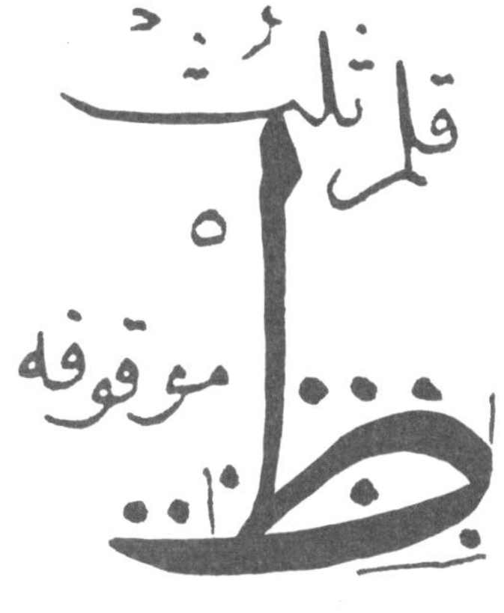

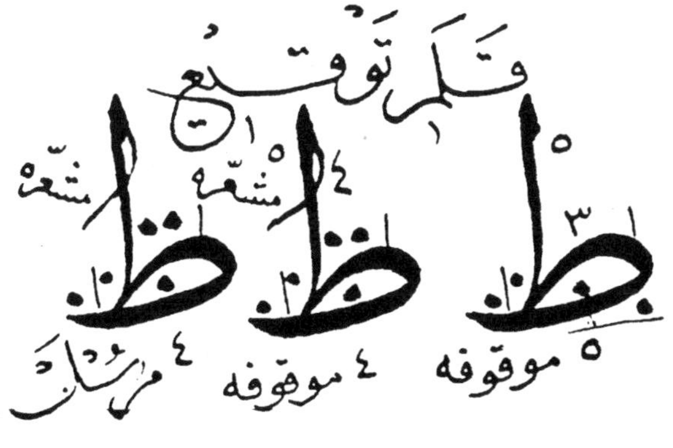

‘AYN

Name: **‘ayn**.

Transliteration: ‘. A strong, guttural sound.

ع

Final	Medial	Initial	Isolated
طع	طعو	عو	ع

ع	Alarz	ع	Diwani	ع	Nastaliq
ع	Al-Waleed	ع	Fairuz	ع	Omar
ع	Al-Qahira	ع	Firdawsi n.	ع	Rabee
ع	Al-Ruha	ع	Hadith	ع	Rouqai
ع	Amin	ع	Hijaz	ع	Shuweifat
ع	Annees	ع	Jarash	ع	Sidon
ع	Baalback	ع	Jiddah	ع	Silwan
ع	Baghdad	ع	Kufic	ع	Sirius
ع	Beirut	ع	Najaf	ع	Suraya
ع	Byblos	ع	Naskh	ع	Tadmur
ع	Dimashk	ع	Naskh cont.	ع	Thuluth

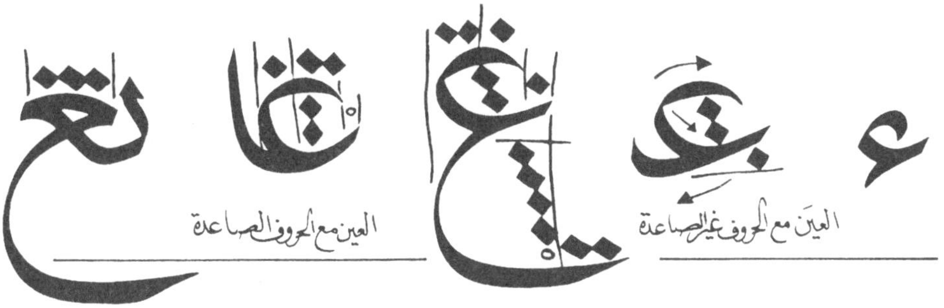

'Ayn is the eighteenth letter of the Arab alphabet and it is guttural.

In the art of reciting the Qur'ān (*tajwīd*) it has the characteristics of sonority, softening, and moderation and the antonymies of lowering and opening.

It is the abbreviation for *'adād* (number).

It symbolizes the source of intellect.

In the "science of the secrets of letters" (*'ilm āl-Ḥurūf*) it represents number seventy and belongs to the element of earth.

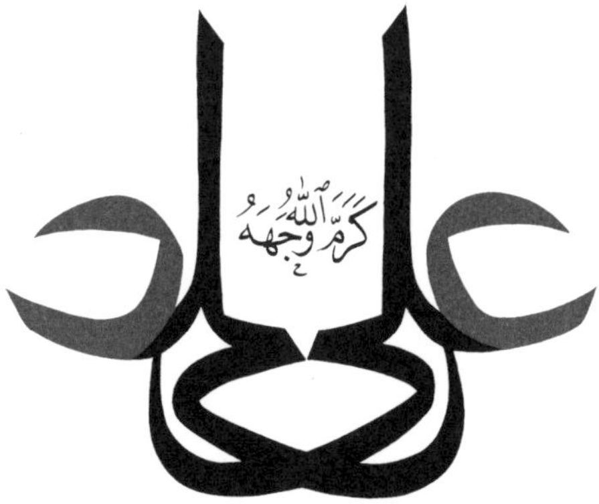

Above: The name of *'Ali* in specular calligraphy.

Below: Examples of some of the oldest versions of the letter *'ayn* in lapidary Kufic.

Left: The name of *'Ali*, son-in-law of the Prophet and the fourth "Righteous Caliph."

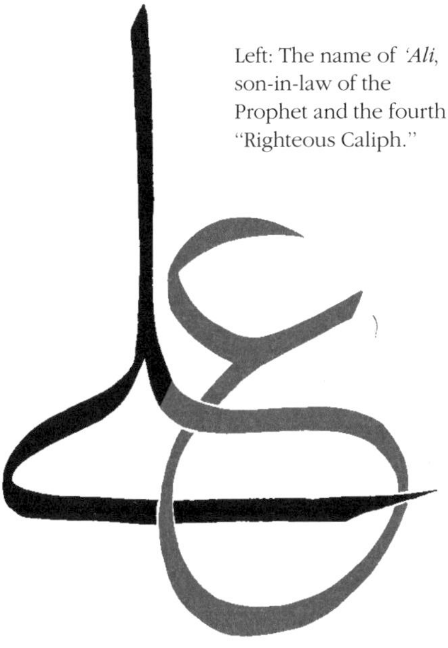

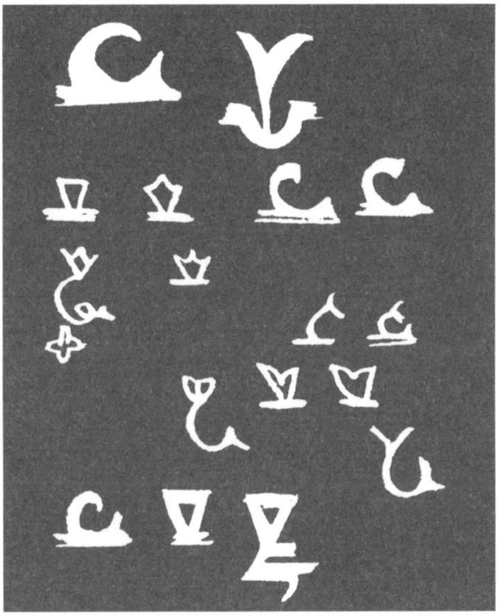

GHAIN

Name: **ghain**.
Transliteration: **gh**.
Pronunciation: a laryngeal-guttural **gr** similar to a gargling sound.

غ

Final	Medial	Initial	Isolated
طغ	طغو	غو	غ

Characters

غ	Alarz	ـغـ	Diwani	غ	Nastaliq
غ	Al-Waleed	ـغـ	Fairuz	غ	Omar
غ	Al-Qahira	ـغـ	Firdawsi n.	غ	Rabee
غ	Al-Ruha	ـغـ	Hadith	غ	Rouqai
غ	Amin	ـغـ	Hijaz	غ	Shuweifat
غ	Annees	ـغـ	Jarash	غ	Sidon
غ	Baalback	ـغـ	Jiddah	غ	Silwan
غ	Baghdad	ـغـ	Kufic	غ	Sirius
غ	Beirut	ـغـ	Najaf	غ	Suraya
غ	Byblos	ـغـ	Naskh	غ	Tadmur
غ	Dimashk	ـغـ	Naskh cont.	غ	Thuluth

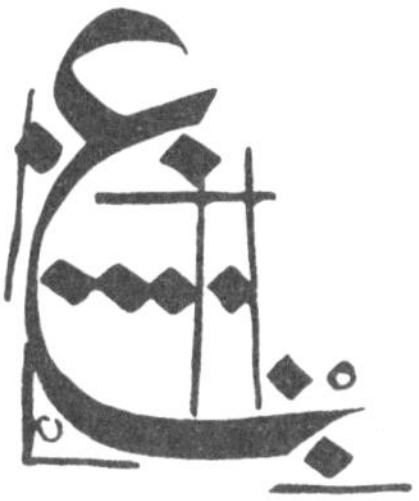
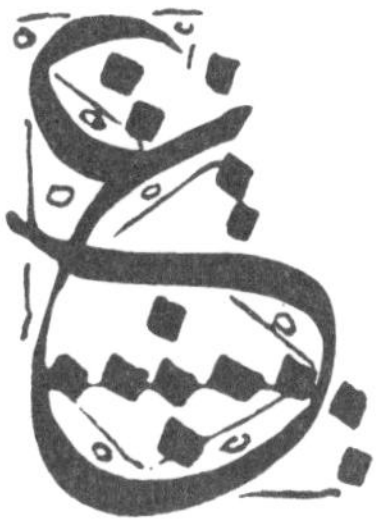
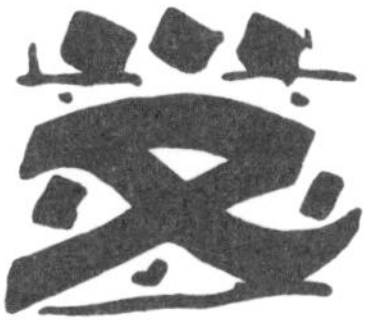
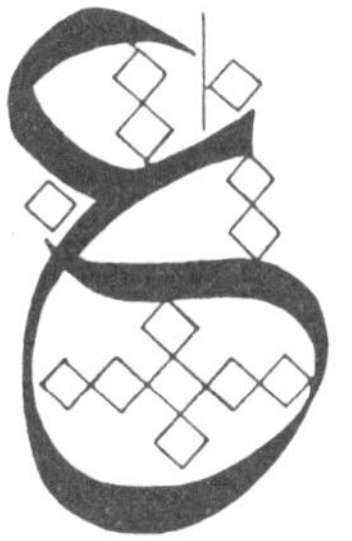

Ghain is the nineteenth letter of the Arab alphabet and it is guttural.

In the art of reciting the Qur'ān (*tajwīd*) it has the characteristics of sonority, elevation, and softening and the antonymies of opening and atony.

It symbolizes total mystery.

In the "science of the secrets of letters" (*'ilm āl-Ḥurūf*) it represents number one hundred and belongs to the element of earth, while in North Africa it is believed to belong to the element of water.

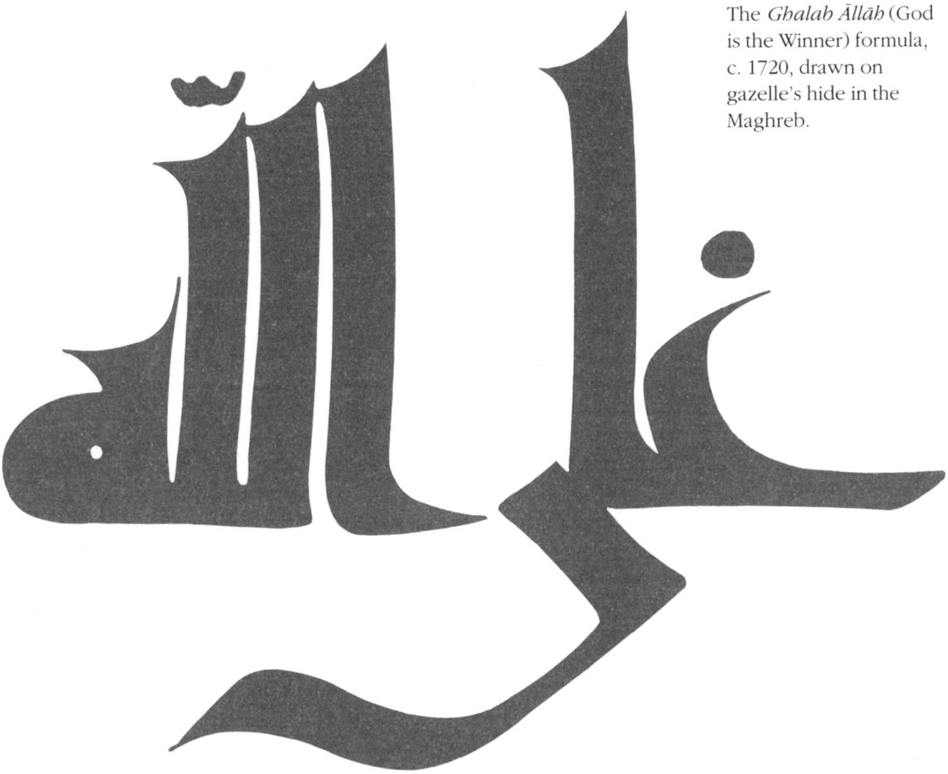

The *Ghalab Āllāh* (God is the Winner) formula, c. 1720, drawn on gazelle's hide in the Maghreb.

FA

ف

Name: **fa**.
Transliteration: **f** (written with a dot underneath in North Africa).
Pronunciation: **f**, as in **f**ool.

Final	Medial	Initial	Isolated
بف	بفو	فو	ف

Characters

ف	Alarz	ف	Diwani	ف	Nastaliq
ف	Al-Waleed	ف	Fairuz	ف	Omar
ف	Al-Qahira	ف	Firdawsi n.	ف	Rabee
ف	Al-Ruha	ف	Hadith	ف	Rouqai
ف	Amin	ف	Hijaz	ف	Shuweifat
ف	Annees	ف	Jarash	ف	Sidon
ف	Baalback	ف	Jiddah	ف	Silwan
ف	Baghdad	ف	Kufic	ف	Sirius
ف	Beirut	ف	Najaf	ف	Suraya
ف	Byblos	ف	Naskh	ف	Tadmur
ف	Dimashk	ف	Naskh cont.	ف	Thuluth

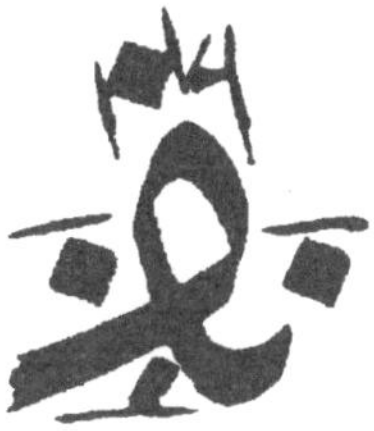

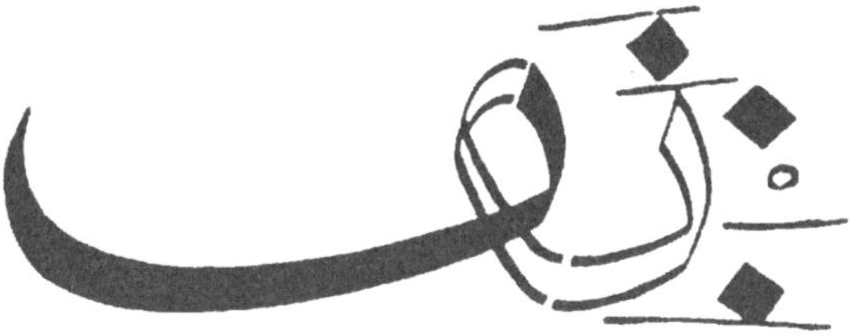

Fa is the twentieth letter of the Arab alphabet; it is an unvoiced, fricative, labio-dental consonant (*rikhwa shafawiyya mahmūsa*).

In the art of reciting the Qur'ān (*tajwīd*) the letter *fa* has no characteristics and its antonymies are whispering, atony, lowering, opening, and volubility.

It serves as the abbreviation for *faddān*, a unit of area measurement equal to 45,217.776 square feet (4,200.833 sq. m).

It symbolizes the tongue.

In the "science of the secrets of letters" (*'ilm āl-Ḥurūf*) it represents number eighty and belongs to the element of fire.

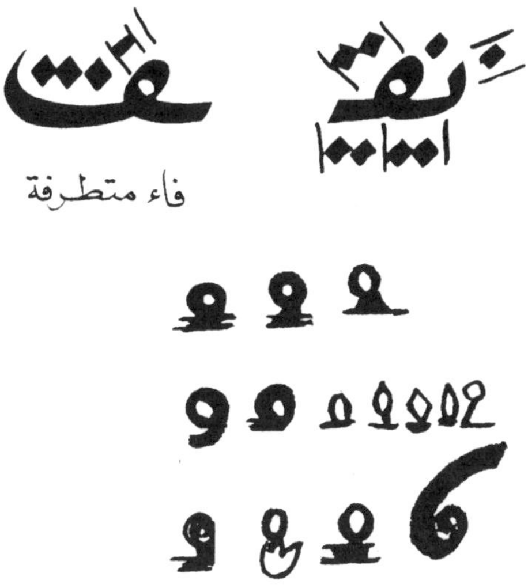

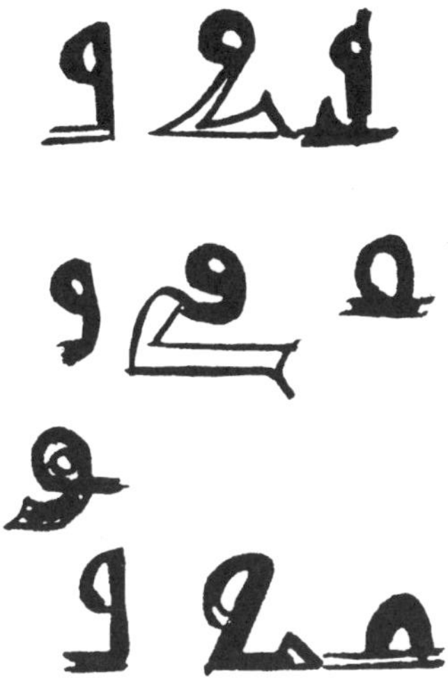

Above and left: Examples of some of the oldest versions of the letter *fa* in lapidary Kufic.

Below: The letter *fa* from a *maghribī* Qur'ān in monumental Kufic of 1023.

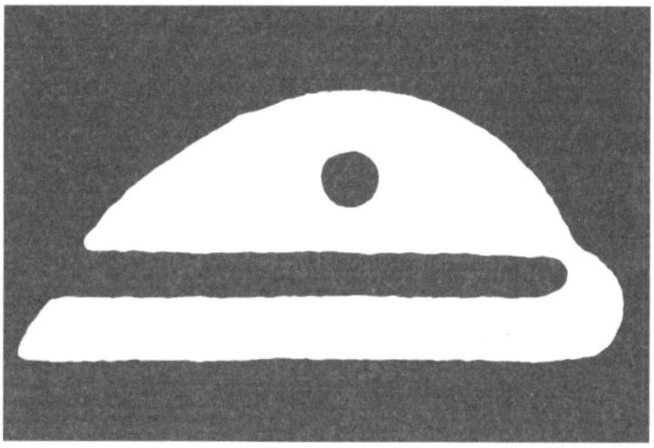

QAF

Name: **qaf**.

Transliteration: **q** (written with only one dot above in North Africa).

Pronunciation: a **k** sound from the back of the throat.

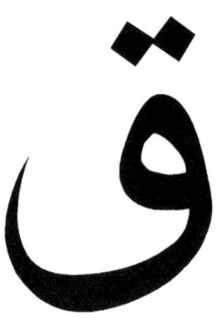

ق

Final	Medial	Initial	Isolated
بق	بقو	قو	ق

ق	Alarz	ق	Diwani	ق	Nastaliq
ق	Al-Waleed	ق	Fairuz	ق	Omar
ق	Al-Qahira	ق	Firdawsi n.	ق	Rabee
ق	Al-Ruha	ق	Hadith	ق	Rouqai
ق	Amin	ق	Hijaz	ق	Shuweifat
ق	Annees	ق	Jarash	ق	Sidon
ق	Baalback	ق	Jiddah	ق	Silwan
ق	Baghdad	ق	Kufic	ق	Sirius
ق	Beirut	ق	Najaf	ق	Suraya
ق	Byblos	ق	Naskh	ق	Tadmur
ق	Dimashk	ق	Naskh cont.	ق	Thuluth

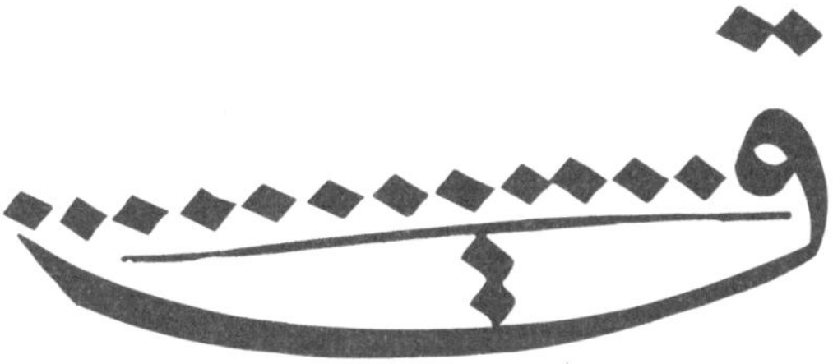

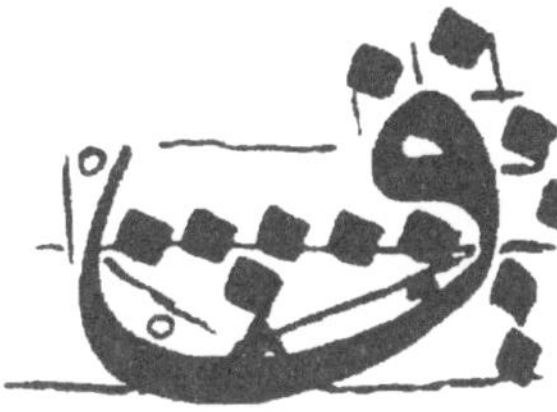

Qaf is the twenty-first letter of the Arab alphabet and it is uvular.

In the art of reciting the Qur'ān (*tajwīd*) it has the characteristics of sonority, elevation, softening, and tonicity and the antonymy of opening.

It serves as the abbreviation for *daqyqat* (minute) or *daqā'iqu* (minutes). *Qaf* is also the name of a legendary mountain.

This is a special letter, since it is the title of the fiftieth sura of the Qur'ān, whose opening verse reads as follows: "Qaf. By the majestic Qur'ān!" In this respect, we note that there are twenty-nine suras that begin with abbreviations (*fawātiḥ Ḥurūf muqatta'a*), composed of either just one letter or groups of from two to five letters. A total of fourteen letters are used, or half of the Arab alphabet: *a, ḥ, r, s, ṣ, t, ', q, k, l, m, n, h, y*. Sometimes the Prophet invoked God by uttering these two phrases: "Oh ka-ḥa-ya-'ain-sād" or "Oh ḥā-mīm-'ayn-sīn-qāf." Some of these letters grouped together give the word *alrḥmn* (*al-Raḥmān*: the Merciful). Commentators have sought many explanations (twelve, according to *Tha'ālibī*, 1:3), though none are totally valid nor satisfactory. Possibly they are initials, abbreviations, clarifying expressions, unknown names or attributes of God, symbols of the Ineffable Names, or names of the Qur'ān. Or maybe they are oaths, formulas of praise, or names of the suras. Some exegetes believe that they might be the initials of the Prophet's scribes, who collected the suras. Since the Qur'ān is recited by singing it psalm-like (*tajwīd*), some see in these letters the rules of psalmody, or kind of psalmody reading key. Finally, it is said: "Every book has its mystery, and the mystery of the Qur'ān is in its initials."

In the "science of the secrets of letters" (*'ilm āl-Ḥurūf*) this letter represents number one hundred and belongs to the element of water.

The formula *Qul āmantu bi-Llāhi* . . . which begins a saying of the Prophet. Drawn in *thuluth* calligraphy in 1924 by Muhyi al-Din Nevevi. Istanbul.

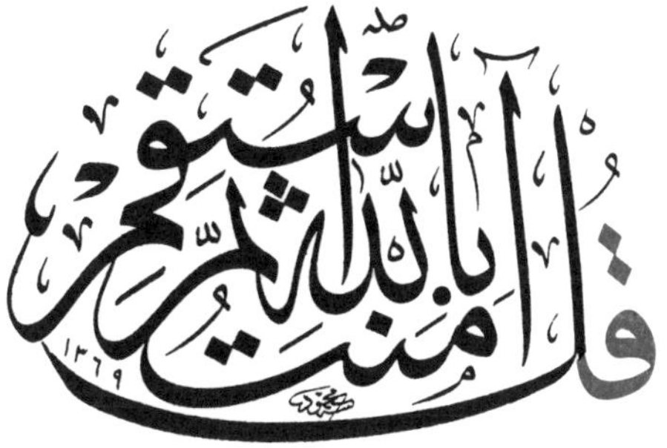

KAF

Name: **kaf**.
Transliteration: **k**.
Pronunciation: **k**, as in **k**itten.

ك

Final	Medial	Initial	Isolated
بك	بكو	كو	ك

ك	Alarz
ك	Al-Waleed
ك	Al-Qahira
ك	Al-Ruha
ك	Amin
ك	Annees
ك	Baalback
ك	Baghdad
ك	Beirut
ك	Byblos
ك	Dimashk
ك	Diwani
ك	Fairuz
ك	Firdawsi n.
ك	Hadith
ك	Hijaz
ك	Jarash
ك	Jiddah
ك	Kufic
ك	Najaf
ك	Naskh
ك	Naskh cont.
ك	Nastaliq
ك	Omar
ك	Rabee
ك	Rouqai
ك	Shuweifat
ك	Sidon
ك	Silwan
ك	Sirius
ك	Suraya
ك	Tadmur
ك	Thuluth

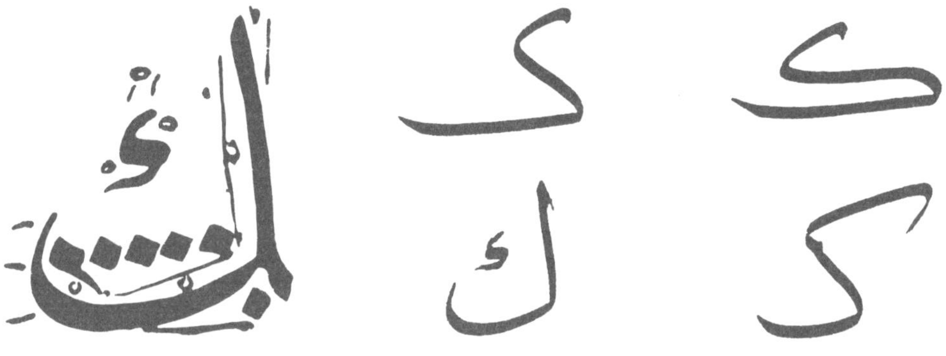

Kaf is the twenty-second letter of the Arabic alphabet and is uvular.

In the art of reciting the Qur'ān (*tajwīd*) it has the characteristics of softening and tonicity and the antonymies of whispering and lowering.

K is the abbreviation of *kīlūmitr* (kilometer). In Syria, Lebanon, Jordan, and Iraq, it is also the abbreviation of *kānūn āl-Āuwal* (the month of December) and of *kānūn āl-Thāniy* (January). In grammar, *ka* is a preposition indicating how, how much, inasmuch as, in the capacity of (*ka ālāuwali*: as before, as in the beginning; *ka al'ādāti*: as usual, as customary).

It symbolizes the verb of creation, *kun* (let there be . . .).

In the "science of the secrets of letters" (*'ilm āl-Ḥurūf*) it represents number twenty and belongs to the element water.

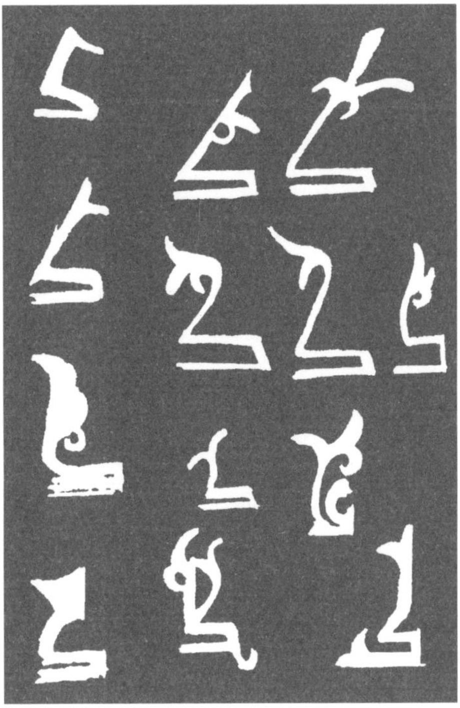

Above: Examples of some of the oldest versions of the letter *kaf* in lapidary Kufic.

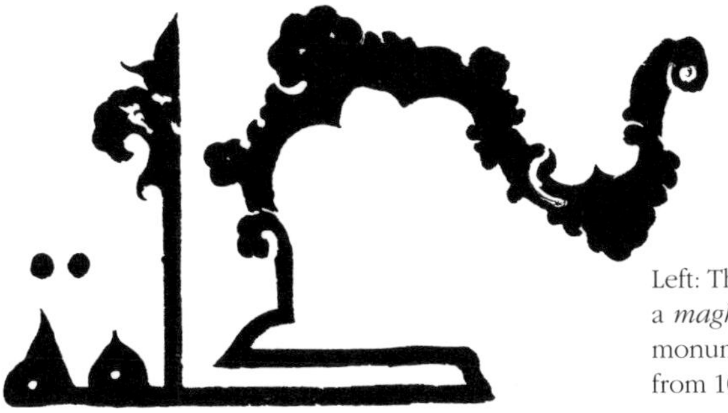

Left: The letter *kaf* from a *maghribī* Qur'ān in monumental Kufic, from 1023.

LAM

Name: **lam**.

Transliteration: **l**.

Pronunciation: **l**, as in **l**ove.

ل

Final	Medial	Initial	Isolated
بل	بلو	لو	ل

Characters

ل	Alarz	ل	Diwani	ل	Nastaliq
ل	Al-Waleed	ل	Fairuz	ل	Omar
ل	Al-Qahira	ل	Firdawsi n.	ل	Rabee
ل	Al-Ruha	ل	Hadith	ل	Rouqai
ل	Amin	ل	Hijaz	ل	Shuweifat
ل	Annees	ل	Jarash	ل	Sidon
ل	Baalback	ل	Jiddah	ل	Silwan
ل	Baghdad	ل	Kufic	ل	Sirius
ل	Beirut	ل	Najaf	ل	Suraya
ل	Byblos	ل	Naskh	ل	Tadmur
ل	Dimashk	ل	Naskh cont.	ل	Thuluth

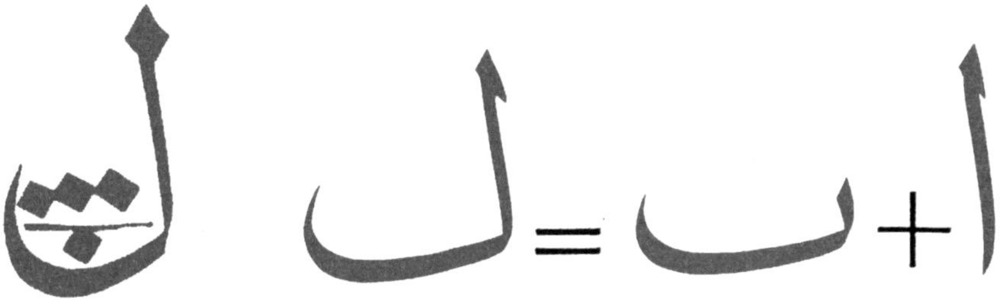

Lam is the twenty-third letter of the Arabic alphabet and is lingual.

In the art of reciting the Qur'ān (*tajwīd*) it has the characteristics of sonority and moderation and the antonymies of lowering and volubility.

L is the abbreviation of *shawwāl*, the tenth month of the Muslim lunar year.

In Arabic, *Lam* is also a person's name.

Grammatically, it is a rich particle. *La* is an adverb used as a prefix, often for the purpose of reinforcing *īnna*, to introduce the predicate, with the meaning of "certainly," "truly," "surely."

La is also the correlative conjunction of *law* and *lawlā*. It is an oath particle, with the meaning of "I swear in the name of." Placed after *ya* it signifies wonder, and its function is similar to that of the exclamation point in English, which does not exist in Arabic.

This letter is vocalized as *la* with the second- and third-person personal pronouns and *li* in the other cases, where it means "to," "for," "of." It signifies the possessive genitive, in particular the author of a text, but also: in favor of, to the benefit of, for the purpose of, on account of. After an infinitive, it introduces the direct object.

Here are some examples: "Īnna rabbiy lasaml'u āl-Du'ā' " (My Lord is so alert to anyone's appeal! Qur'ān 14:39); "law kunta taf'alu hadhā lakāna ānfa'a" (it would have been more useful if you had done such-and-such); "la'amruka" ([I swear] on your life); "yā lal'ajabi" (how wonderful!); "yā lahu'amalin ḥasanin" (what a lovely deed!).

It symbolizes perfect understanding.

In the "science of the secrets of letters" (*'ilm āl-Ḥurūf*) it represents number thirty and belongs to the element earth.

Examples of some of the oldest versions of the letter *lam* in lapidary Kufic.

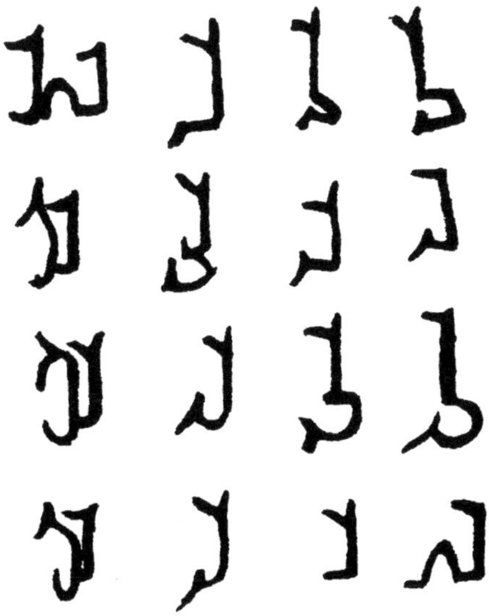

MIM

Name: **mim**.

Transliteration: **m**.

Pronunciation: **m**, as in **m**ask.

م

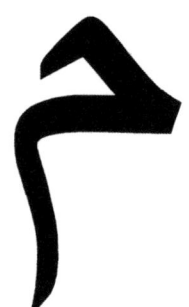

Final	Medial	Initial	Isolated
بم	بمو	مو	م

Characters

م	Alarz	م	Diwani	م	Nastaliq
م	Al-Waleed	م	Fairuz	م	Omar
م	Al-Qahira	م	Firdawsi n.	م	Rabee
م	Al-Ruha	م	Hadith	م	Rouqai
م	Amin	م	Hijaz	م	Shuweifat
م	Annees	م	Jarash	م	Sidon
م	Baalback	م	Jiddah	م	Silwan
م	Baghdad	م	Kufic	م	Sirius
م	Beirut	م	Najaf	م	Suraya
م	Byblos	م	Naskh	م	Tadmur
م	Dimashk	م	Naskh cont.	م	Thuluth

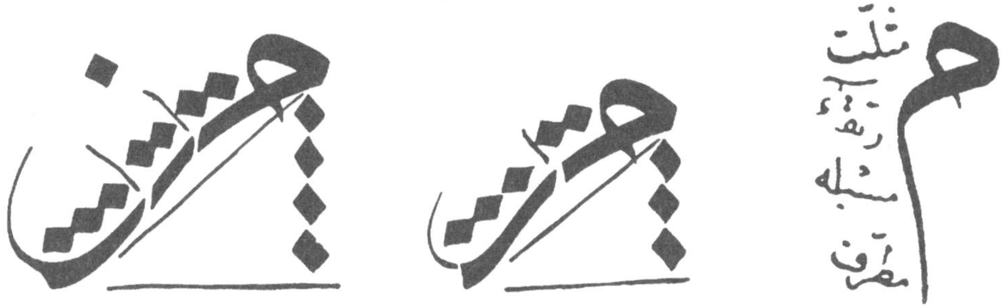

Mim is the twenty-fourth letter of the Arabic alphabet and is labial.

In the art of reciting the Qur'ān (*tajwīd*) it has the characteristics of sonority and moderation and the antonymies of lowering, opening, nasalization, and volubility.

M is the abbreviation of *muḥarram,* a month in the Muslim lunar year, and of *millym,* a coin worth one thousand Egyptian lira; of *tamma* ("the end"—said of a book or a thing); of *sanat mylādyyat,* a year in the Christian age. We also find this letter in the acronym *sh.m.m.,* which stands for *maḥdwdat* (limited) *maswwlyyt* (liability), which are parts of the expressions "limited liability company" and "joint stock company."

Grammatically, *ma* has the function of *mā* after prepositions, and it means "what?" (*īlā ma*: toward where? from where? for what purpose?; *bima*: with what?; *ḥattā ma*: until where?, until when?, up to what point?; *lima*: why?, for what?).

In "the science of the secrets of letters" (*'ilm āl-Ḥurūf*) it represents number forty and belongs to the element of fire. For the Hurufi esoteric sect it symbolizes the duality power of matter—power of God.

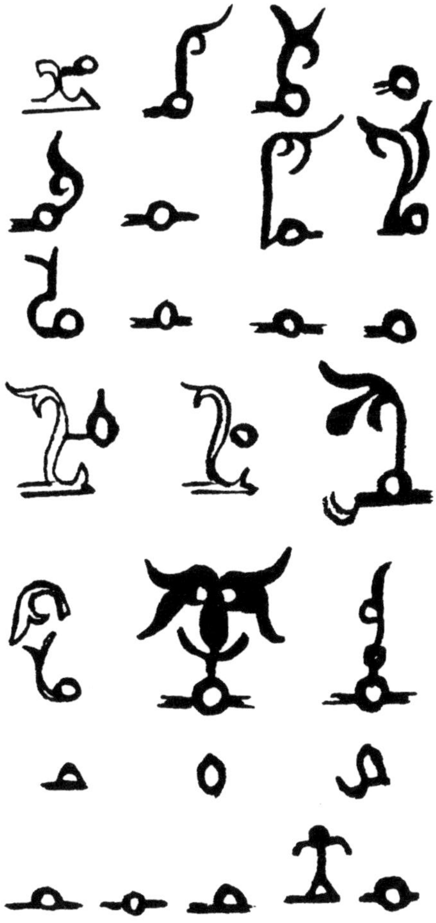

Examples of some of the oldest versions of the letter *mim* in lapidary Kufic.

NUN

Name: **nun**.
Transliteration: **n**.
Pronunciation: **n**, as in **n**ever.

ن

Final	Medial	Initial	Isolated
طن	طنو	نو	ن

ن	Alarz	ن	Diwani	ن	Nastaliq
ن	Al-Waleed	ن	Fairuz	ن	Omar
ن	Al-Qahira	ن	Firdawsi n.	ن	Rabee
ن	Al-Ruha	ن	Hadith	ن	Rouqai
ن	Amin	ن	Hijaz	ن	Shuweifat
ن	Annees	ن	Jarash	ن	Sidon
ن	Baalback	ن	Jiddah	ن	Silwan
ن	Baghdad	ن	Kufic	ن	Sirius
ن	Beirut	ن	Najaf	ن	Suraya
ن	Byblos	ن	Naskh	ن	Tadmur
ن	Dimashk	نْ	Naskh cont.	ن	Thuluth

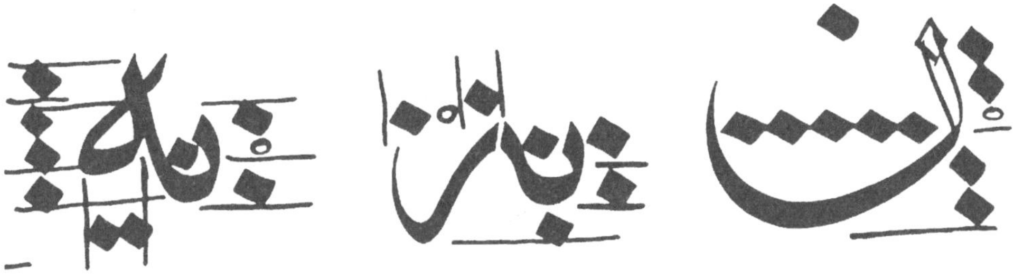

Nun is the twenty-fifth letter of the Arab alphabet and it is lingual.

In the art of reciting the Qur'ān *(tajwīd)* it has the characteristics of sonority and moderation and the antonymies of lowering, opening, nasalization, and volubility.

N is the abbreviation of *ramadan*, the name of the Muslim lunar month when ritual fasting is observed.

Nun also means "whale," therefore the prophet Jonah is also called *dḥu āl-Nūn* (he of the whale). Gramatically, *nun* can be used to reinforce; in that case, it is called *nūn āl-Ta'kid*; and *tanūyn* refers to nunnation, which is the indeterminate form of a noun or an adjective formed by adding a final *nun*. It corresponds to the indeterminate English articles a, an, some. Finally, a *nun* rhyme, or something having the shape of a *nun*—a crescent or half-moon—is called *nūniyya*.

In the "science of the secrets of letters" (*'ilm āl-Ḥurūf*) it represents number twenty-five and belongs to the element of air.

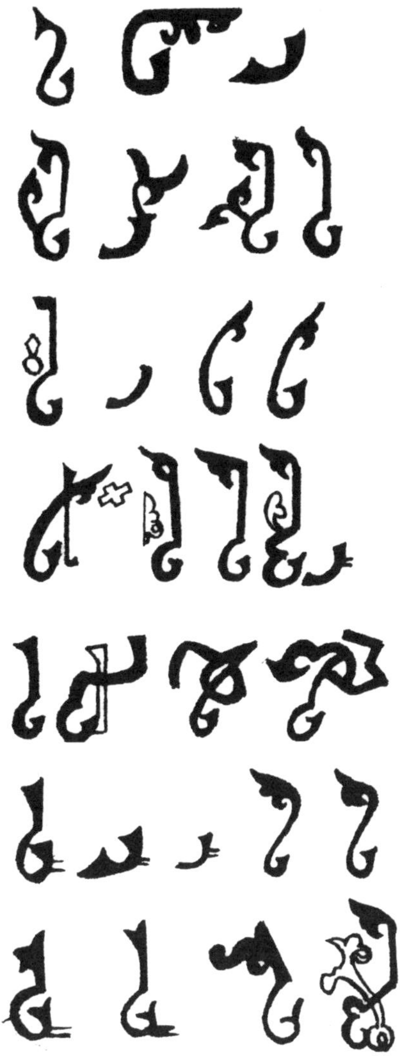

Examples of some of the oldest versions of the letter *nun* in lapidary Kufic.

HA

Name: **ha**.
Transliteration: **h**.
Pronunciation: an almost silent **h**, as in **h**appy.

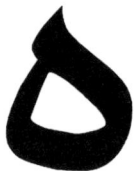

ه

Final	Medial	Initial	Isolated
طه	طهو	هو	ه

Characters

ه	Alarz	ه	Diwani	ه	Nastaliq
ه	Al-Waleed	ه	Fairuz	ه	Omar
ه	Al-Qahira	ه	Firdawsi n.	ه	Rabee
ه	Al-Ruha	ه	Hadith	ه	Rouqai
ه	Amin	ه	Hijaz	ه	Shuweifat
ه	Annees	ه	Jarash	ه	Sidon
ه	Baalback	ه	Jiddah	ه	Silwan
ه	Baghdad	ه	Kufic	ه	Sirius
ه	Beirut	ه	Najaf	ه	Suraya
ه	Byblos	ه	Naskh	ه	Tadmur
ه	Dimashk	ه	Naskh cont.	ه	Thuluth

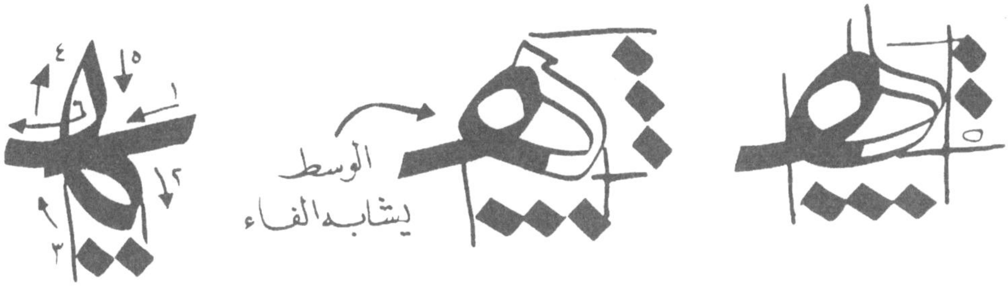

Ha is the twenty-sixth letter of the Arab alphabet, and is guttural.

In the Arabic system of pronunciation it is a glottal, unvoiced spirant consonant: *rikhwa mahmūsa* or *aqṣā āl-Ḥalq*.

In the art of reciting the Qur'ān (*tajwīd*) it has the characteristic of softening and the antonymies of whispering, lowering, opening, and atony.

This letter is the abbreviation of *sanat hijryyat*: the year of Hegira. It is the symbol of orientation to God.

In the "science of the secrets of letters" (*'ilm āl-Ḥurūf*) it represents number five, just as in the Syriac and Canaanite alphabets, and belongs to the element of fire.

Below: The term *Hw* (He) in specular calligraphy, the principal Sufi script.

Right: Examples of some of the oldest versions of the letter *ha* in lapidary Kufic.

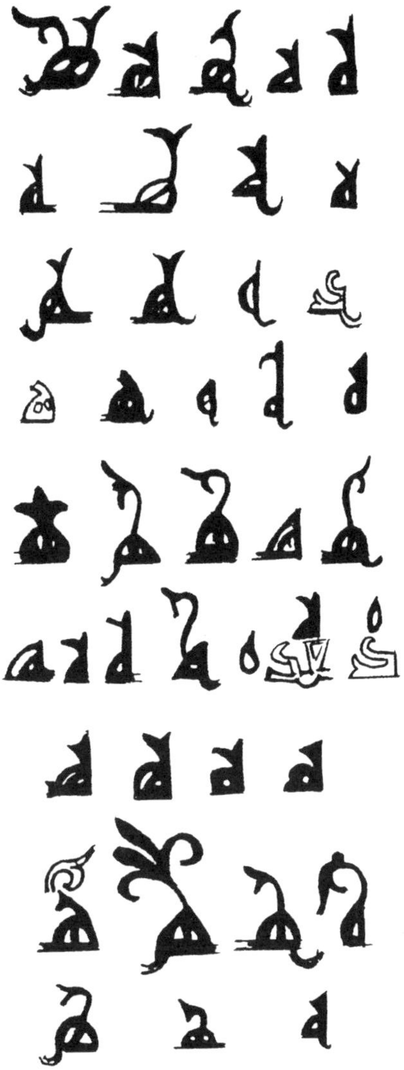

WAW

Name: **waw**.
Transliteration: **w**.
Pronunciation: long, semi-vocalic, as in **w**hile.

و

Final	Medial	Initial	Isolated
طو			و

Characters

و	Alarz	و	Diwani	و	Nastaliq
و	Al-Waleed	و	Fairuz	و	Omar
و	Al-Qahira	و	Firdawsi n.	و	Rabee
و	Al-Ruha	و	Hadith	و	Rouqai
و	Amin	و	Hijaz	و	Shuweifat
و	Annees	و	Jarash	و	Sidon
و	Baalback	و	Jiddah	و	Silwan
و	Baghdad	و	Kufic	و	Sirius
و	Beirut	و	Najaf	و	Suraya
و	Byblos	و	Naskh	و	Tadmur
و	Dimashk	وَ	Naskh cont.	و	Thuluth

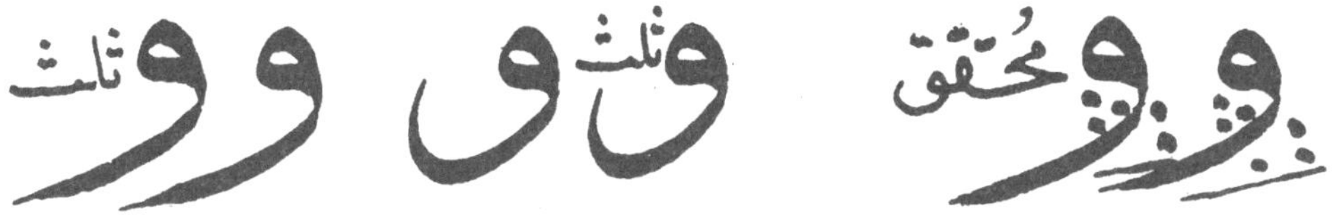

Waw is the twenty-seventh letter of the Arab alphabet and is labial.

In the art of reciting the Qur'ān (*tajwīd*) it has the characteristics of sonority and softening and the antonymies of lowering, opening, atony, softness, and concealment.

Wa is a conjunction; it means "plus"; it is also an adversative conjunction meaning "instead" and a temporal conjunction meaning "meanwhile, while." When followed by a genitive, it introduces an oath: by, in the name of (*wa Āllāh*: by God!, in God's name!) or gives an exclamative tone to a phrase: so much!, so many!, as in *wa kāsin sharibtu* (I drank so many glasses!). Followed by an accusative, it expresses a relationship of company, contemporaneity, concomitance, as in *dhahaba wa iyyāhu* (he left together with him).

For the Sufi masters, this letter symbolizes the mystical promise of total assent to God (*wujūd mutlaq*).

In the "science of the secrets of letters" (*'ilm āl-Ḥurūf*) it represents number six and belongs to the element of air.

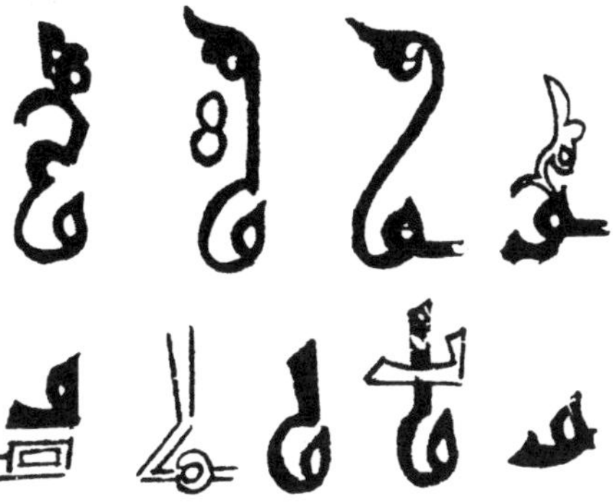

Below: Decoration consisting of the letter *waw* highlighted six times.

Above: Examples of some of the oldest versions of the letter *waw* in lapidary Kufic.

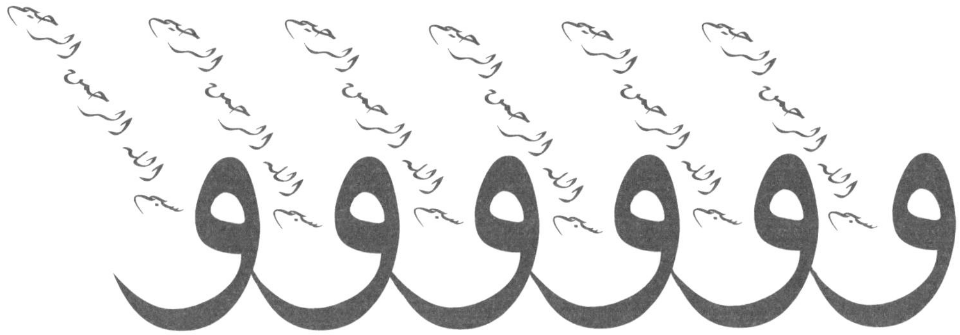

COMPOSITIONS CONTAINING THE LETTER *WAW*

1

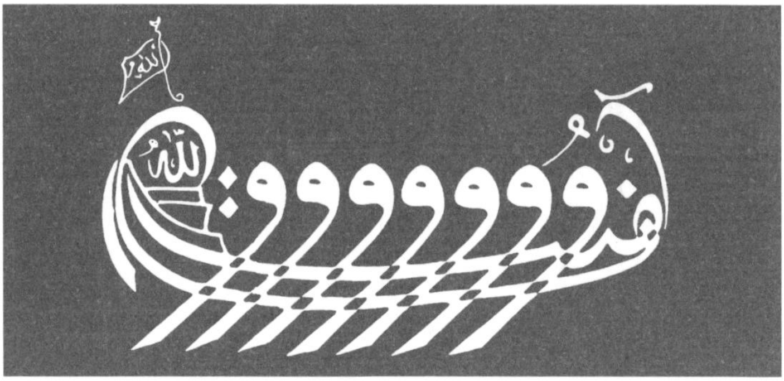

2

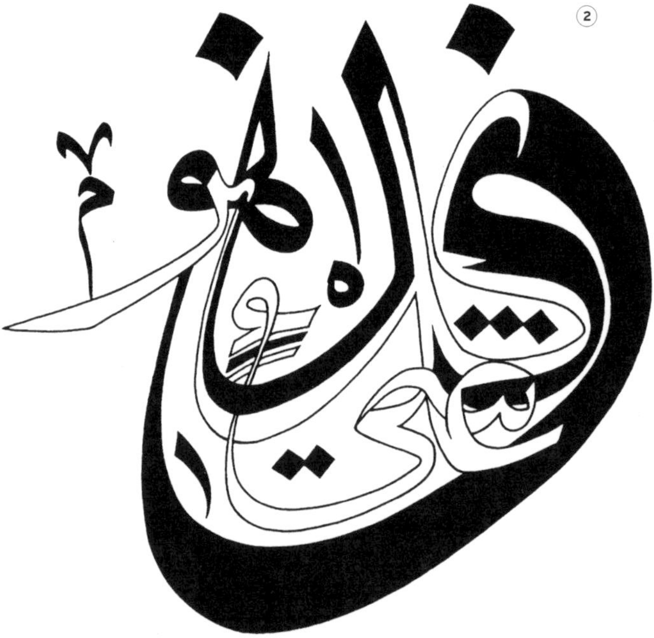

1. Design in the shape of a boat in which the letter *waw* used in the phrase *Hū, Ālläh* (God, Himself) is highlighted. From the Mehmet Shevki Efendi (1829–1887) school in Istanbul.

2. From a drawing by Hassan Massoudi: elements of the mural decoration in the Ulu Jami'. Bursa, Turkey.

3. Boat-shaped composition by Abd al-Kader. Tunisia, twentieth century.

4. Page from a text in which the letter *waw* is emphasized by lengthening it. Calligraphy by Hassan Massoudi.

3

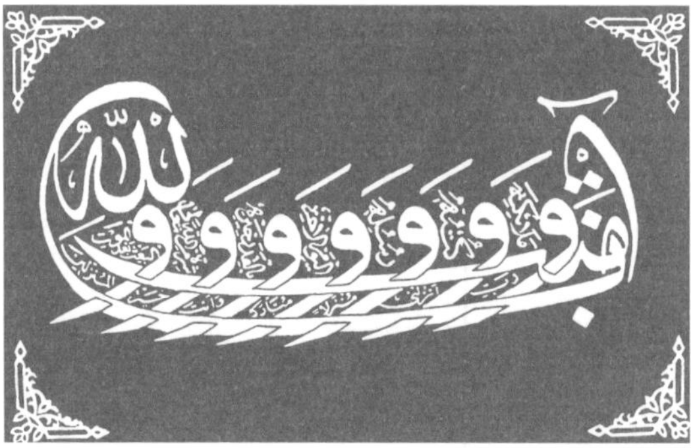

4

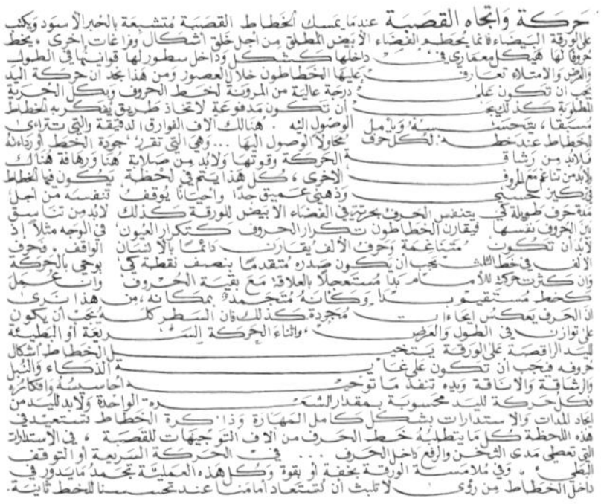

5

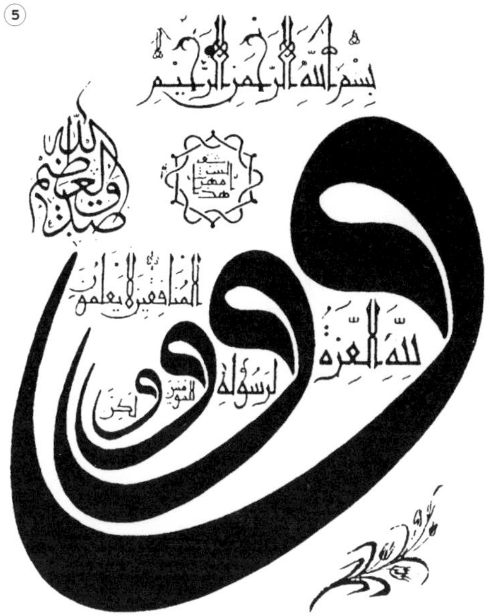

6

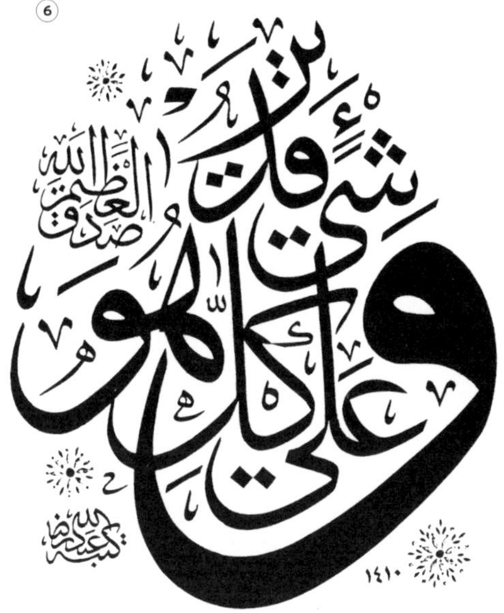

7

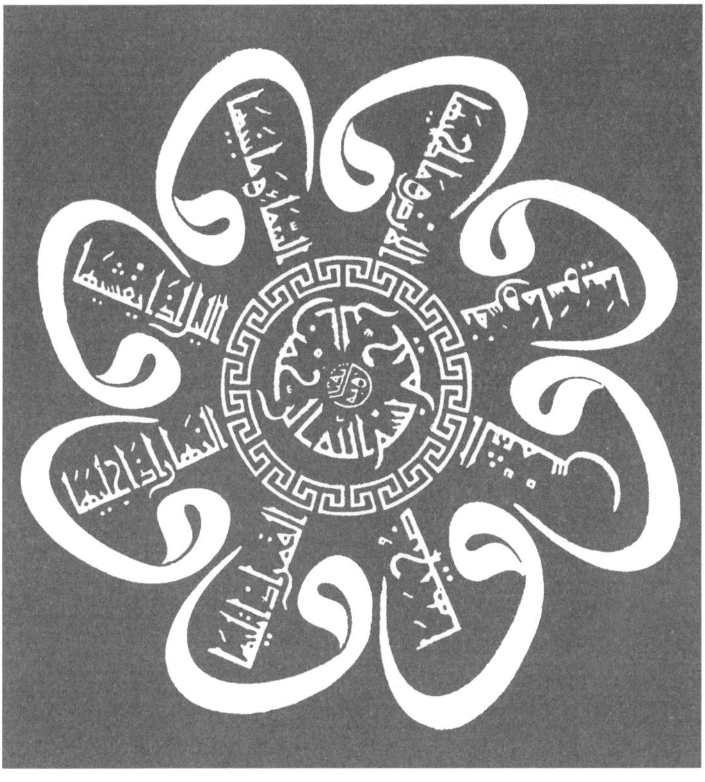

5. Excerpt from the eighth verse of the sixty-third sura with four emphasized *waws*: "*Wa* Lillāh āl-izzat *wa* liraswlihi *wa* lilmwminīn *wa* lākinna āl-Munāfiqīna lā īa'lamwn" ("Yet influence belongs to God, his messenger, and believers, even though hypocrites do not realize it"). Ulu Jami', Bursa, Turkey.

6. The phrase *Ṣadaq Āllāh* (The Word of God) with a verse from the Qur'ān, drawn on a wall of the Ulu Jami', Bursa, Turkey, by Mehmet Shefik Bey (1819–1879).

7. Beginning of the "Sun Verse" (ninety-first sura): The first seven verses each begin with the letter *waw*. Mural fresco from the Ulu Jami', Bursa, Turkey, built between 1379 and 1421; thanks to its numerous murals and paintings it is considered a museum of Turkish calligraphy.

YA

Name: **ya**.
Transliteration: **y**.
Pronunciation: long, semi-vocalic, as in **y**ell, br**ee**ze.

ي

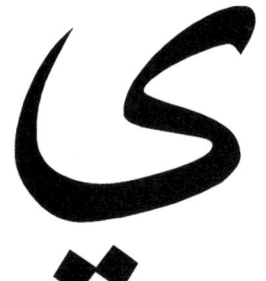

Final	Medial	Initial	Isolated
يو	طيو	يو	ي

Characters

ي	Alarz	ي	Diwani	ي	Nastaliq
ي	Al-Waleed	ي	Fairuz	ي	Omar
ي	Al-Qahira	ي	Firdawsi n.	ي	Rabee
ي	Al-Ruha	ي	Hadith	ي	Rouqai
ي	Amin	ي	Hijaz	ي	Shuweifat
ي	Annees	ي	Jarash	ي	Sidon
ي	Baalback	ي	Jiddah	ي	Silwan
ي	Baghdad	ي	Kufic	ي	Sirius
ي	Beirut	ي	Najaf	ي	Suraya
ي	Byblos	ي	Naskh	ي	Tadmur
ي	Dimashk	ي	Naskh cont.	ي	Thuluth

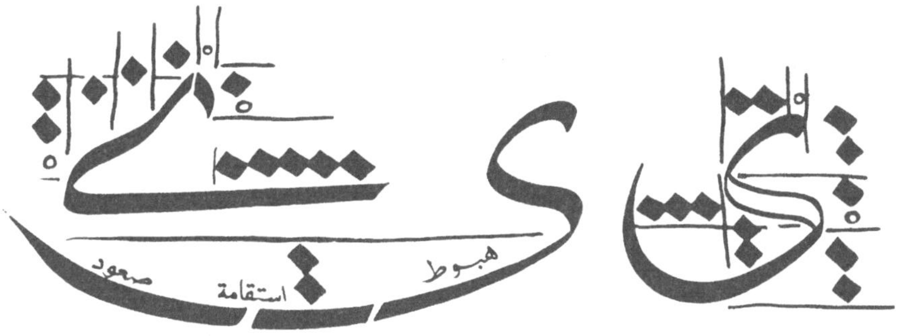

Ya is the twenty-eighth letter of the Arabic alphabet and it is subpalatal.

In the art of reciting the Qur'ān (*tajwīd*) it has the characteristics of sonority and softening and the antonymies of lowering, opening, softness, concealment, and atony.

It symbolizes God's help.

In the "science of the secrets of letters" (*'ilm āl-Ḥurūf*) it represents number ten and belongs to the element of air.

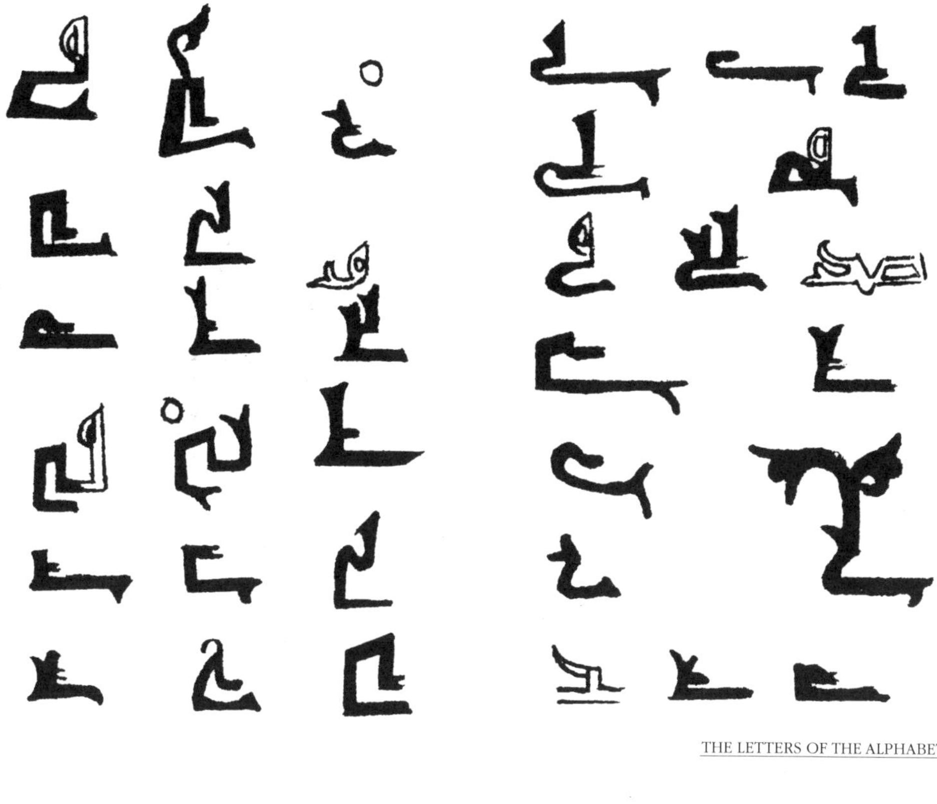

TA MARBŪṬA

Transliteration: **h** or **t**.

ة

Final	Medial	Initial	Isolated
طة			ة

ة	Alarz	ة	Diwani	ة	Nastaliq
ة	Al-Waleed	ة	Fairuz	ة	Omar
ة	Al-Qahira	ة	Firdawsi n.	ة	Rabee
ة	Al-Ruha	ة	Hadith	ة	Rouqai
ة	Amin	ة	Hijaz	ة	Shuweifat
ة	Annees	ة	Jarash	ة	Sidon
ة	Baalback	ة	Jiddah	ة	Silwan
ة	Baghdad	ة	Kufic	ة	Sirius
ة	Beirut	ة	Najaf	ة	Suraya
ة	Byblos	ة	Naskh	ة	Tadmur
ة	Dimashk	ة	Naskh cont.	ة	Thuluth

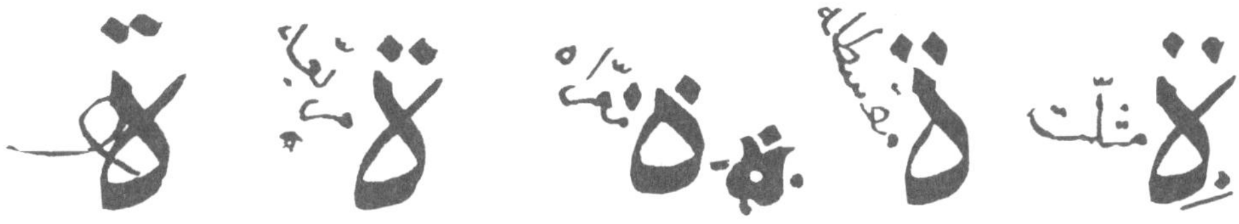

Ta marbūṭa is a tied *ta*, since it is like a *ta* but with crossed endings. It is used only as a suffix. It is transliterated as *a* when the word has no desinence, *at* when the word is followed by a desinence.

This letter is really a grammatical tool, a ligature that often defines the feminine gender, and is pronounced only when a word is tied to the following word. For example: *madinat* is pronounced *madinah* (the *t* is silent); *madinat āl-Nabi* is read *madinat-ānnabi.*

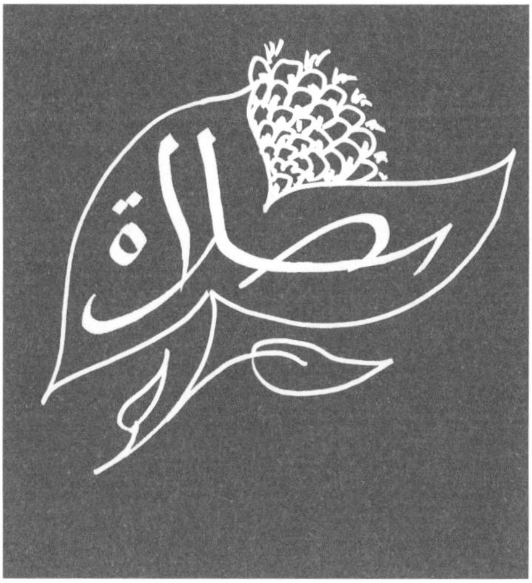

Right: The term *ṣalāt* (prayer) with the *ta marbūṭa* ending, from a book of *Wirde* (sacred invocations) from Morocco.

Below: The phrase *Yūladu āl-Nāsu āḥrāran sawāsiyatan* (All men are born free and equal), which ends with a *ta marbūṭa*.

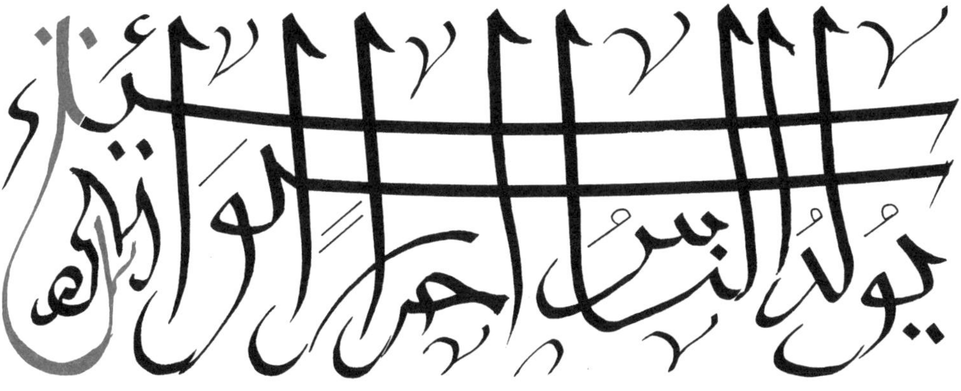

SHORT VOWELS AND DIACRITICAL MARKS

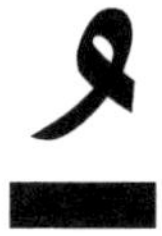

ḍamma: A miniature *waw* above the consonant; it signifies a short *u* vowel, as in "b**u**ll."

fatḥa: A slanted stroke, similar to an acute accent, above the consonant; it signifies a short *a* vowel such as the *a* in "Frenchm**a**n" or the *u* in "b**u**n."

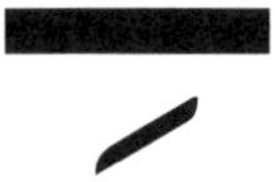

kasra: A slanted stroke, similar to an acute accent, below the consonant; it signifies a short *i* vowel, such as the *i* in "b**i**d."

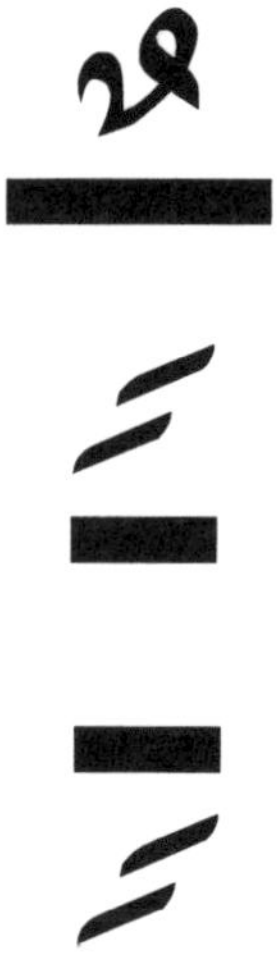

tanwīn (nunnation): Doubling of *ḍamma*, *fatḥa* and *kasra* (short *a*, *i*, and *u* vowels) at the end of a word; it gives the pronunciation of "un," "an," and "in," indicating the indeterminate article respectively in the nominative, accusative, and indirect cases.

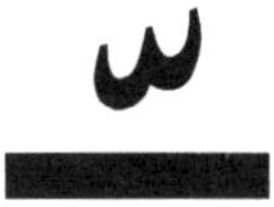

tashdīd (reinforcement, also called *shadda*): A mark signifying the doubling of a consonant; it is a small initial *s* placed above the consonant. The term is derived from the verb *ishtadda* (to be strong, robust, intense; to grow more emphatic or intense).

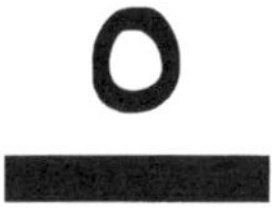

sukūn (silence; also called *jazm*: truncation): A small circle placed above the consonant; it signifies the absence of a short vowel.

hamza (*al-Qaṭ'i* when disjunctive; *al-Waṣli* when conjunctive): A sort of small initial *'ayn* (ʿ) placed above the consonant. Some grammarians treat it as a consonant and thus place it at the beginning of the alphabet, where the *alif* normally is. When accompanied by a short vowel (*ḍamma, fatḥa,* or *kasra*) it is read, respectively, as *ū, ā, ī.* When it occurs at the beginning of a word—only above the *alif*—it indicates a glottal stop, a sound immediately blocked by the glottis. When it occurs in the middle of a word (with a purely orthographic support from an underlying *alif, waw,* or *ya* without the two diacritical marks, read as *ā*), it signifies a net pause after the preceding syllable, or a suspension of the voice. When it occurs at the end of a word, it is written directly on the line without an underlying consonant, and is pronounced *a'.*

madda (lengthening, also called *alif madda*): When two initial *alifs* follow each other, or when a final *alif* is followed by a *hamza*, only one is written, with the *madda* sign on top; it is a tiny horizontal *alif,* not unlike the Spanish tilde (˜). It signifies a long *ā.*

waṣla (ligature, also called *alif wasla*): A sign that ties the pronunciation of the last short vowel declension of the preceding word to the first syllable of the following word that has this initial sign (the *alif* is silent).

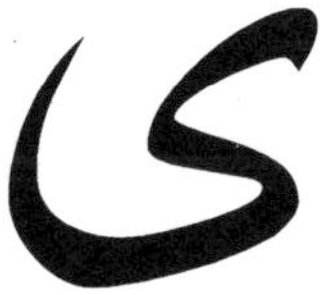

maqsūra (restricted, also called *alif maqsūra*): The letter *ya* without the two diacritical marks, placed at the end of a word; it is read *ā.* It is equivalent to an *alif madda.*

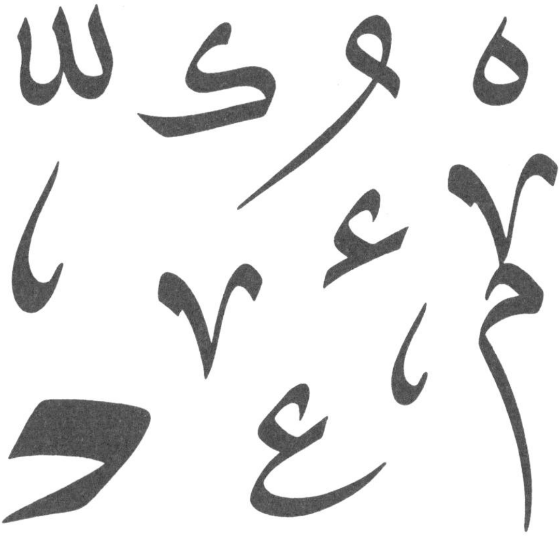

Orthographic, vocalic, and ornamental additional symbols of the Arabic alphabet, taken from the large roundels drawn by Kazasker Mustafa Izzet (1801–1876). Basilica of Saint Sophia, Istanbul.

LAM-ALIF

Name: **lam-alif**.
Transliteration: **la**.
Pronunciation: **lah**.

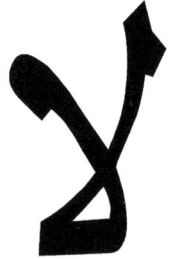

لا

Final	Medial	Initial	Isolated
طلا			لا

لا	Alarz	لا	Diwani	لا	Nastaliq
لا	Al-Waleed	لا	Fairuz	لا	Omar
لا	Al-Qahira	لا	Firdawsi n.	لا	Rabee
لا	Al-Ruha	لا	Hadith	لا	Rouqai
لا	Amin	لا	Hijaz	لا	Shuweifat
لا	Annees	لا	Jarash	لا	Sidon
لا	Baalback	لا	Jiddah	لا	Silwan
لا	Baghdad	لا	Kufic	لا	Sirius
لا	Beirut	لا	Najaf	لا	Suraya
لا	Byblos	لا	Naskh	لا	Tadmur
لا	Dimashk	لا	Naskh cont.	لا	Thuluth

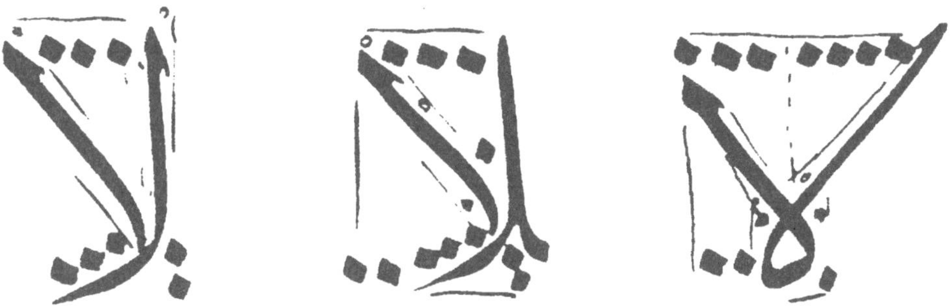

The *lam-alif* is not part of the traditional alphabet sequence, but it is included because of a hadith (that is, a saying of the prophet Muhammad), though that authenticity is not very credible according to the preeminent collector of such sayings, the Turkish Bukhari. Abd-al-Rahman ibn al-Saygh (1441) reported the saying as follows: "Abu Dharr al-Ghifari asked the Prophet: 'How many letters are there?' The Prophet replied: 'Twenty-nine.' His companion wondered, then counted them all one by one and triumphantly exclaimed, 'There are twenty-eight.' But the Prophet retorted: 'No, there are twenty-nine, there is also the *lam-alif*.' "

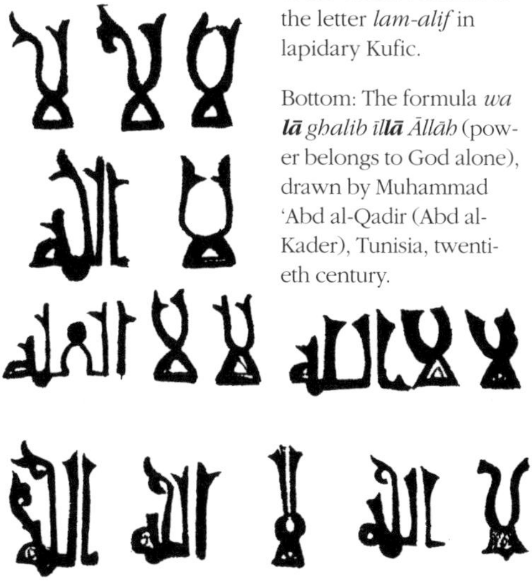

Left: Examples of some of the oldest versions of the letter *lam-alif* in lapidary Kufic.

Bottom: The formula *wa **lā** ghalib il**lā** Āllāh* (power belongs to God alone), drawn by Muhammad 'Abd al-Qadir (Abd al-Kader), Tunisia, twentieth century.

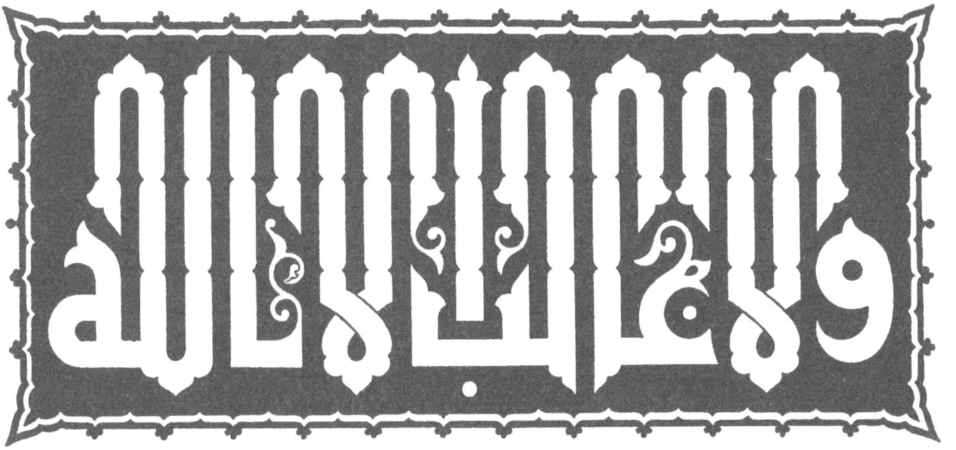

VARIANTS OF THE *LAM-ALIF* LETTER

1

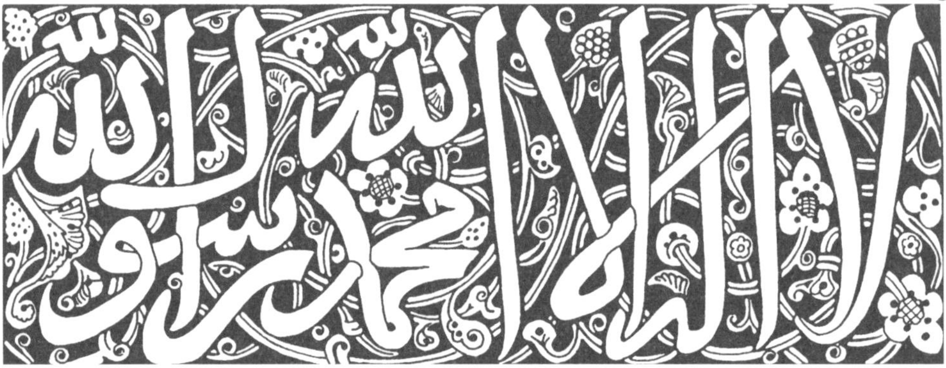

2

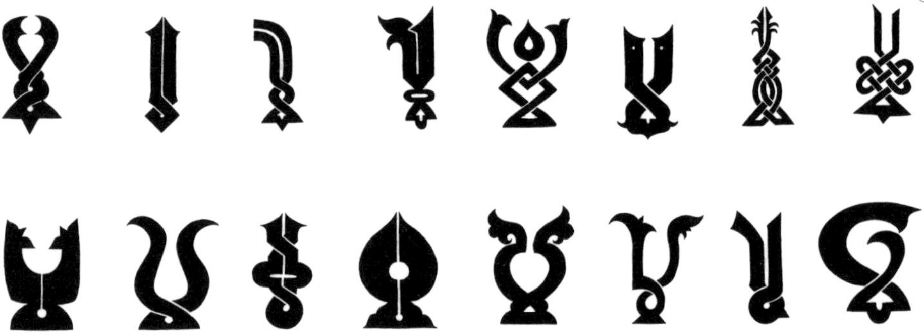

3

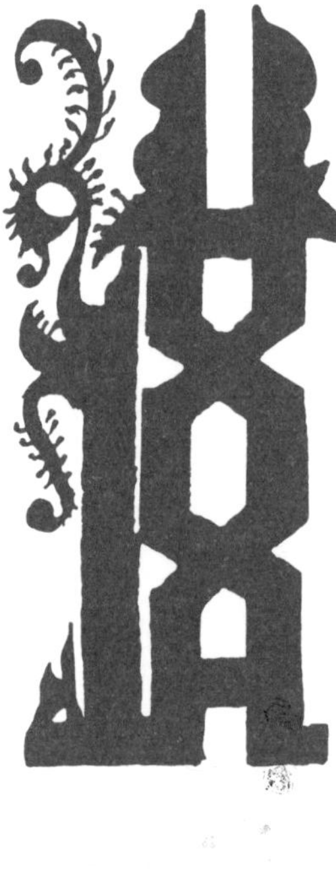

4

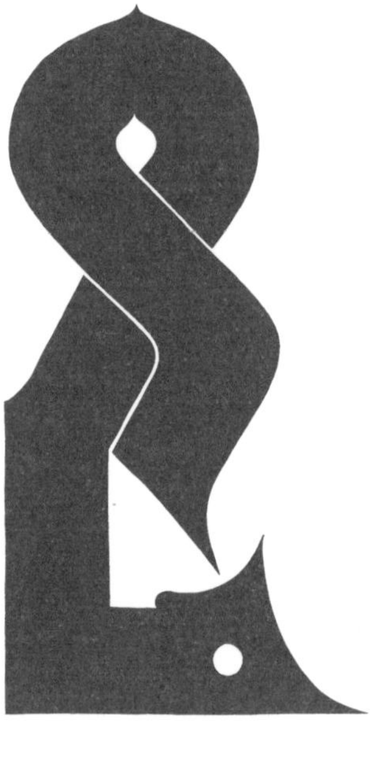

1. The *shahāda* (***Lā** Īlāha il**lā** Āllāh, Muḥammad rasūl Āllāh*), from a 1588 relief in the Jami' Masjid of Bukhara, Uzbekistan.

2. Various examples of the *lam-alif* collected by Hassan Massoudi.

3, 4. Examples of the *lam-alif* from a Qur'ān drawn in Kufic in the Middle Ages.

THE SUPPLEMENTAL LETTERS

پ	چ	ژ
pa	çim	zha
ڤ	گ	ڭ
vaf	gaf	gli

These six letters are used only in non-Arabic languages that use the Arab alphabet.

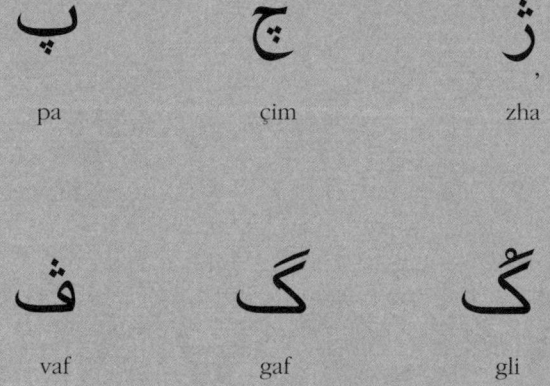

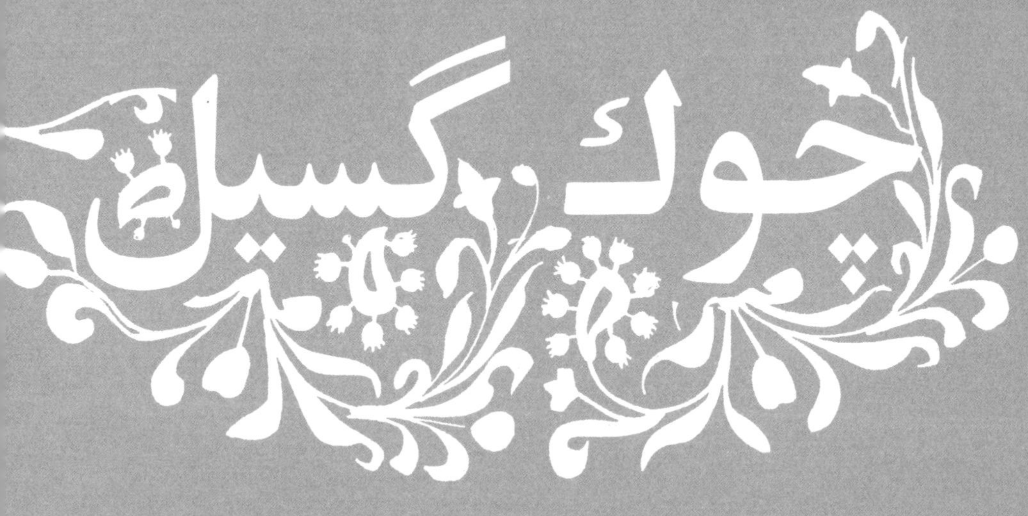

The letters *c* and hard *g* in the Turkish phrase *Çiok güsel* (Very pretty!).

PA

پ

Name: **pa**.

Transliteration: **p**.

Pronunciation: **p**,
as in **P**eter.

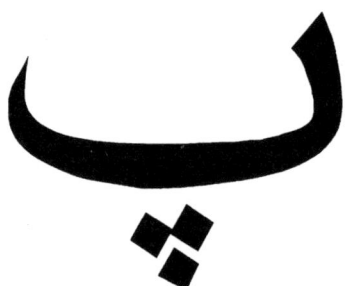

Final	Medial	Initial	Isolated
طپ	طپو	پو	پ

	Alarz	پ	Diwani	پ	Nastaliq
	Al-Waleed	پ	Fairuz		Omar
	Al-Qahira	پ	Firdawsi n.		Rabee
	Al-Ruha		Hadith		Rouqai
	Amin		Hijaz	پ	Shuweifat
	Annees		Jarash		Sidon
	Baalback		Jiddah	پ	Silwan
	Baghdad	پ	Kufic		Sirius
پ	Beirut		Najaf		Suraya
	Byblos	پ	Naskh		Tadmur
پ	Dimashk		Naskh cont.		Thuluth

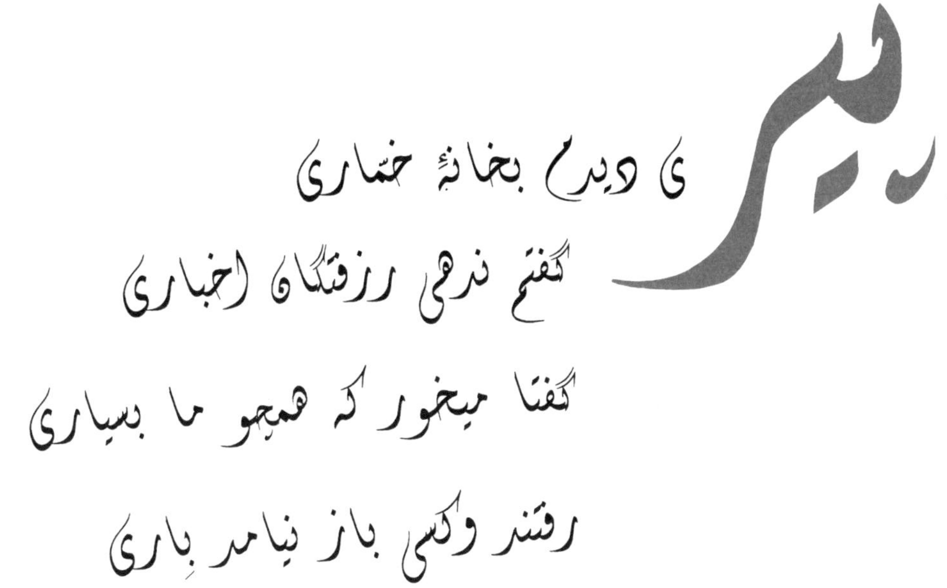
پیری دیدم بخانهٔ خماری
گفتم ندهی ز رفتگان اخباری
گفتا میخور که همچو ما بسیاری
رفتند وکسی باز نیامد باری

To the wine-house I saw the sage repair,
Bearing a wine-cup, and a mat for prayer;
I said, "O Shaikh, what does this conduct mean?"
Said he, "Go drink! The world is naught but air."

(Quatrain No. 80, from *The Sufistic Quatrains of Omar Khayyam,* translated by E. H. Whinfield, p. 161.)

Above: Quatrain beginning with the letter *pa,* by Persian mathematician and poet Omar Khayyam (1048–1131).

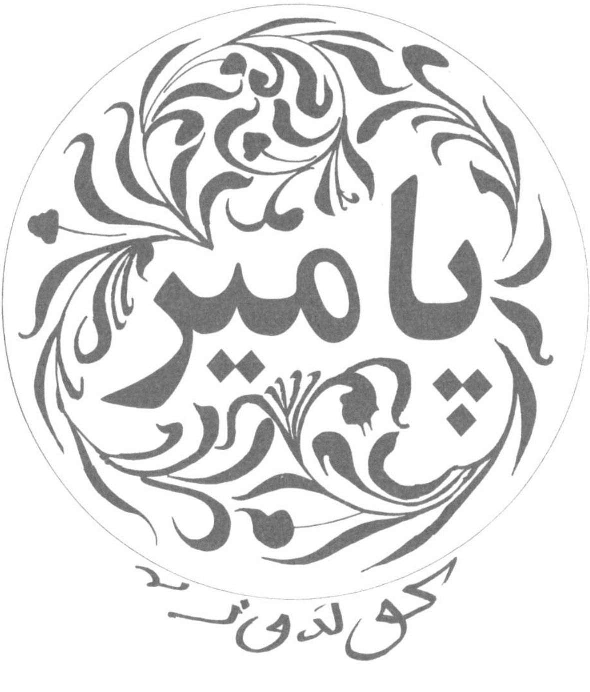
پامیر

Left: The letter *p* in the word *Pamir.* From a sign in the Shahar Shata market in Kabul, Afghanistan, twentieth century.

ÇIM

Name: **çim**.
Transliteration: **ç**.
Pronunciation: **ch**, as in **Ch**ina.

چ

Final	Medial	Initial	Isolated
طچ	طچو	چو	چ

Glyph	Font	Glyph	Font	Glyph	Font
	Alarz	چ	Diwani	چ	Nastaliq
	Al-Waleed	چ	Fairuz		Omar
	Al-Qahira		Firdawsi n.		Rabee
	Al-Ruha		Hadith		Rouqai
	Amin		Hijaz	چ	Shuweifat
	Annees		Jarash		Sidon
	Baalback		Jiddah	چ	Silwan
	Baghdad	چ	Kufic		Sirius
چ	Beirut		Najaf		Suraya
	Byblos	چ	Naskh		Tadmur
چ	Dimashk		Naskh cont.		Thuluth

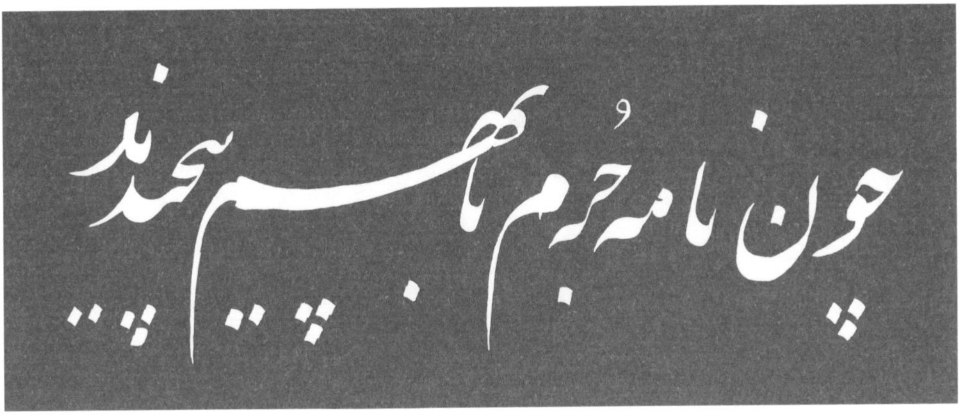

Top: One verse and two quatrains by Omar Khayyam that begin with the letter *çim*.

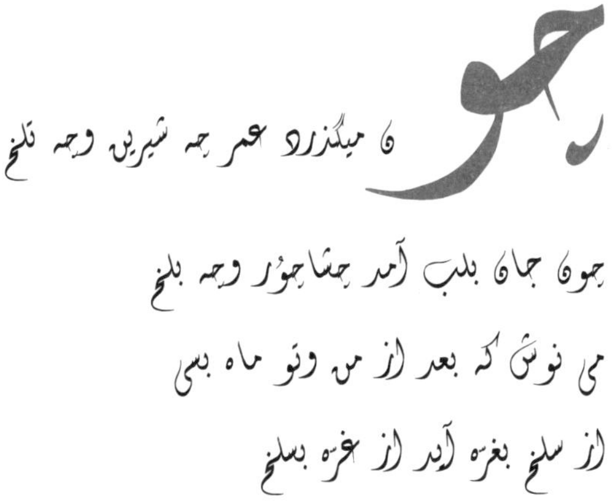

When life is spent, what's Balkh or Nishapore?
What sweet or bitter, when the cup runs o'er?
Come drink! Full many a moon will wax and wane
In times to come, when we are here no more.

(Quatrain No. 134, p. 174)

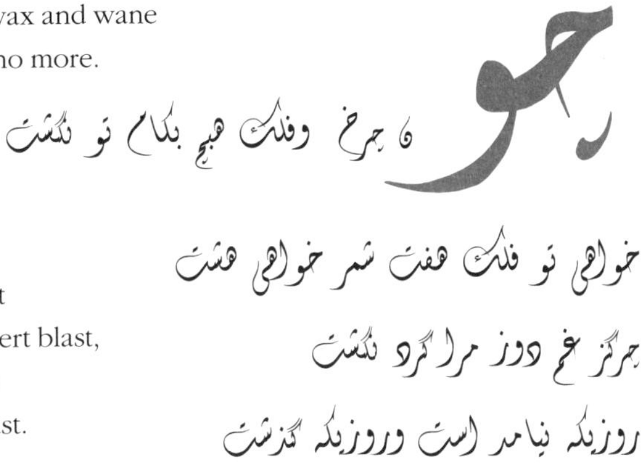

My life lasts but a day or two, and fast
Sweeps by, like torrent stream or desert blast,
Howbeit, of two days I take no heed:
The day to come, and that already past.

(Quatrain No. 26, p. 147)

(From *The Sufistic Quatrains of Omar Khayyam,* translated by E. H. Whinfield.)

ZHA

Name: **zha**.
Transliteration: **zh**.
Pronunciation: **zh**.

ژ

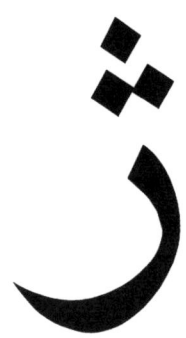

Final	Medial	Initial	Isolated
ـژ			ژ

Characters

	Alarz	ژ	Diwani	ژ	Nastaliq
	Al-Waleed	ژ	Fairuz		Omar
	Al-Qahira	ژ	Firdawsi n.		Rabee
	Al-Ruha		Hadith		Rouqai
	Amin		Hijaz	ژ	Shuweifat
	Annees		Jarash		Sidon
	Baalback		Jiddah	ژ	Silwan
	Baghdad	ژ	Kufic		Sirius
ژ	Beirut		Najaf		Suraya
	Byblos	ژ	Naskh		Tadmur
ژ	Dimashk		Naskh cont.		Thuluth

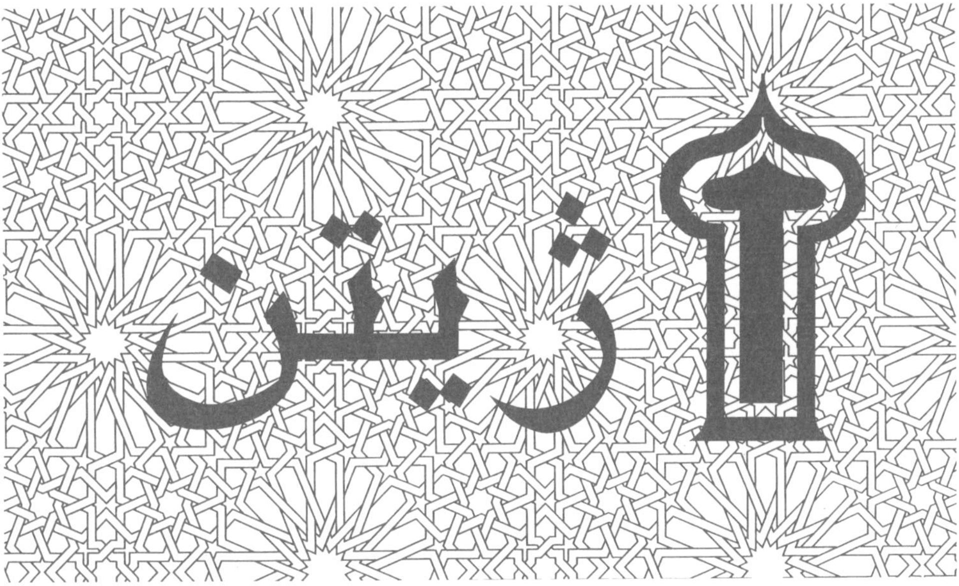

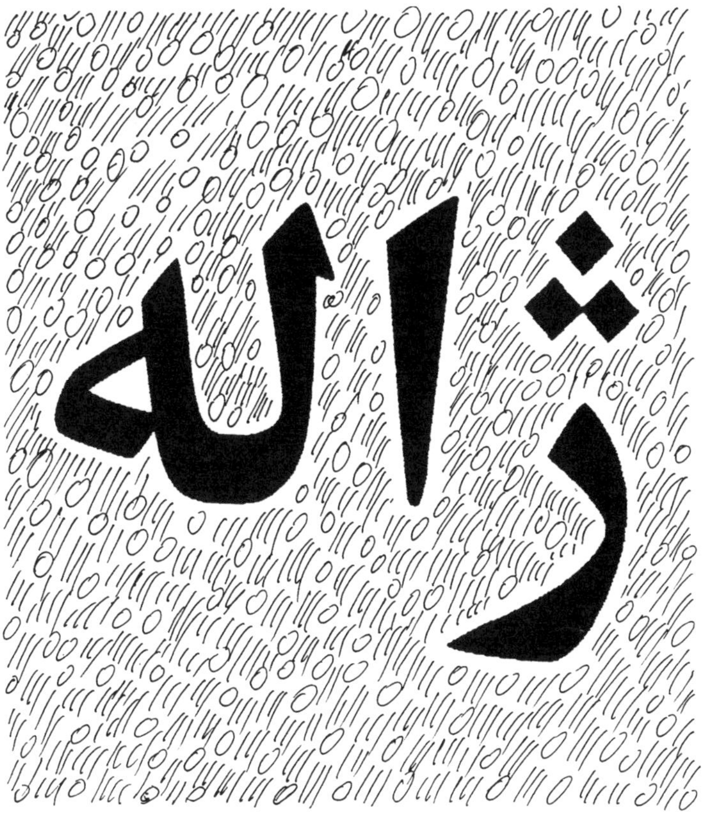

Above: The letter *zha*, the beginning of *Zhaytun*, a man's name. From the frontispiece of a volume of poetry published in Hyderabad in 1968.

Left: One of the extremely rare words in the Urdu language that begin with the letter *zha*: *ẓhāla* (hail).

VAF

Name: **vaf**.

Transliteration: **v**.

Pronunciation: **v**, as in **v**ase.

ڤ

Final	Medial	Initial	Isolated
بڤ	بڤو	ڤو	ڤ

Characters

	Alarz	ڤ	Diwani	ڤ	Nastaliq
	Al-Waleed	ڤ	Fairuz		Omar
	Al-Qahira	ڤ	Firdawsi n.		Rabee
	Al-Ruha		Hadith		Rouqai
	Amin		Hijaz	ڤ	Shuweifat
	Annees		Jarash		Sidon
	Baalback		Jiddah	ڤ	Silwan
	Baghdad	ڤ	Kufic		Sirius
ڤ	Beirut		Najaf		Suraya
	Byblos	ڤ	Naskh		Tadmur
ڤ	Dimashk		Naskh cont.		Thuluth

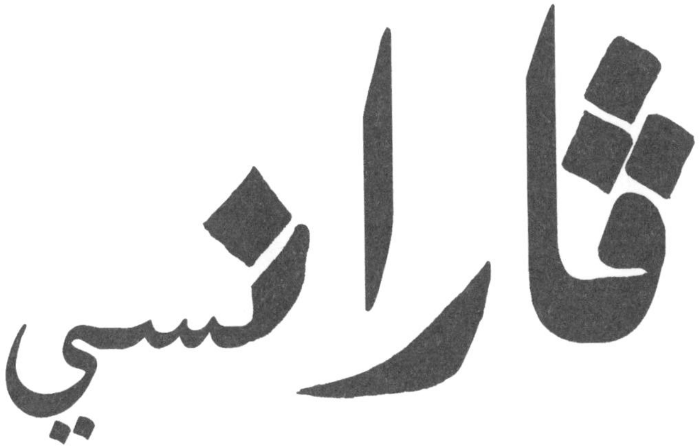

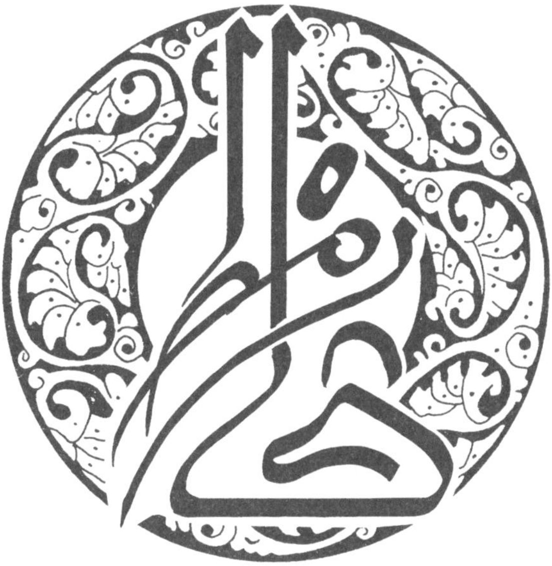

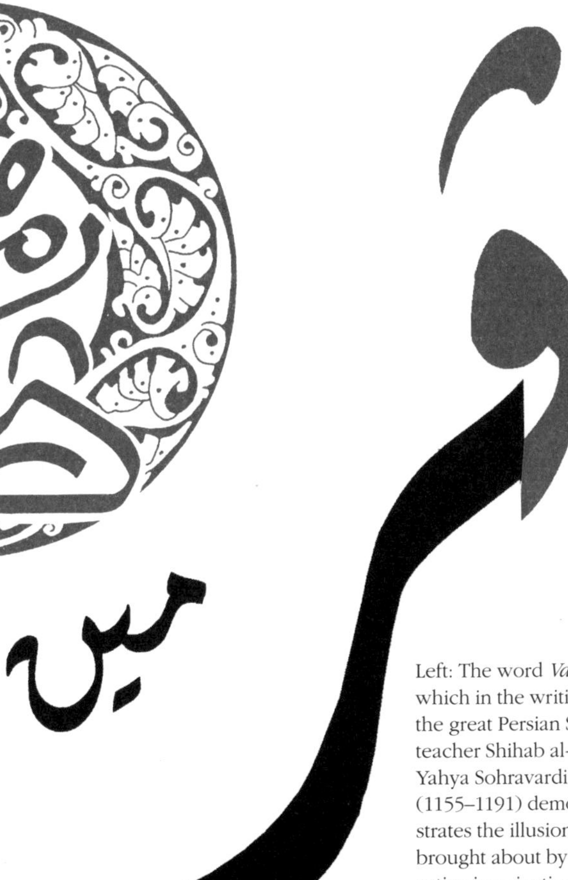

Top: The name of the Indian city Vārānāsī (Benares).

Above: The letter *v*, the beginning of the last name Varimtov, a famous ceramist from Khiva, Uzbekistan, twentieth century.

Left: The word *Varamīn*, which in the writings of the great Persian Sufi teacher Shihab al-Din Yahya Sohravardi (1155–1191) demonstrates the illusions brought about by an active imagination (*barzakh*).

GAF

Name: **gaf**.
Transliteration: **g**.
Pronunciation: hard **g**, as in **g**oat.

گ

Final	Medial	Initial	Isolated
بگ	بگو	گو	گ

	Alarz	گ	Diwani	گ	Nastaliq
	Al-Waleed	گ	Fairuz		Omar
	Al-Qahira	گ	Firdawsi n.		Rabee
	Al-Ruha		Hadith		Rouqai
	Amin		Hijaz	گ	Shuweifat
	Annees		Jarash		Sidon
	Baalback		Jiddah	گ	Silwan
	Baghdad	گ	Kufic		Sirius
گ	Beirut		Najaf		Suraya
	Byblos	گ	Naskh		Tadmur
گ	Dimashk		Naskh cont.		Thuluth

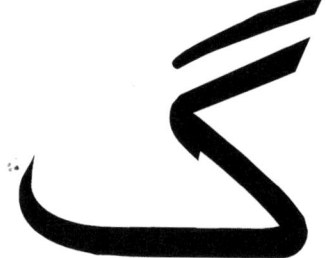

گ

می نخوری طعنه مزن مستانرا
گر توبه دهد توبه کُنم یزدانرا
تو فخر بآن کنی که من می نخورم
صد کار کنی که می غُلامست آنرا

Blame not the drunkards, you who wine eschew,
Had I but grace, I would abstain like you,
And mark me, vaunting zealot, you commit
A hundredfold worse sins than drunkards do.

(Quatrain No. 11, from *The Sufistic Quatrains of Omar Khayyam*, translated by E. H. Whinfield, p. 143.)

گه

گشته نهان رُو بکسی ننمایٔ
گه در صُور کون ومکان پیدایٔ
این جلوه گری بجویشتن بنمایٔ
خود عین عیان خودی وبینایٔ

Now Thou art hidden, unseen of all that be;
Now Thou art fully display'd that all may see:
Being, as Thou art, the Player and the Play,
And playing for Thine own pleasure, carelessly.

(Quatrain No. 15, from *Quatrains from Omar Khayyam*, translated by F. York Powell.)

Two quatrains by Omar Khayyam beginning with the letter *gaf.*

Name: **none**.
Transliteration: **none**.
Pronunciation: **li**, as in mil**li**on.

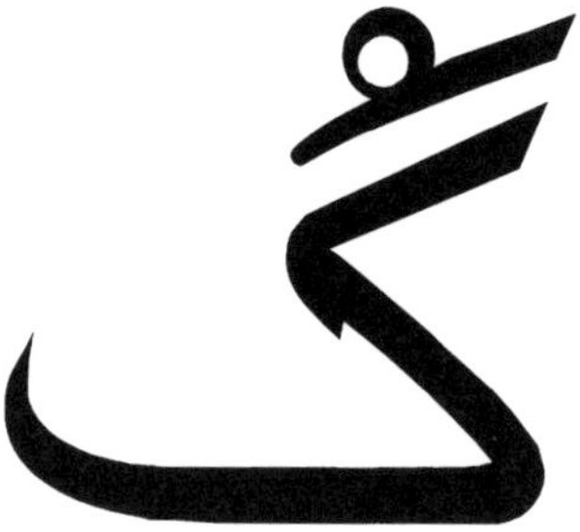

Final		Medial		Initial		Isolated
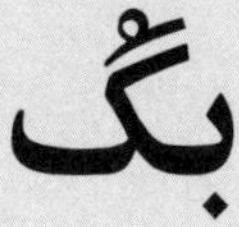		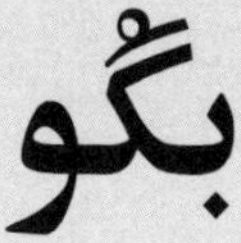		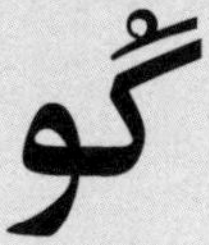		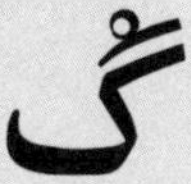

	Alarz	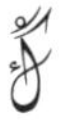	Diwani	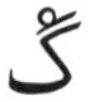	Nastaliq
	Al-Waleed		Fairuz		Omar
	Al-Qahira		Firdawsi n.		Rabee
	Al-Ruha		Hadith		Rouqai
	Amin		Hijaz		Shuweifat
	Annees		Jarash		Sidon
	Baalback		Jiddah		Silwan
	Baghdad	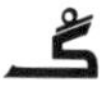	Kufic		Sirius
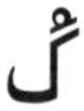	Beirut		Najaf		Suraya
	Byblos	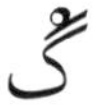	Naskh		Tadmur
	Dimashk		Naskh cont.		Thuluth

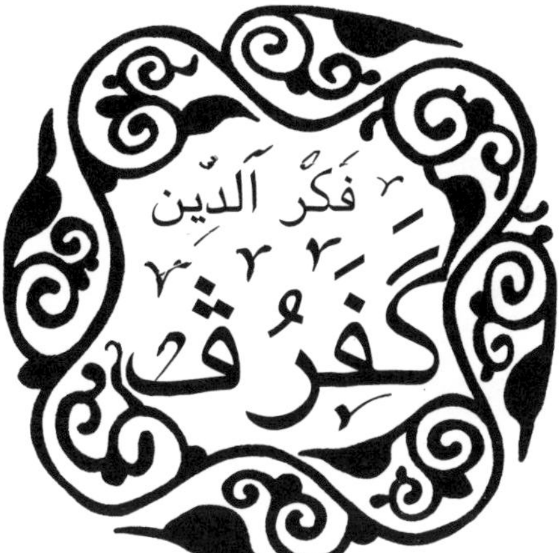

Left: The letters *g* (hard) and *v*, as seen in the name of the Azerbaijani musician Fakraddin Gafarov. From a concert program. Baku, Azerbaijan, twentieth century.

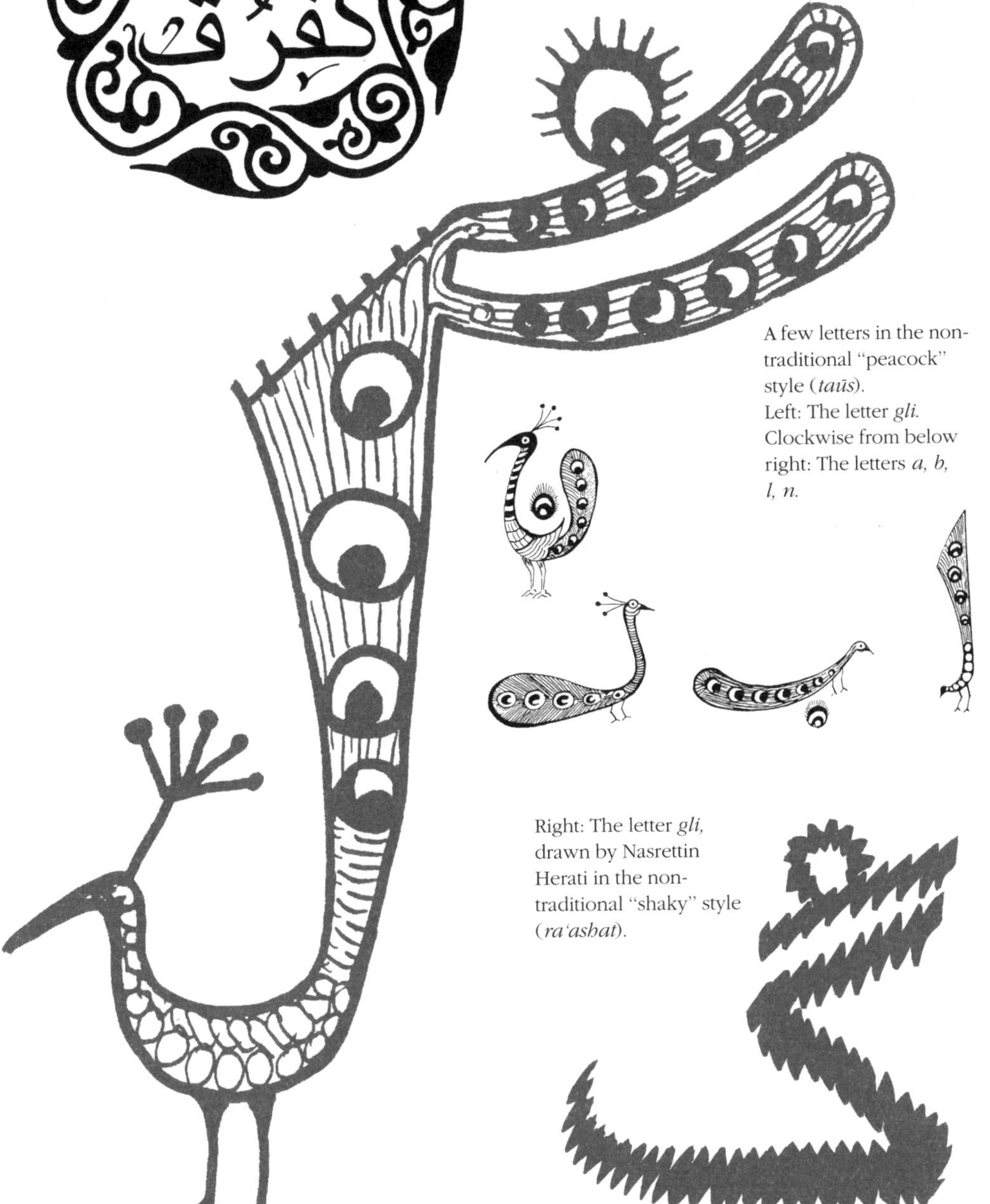

A few letters in the non-traditional "peacock" style (*taūs*).
Left: The letter *gli*.
Clockwise from below right: The letters *a, b, l, n*.

Right: The letter *gli*, drawn by Nasrettin Herati in the non-traditional "shaky" style (*ra'ashat*).

يولد الناس أحرارا سواسية

يولد الناس أحرارا سواسية

يولد الناس أحرارا سواسية

يولد الناس أحرارا سواسية

يولد الناس أحرارا سواسية

يولد الناس أحرارا سواسية

يولد الناس أحرارا سواسية

يولد الناس أحرارا سواسية

يُولد الناس أحرارا سواسية

يُولد الناس أحرارا سواسية

يُولد الناس أحرارا سواسية

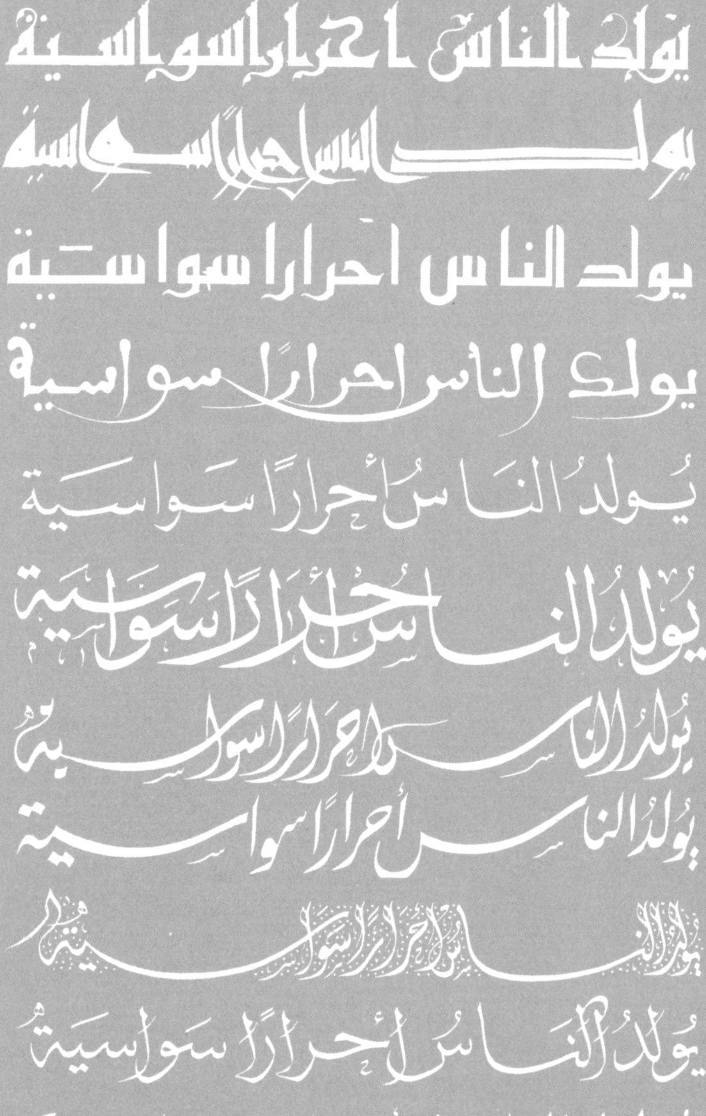

The first phrase of the
Human Rights Charter
("All men are born free
and equal"), drawn by
Hassan Massoudi (Paris,

twentieth century) in
eleven different styles.
From top to bottom:
Classic Kufic, Qarmatian
Kufic, modern Kufic,

*maghribī, thuluth,
naskhī, dīwānī,* Farsi,
dīwānī jalī, ijāza, ruqa.

STYLES, VARIANTS, AND CALLIGRAPHIC ADAPTATIONS

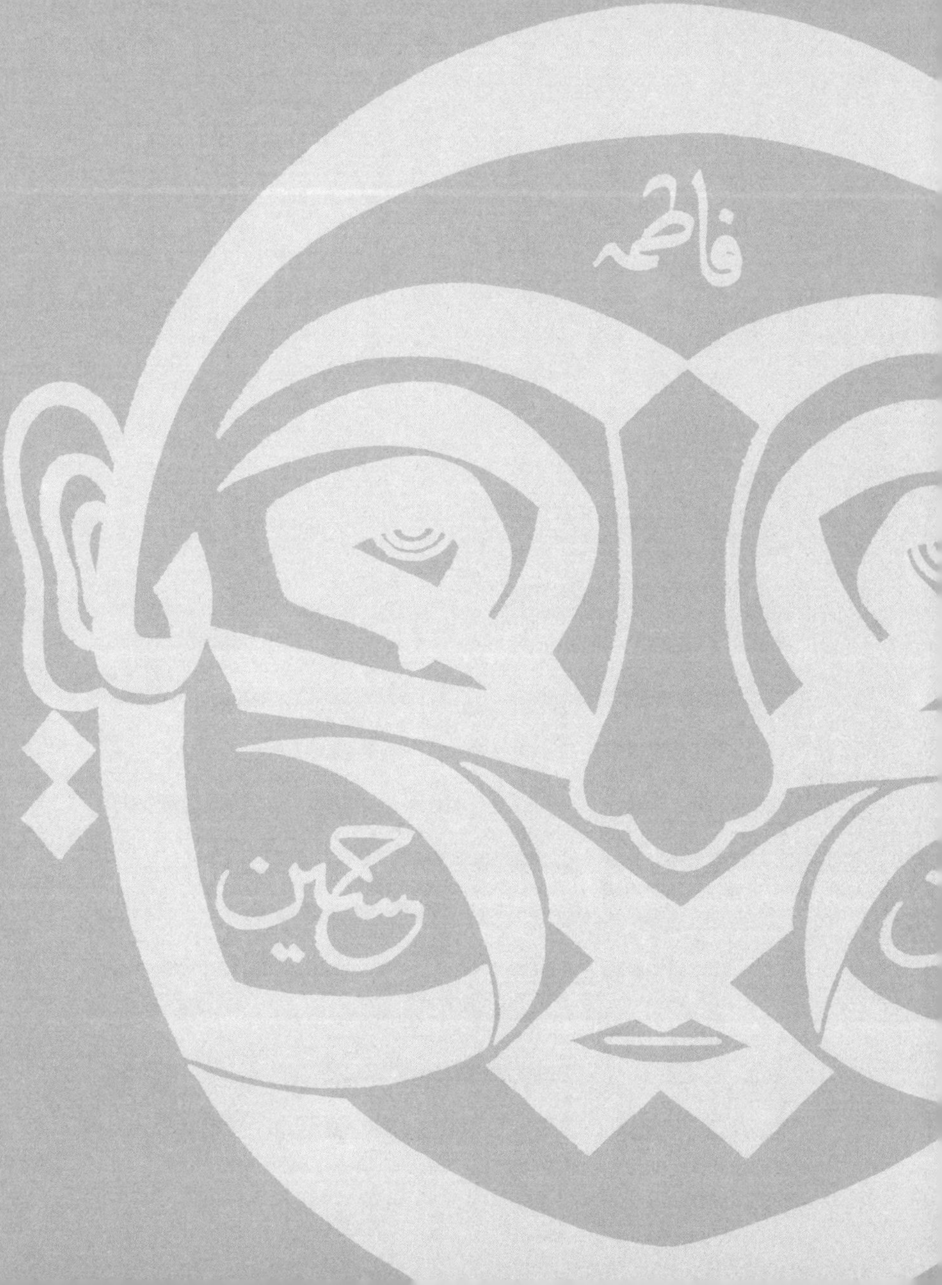

EXAMPLES OF CLASSIC SEVENTH- TO NINTH-CENTURY KUFIC STYLE

1

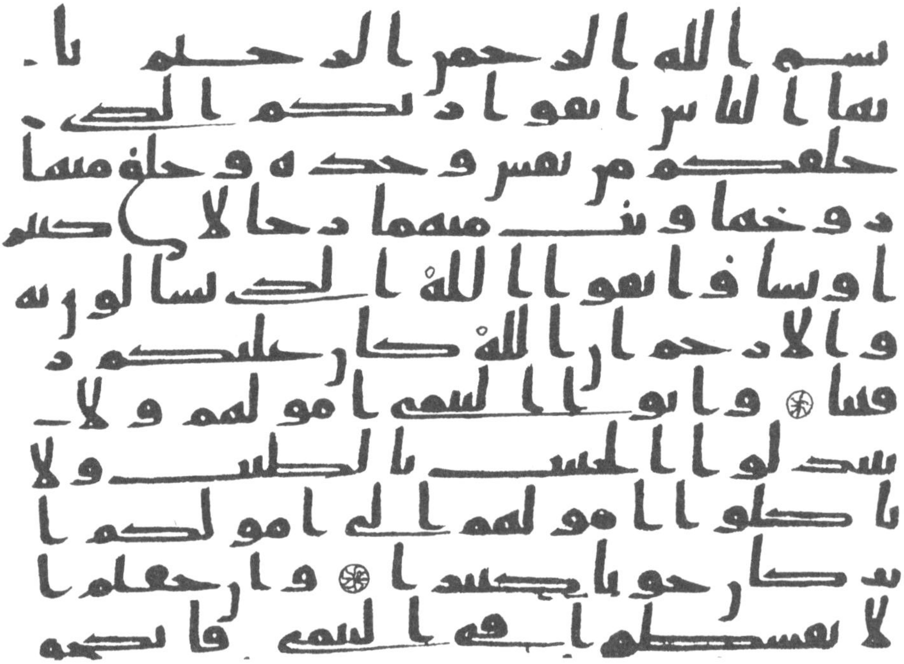

2

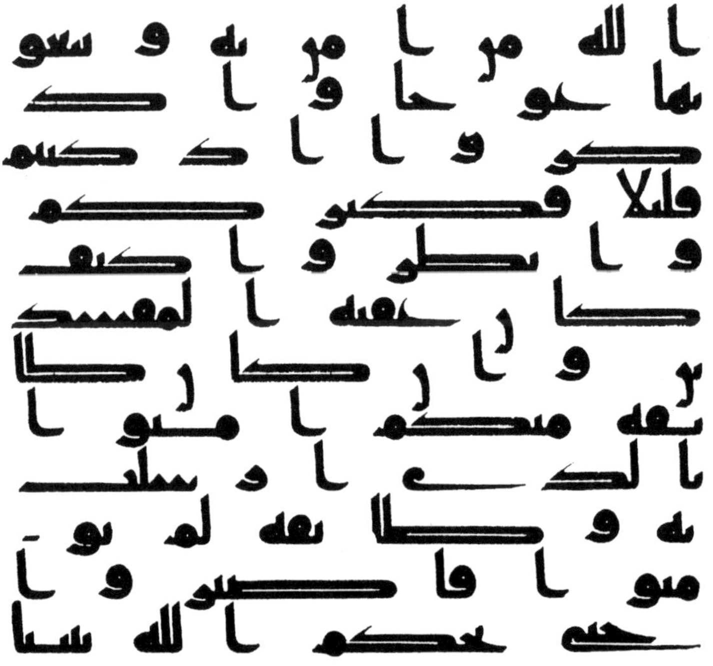

1. Excerpt from the Qur'ān commissioned by Caliph Uthman (d. 656). Istanbul, Topkapi Sarayë Museum.

2. Excerpt from a Qur'ān from the period of Caliph Uthman (d. 656). St. Petersburg, National Library.

3. Excerpt taken from an eighth-century Qur'ān. St. Petersburg, Library of Oriental Studies, 322.

4. Excerpt from a ninth-century Qur'ān, written in Iran or Iraq. Tehran, Bastan Museum, 4289.

3

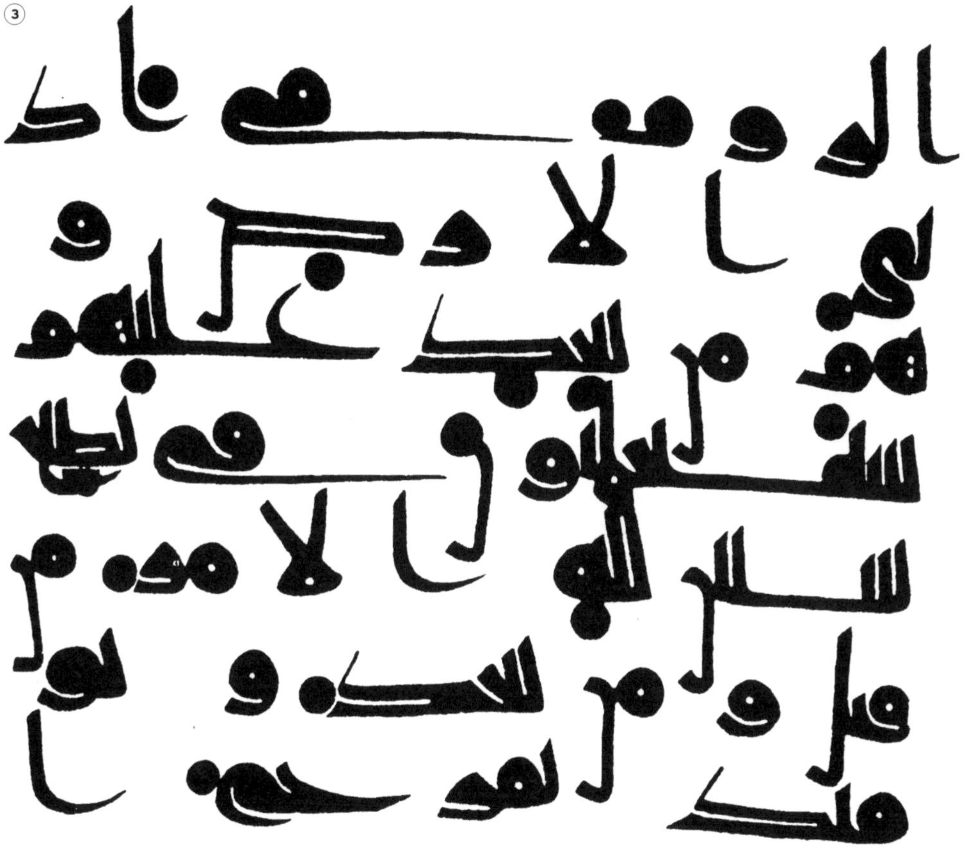

4

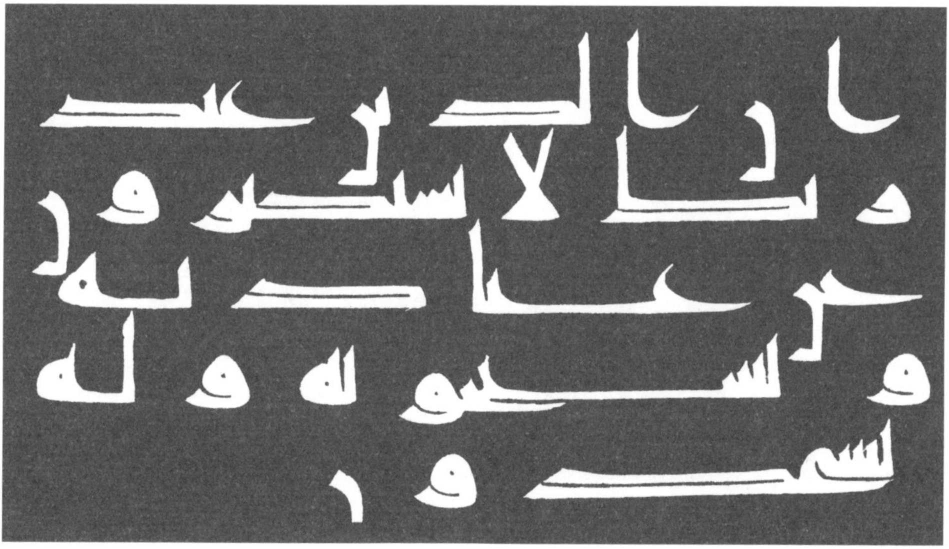

EXAMPLES OF QARMATIAN KUFIC

1
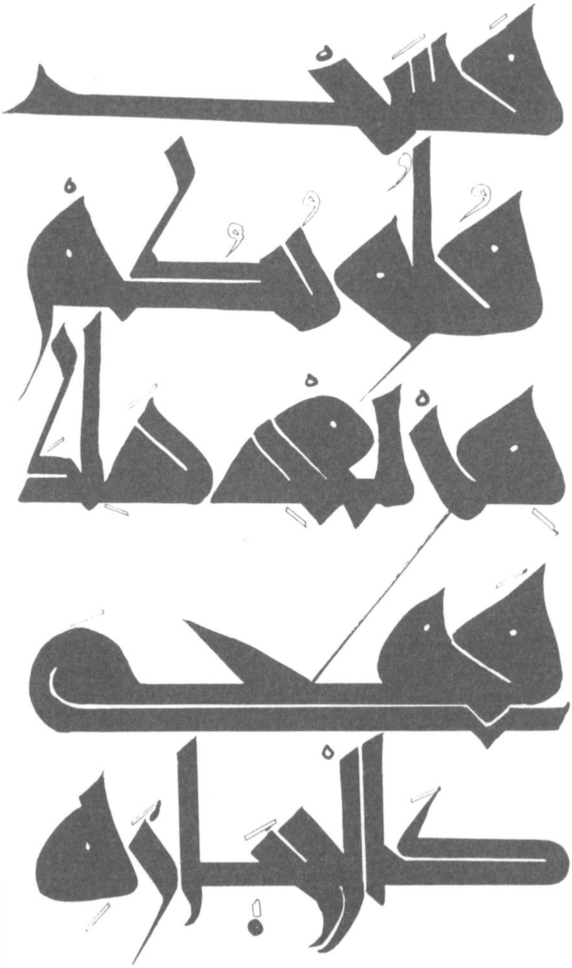

1. Excerpt from a Qur'ān composed by Ali al-Warraq between 1019 and 1020, probably in Kairouan, Tunisia. This Qur'ān is associated with the name of *Mushaf āl-Ḥāḍinah*. Kairouan, Tunisia, Ibrahim ibn al-Aghlab Museum.

2. A phrase written in *nissabāri* Kufic.

3. Page from an eleventh-century Qur'ān, written in either Iran or Iraq. Geneva, H. H. Sadruddin Agha Khan Collection.

2
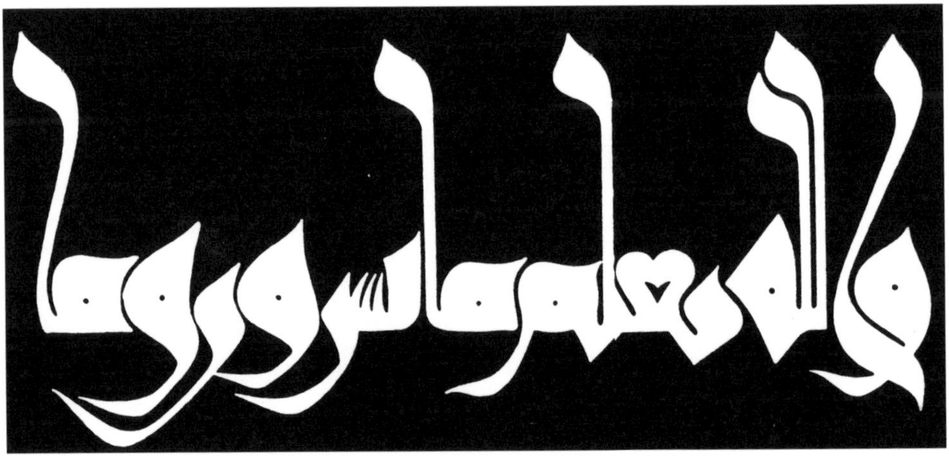

3

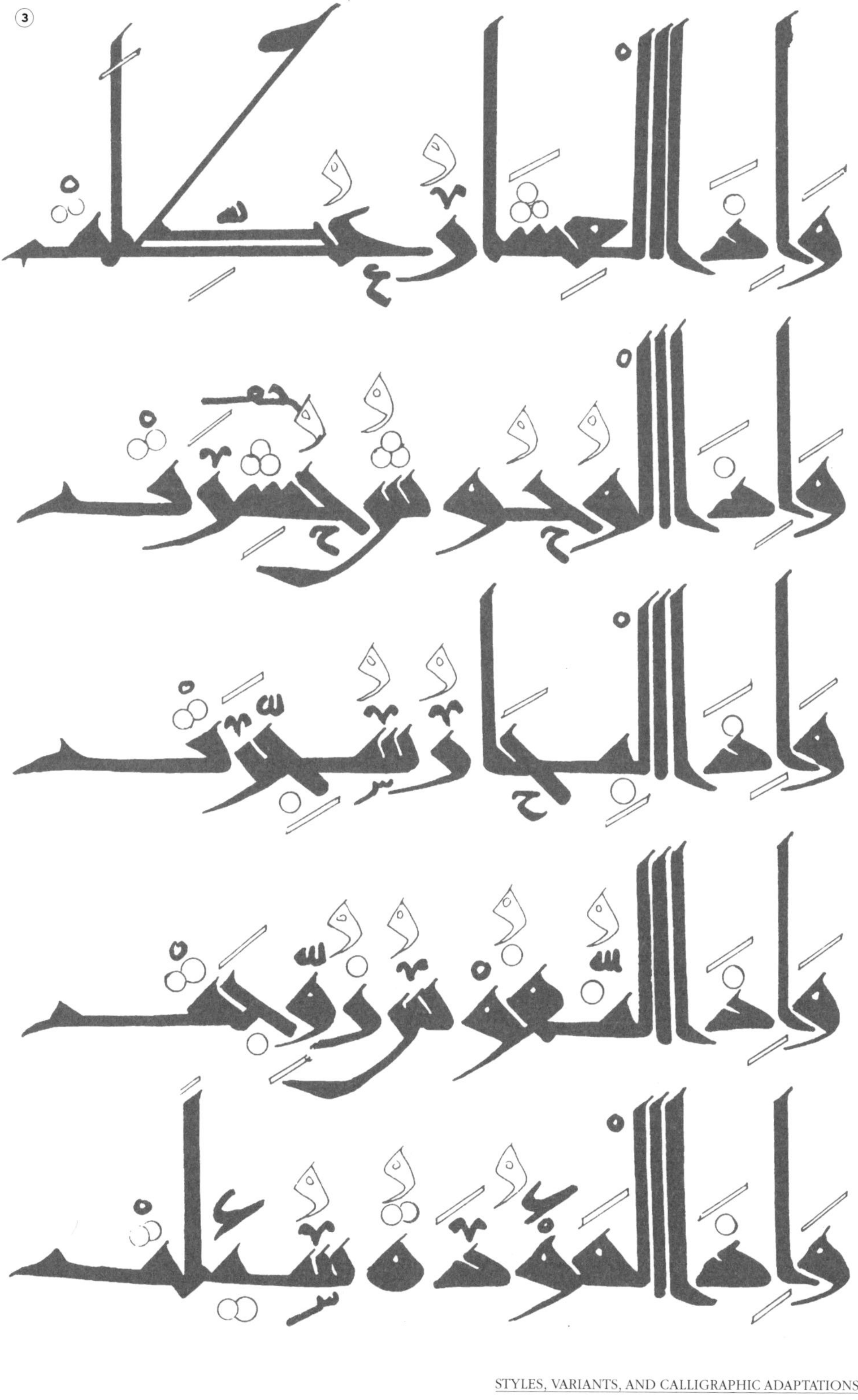
وإذا العشار عطلت
وإذا الوحوش حشرت
وإذا البحار سجرت
وإذا النفوس زوجت
وإذا الموءودة سئلت

EXAMPLES OF FOLIATED AND PLAITED KUFIC

1

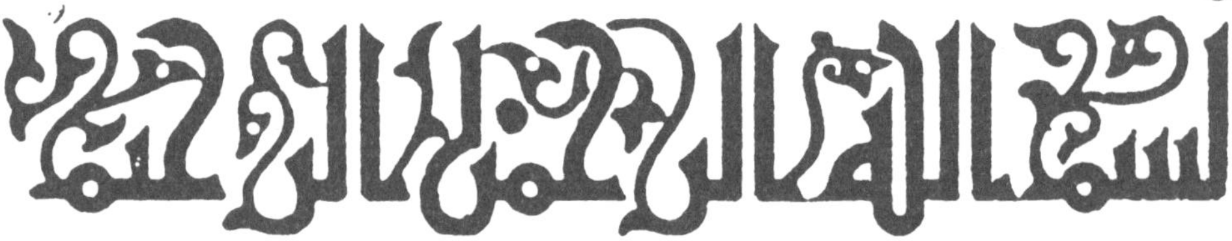

2

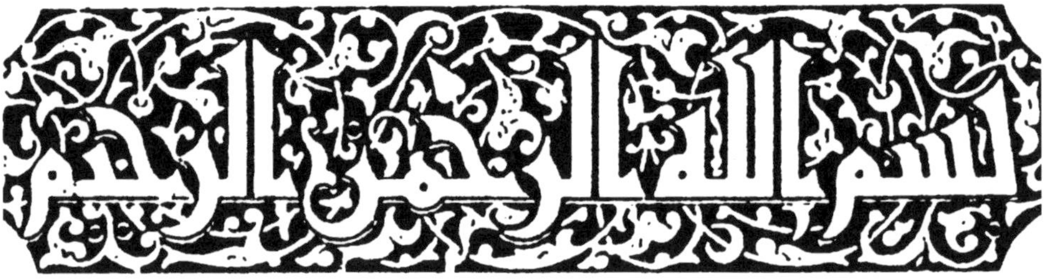

1. *Basmala* drawn in foliated Kufic. Córdoba, Spain, Grand Mosque.

2. *Basmala* in foliated Kufic. Granada, Spain, Alhambra.

3. A relief of 1107, from the Qasma Kazi mosque of Zanzibar, Africa.

4. *Basmala* in plaited Kufic.

5. *Basmala* in plaited Kufic.

6. *Basmala* in plaited Kufic by Izzet Necmeddin, 1946.

3

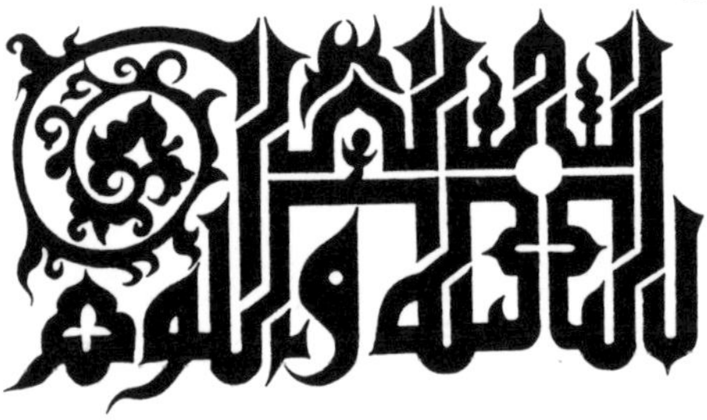

5

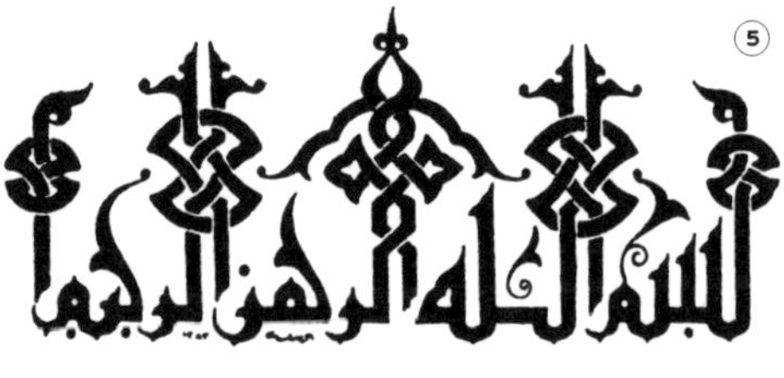

4

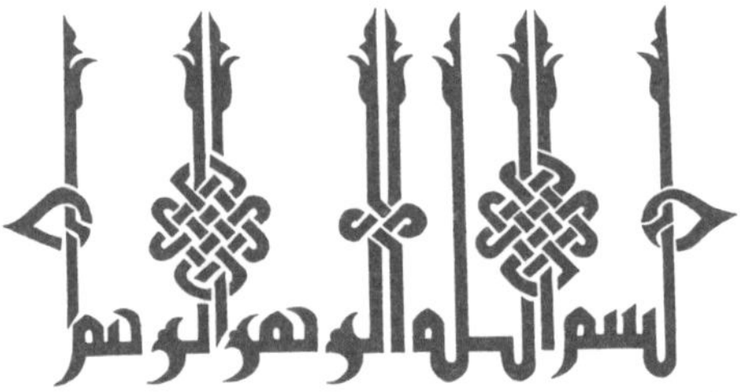

6

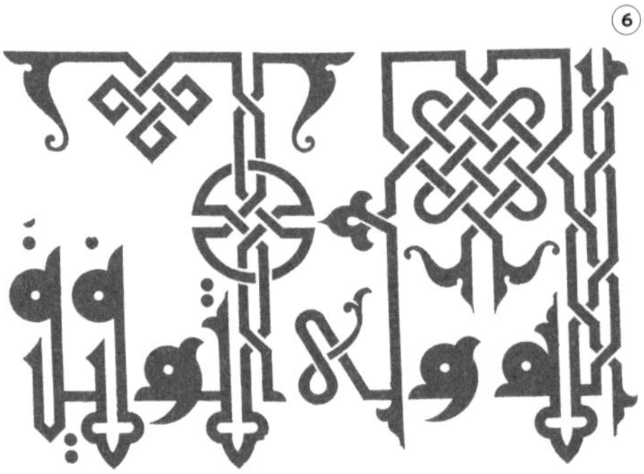

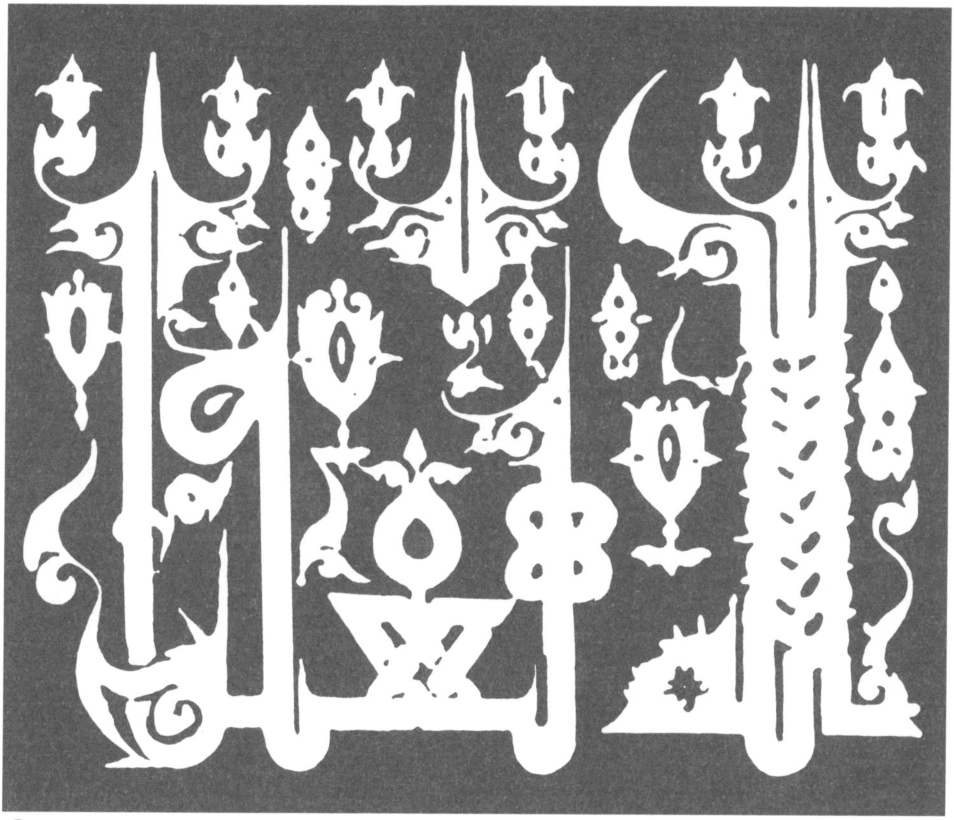

(7)

7. Plaited and flowered Kufic, fifteenth century. Hetimandel Palace, Tar-o Sār, Afghanistan.

8. Plaited and flowered Kufic, eighteenth century. Afghanistan.

(8)

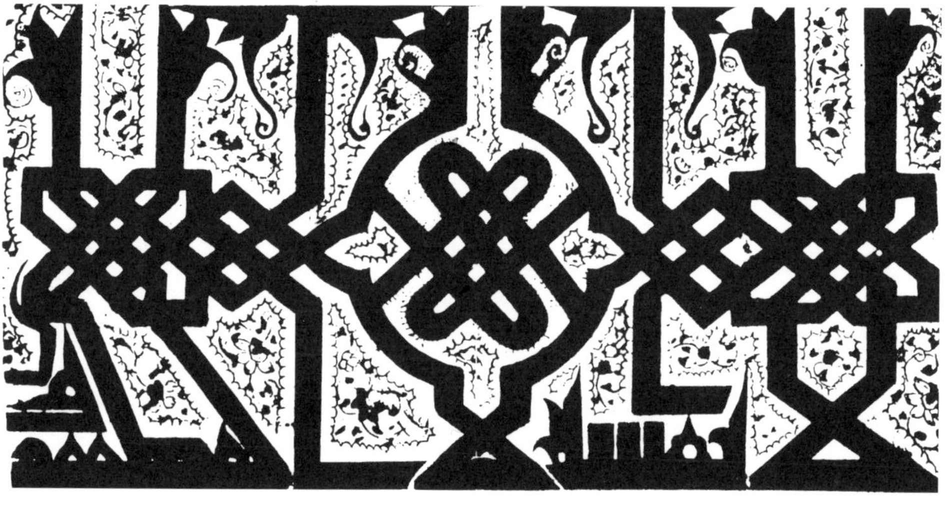

CONTEMPORARY USES OF CLASSIC KUFIC

1

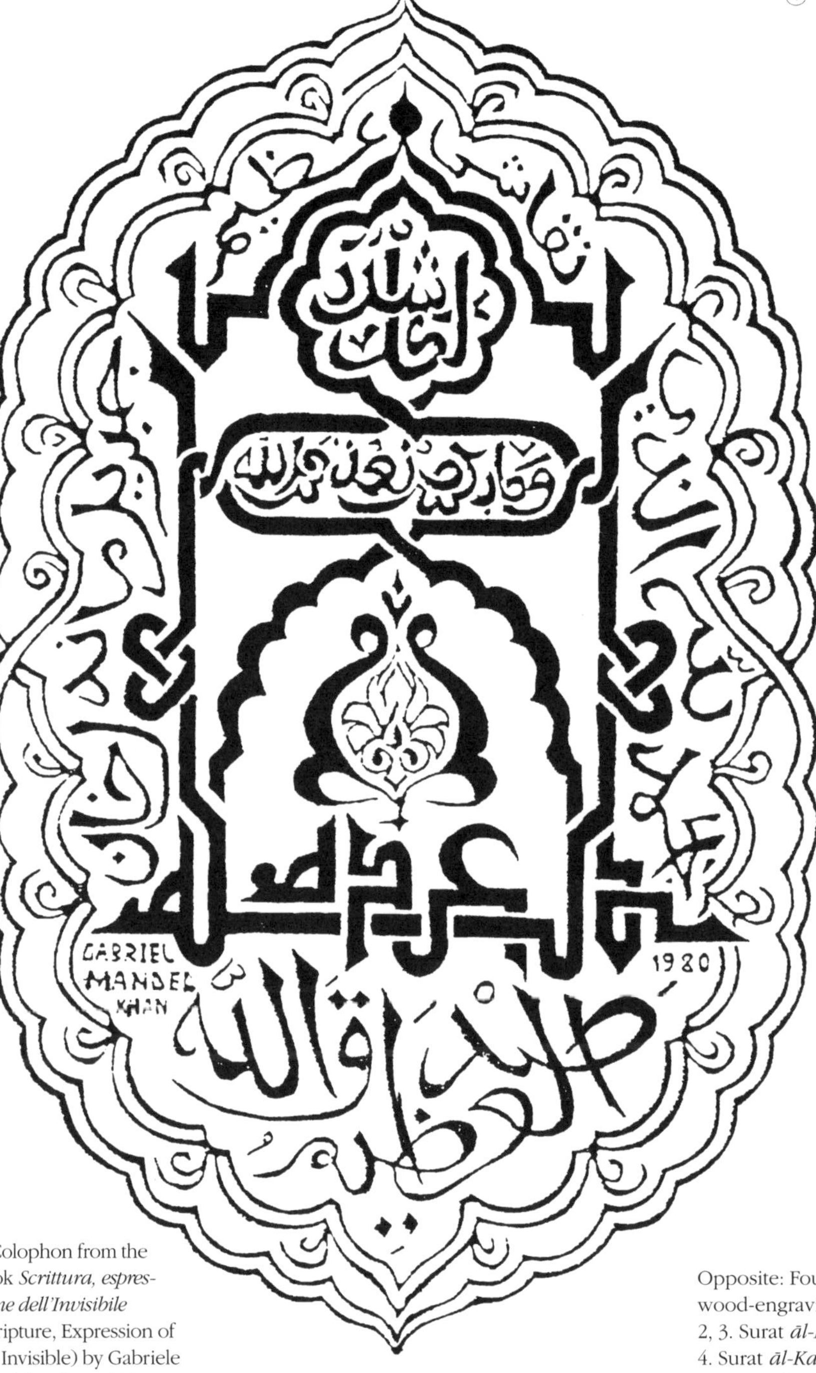

1. Colophon from the book *Scrittura, espressione dell'Invisibile* (Scripture, Expression of the Invisible) by Gabriele Mandel. Milan, 1980.

Opposite: Four pages of wood-engraving.
2, 3. Surat *āl-Fātiḥa*.
4. Surat *āl-Kawthar*.
5. Surat *āl-'Aṣr*.

2

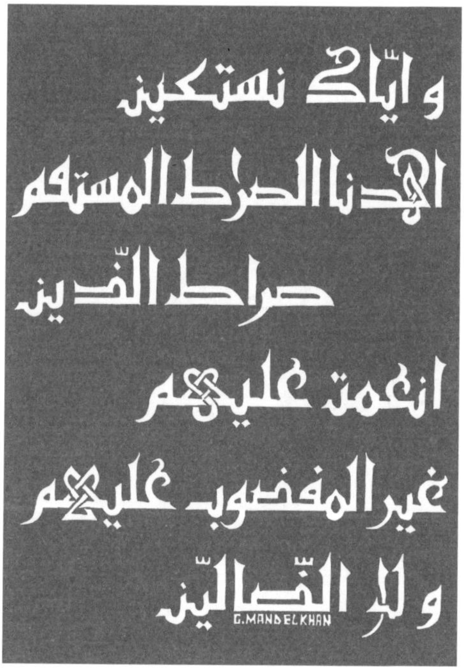
وإياك نستعين
اهدنا الصراط المستقيم
صراط الذين
انعمت عليهم
غير المغضوب عليهم
ولا الضالين
G.MANDELKHAN

3

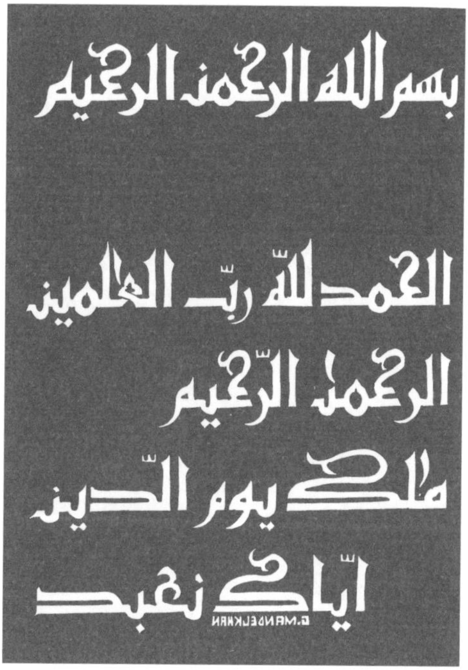
بسم الله الرحمن الرحيم
الحمد لله رب العلمين
الرحمن الرحيم
ملك يوم الدين
اياك نعبد
G.MANDELKHAN

4

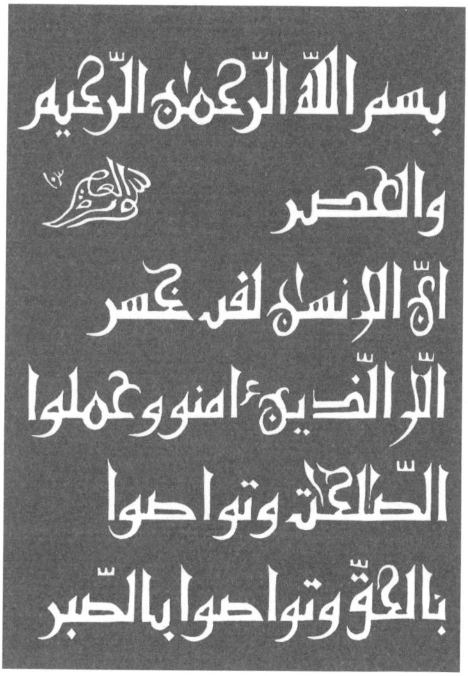
بسم الله الرحمن الرحيم
والعصر
ان الانسان لفي خسر
الا الذين امنوا وعملوا
الصلحت وتواصوا
بالحق وتواصوا بالصبر

5

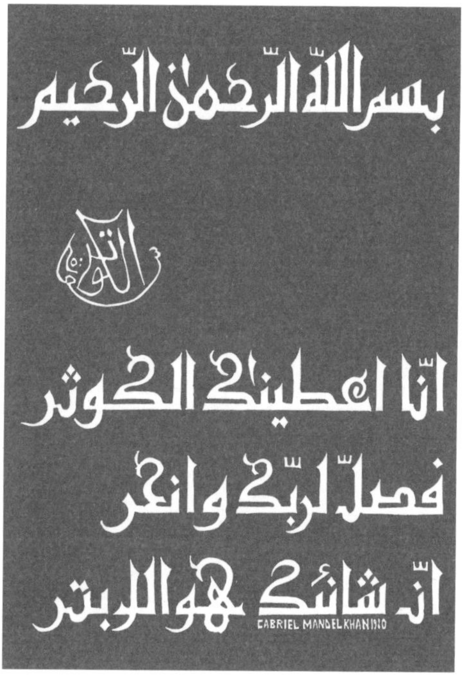
بسم الله الرحمن الرحيم
انا اعطينك الكوثر
فصل لربك وانحر
ان شانئك هو الابتر
GABRIEL MANDELKHAN 1980

SOME ASPECTS OF THE DĪWĀNĪ STYLE

1

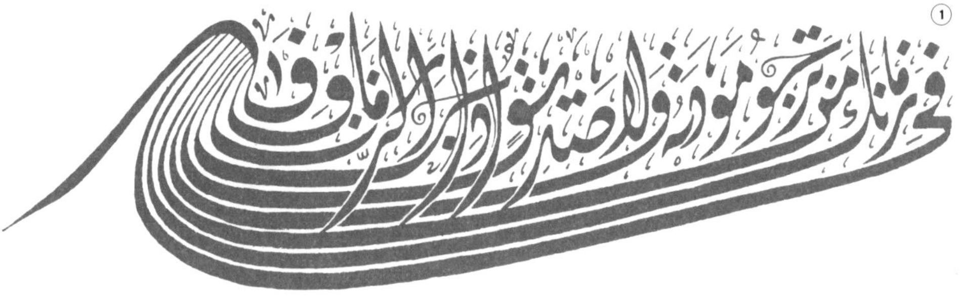

2

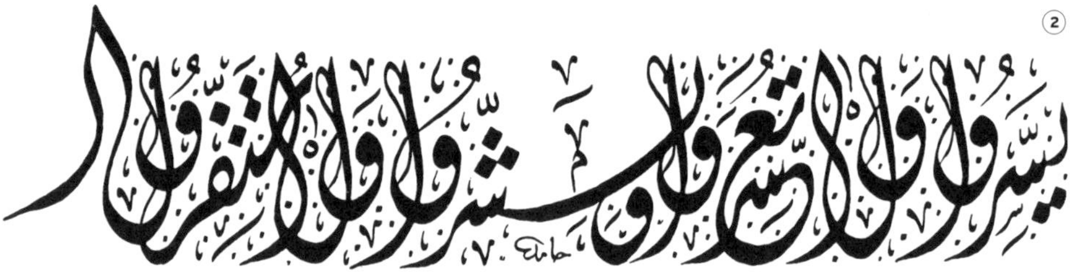

1. Boat-shaped composition in *dīwānī jalī*, by Mulla 'Ali. Istanbul, 1826.

2. A title from *Kirk Hadīs Tercümen* by Usuli. Istanbul, Suleymaniye Fatih Kutuphanesi, 5427.

3. Boat-shaped composition by Mehmet Izzet al-Karkuki (Turkish, 1841–1904).

3

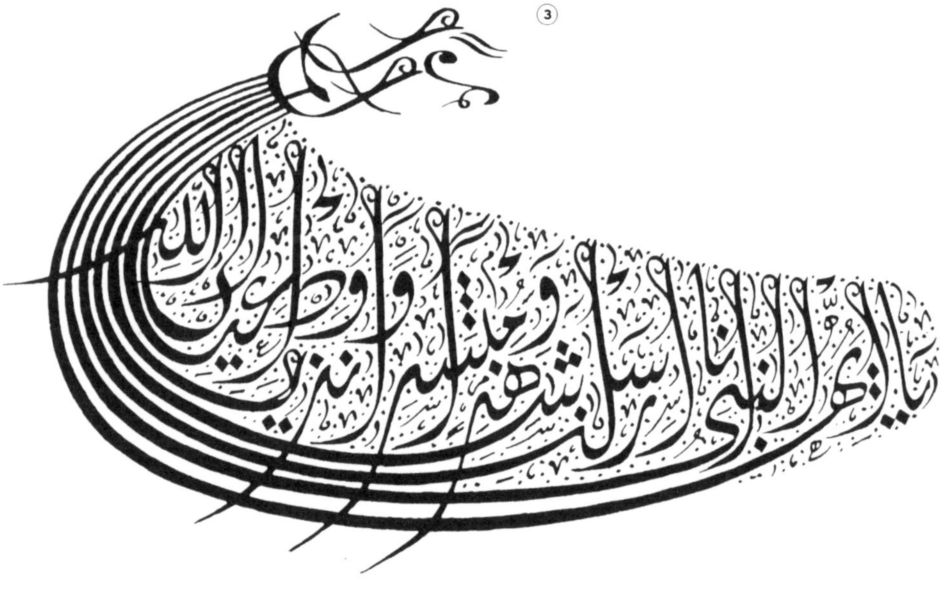

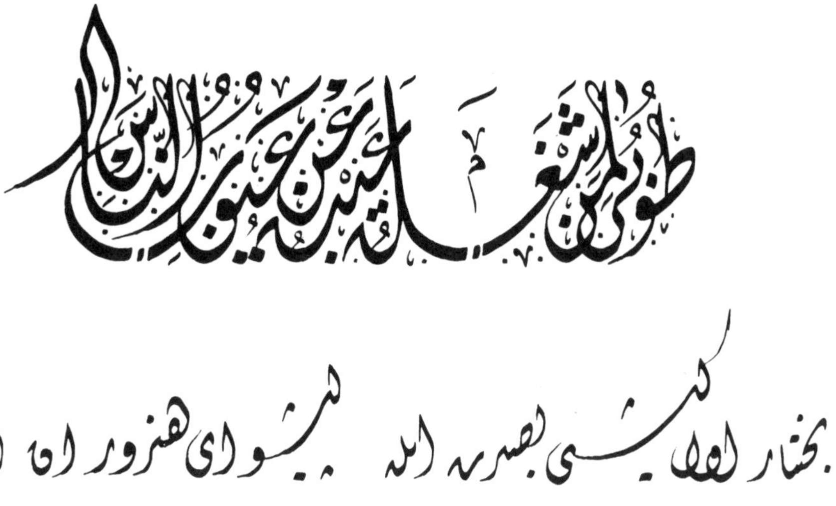

4

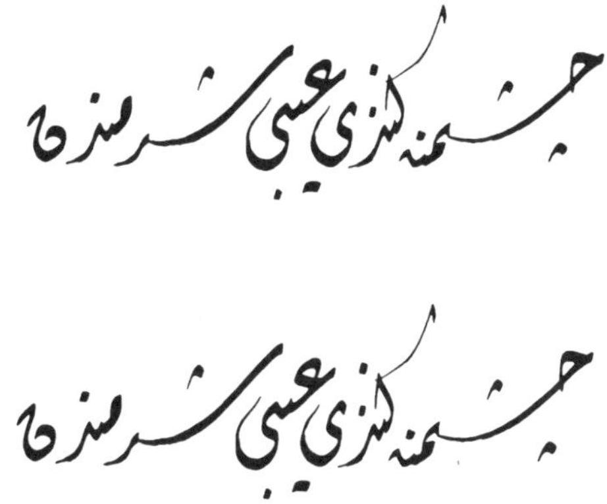

5

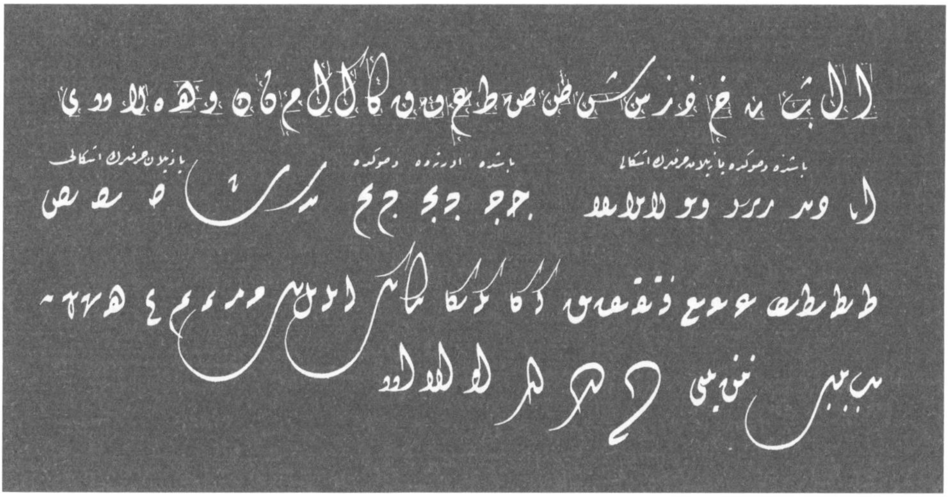

4. A page in *dīwānī jalī*. Istanbul, Suleymaniye Fatih Kutuphanesi.

5. A page from a calligraphic essay from the *Code* by Mehmet Evki Efendi (Turkish, 1804–1887).

COMPOSITIONS IN THE DĪWĀNĪ JALĪ STYLE

1

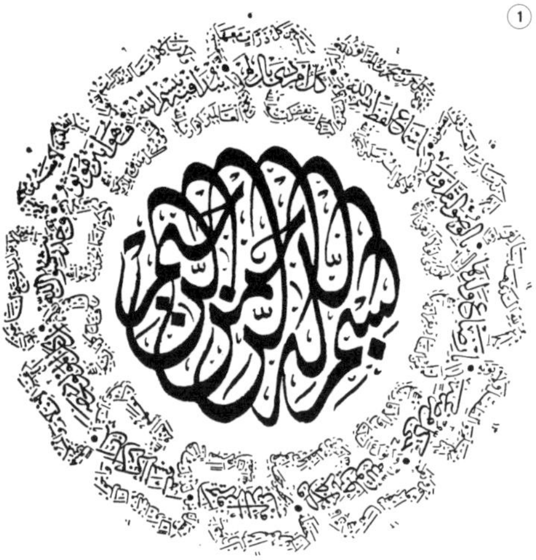

2

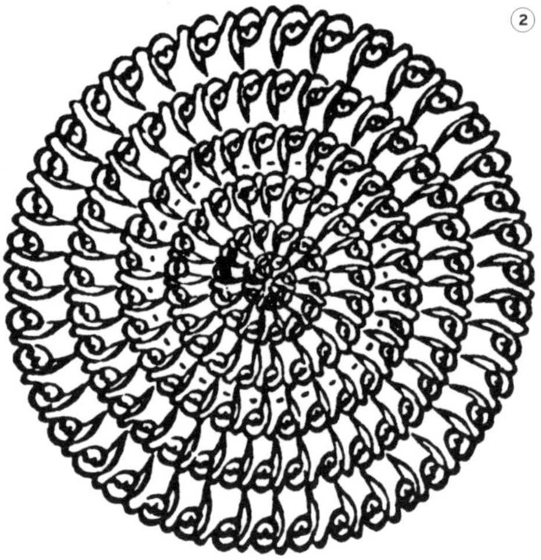

1. Composition by Abd al-Kader. The center is in *dīwānī jalī*, and the border in *thuluth* and *naskhī*. Tunisia, twentieth century.

2. Composition by Umar Yusuf al-Najjar, 1961. Jerusalem.

3. Composition by Abd al-Kader. Tunisia, twentieth century.

4. The *shahāda* by Mohamed Aziza. Tunisia, twentieth century.

5. Logo of the Sufi Jerrahi-Halveti brotherhood: *Ḥānqāh ḥaḍrat Sulṭān Muḥammad Nūr āl-Dīn āl-Jerraḥi āl-Khalwātī*. Istanbul, c. 1720.

3

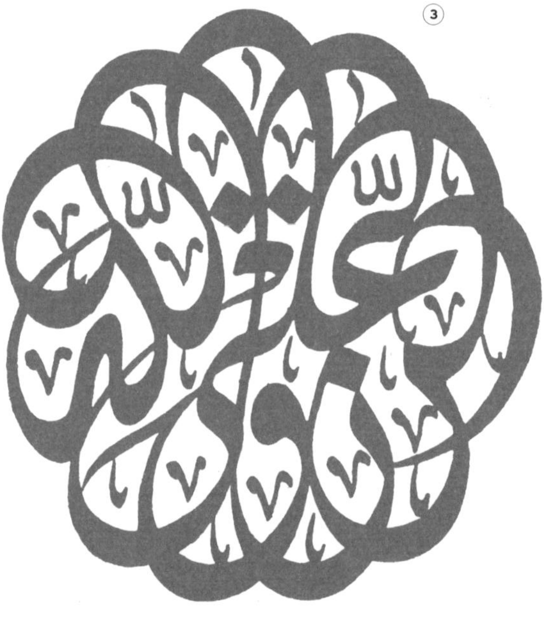

4

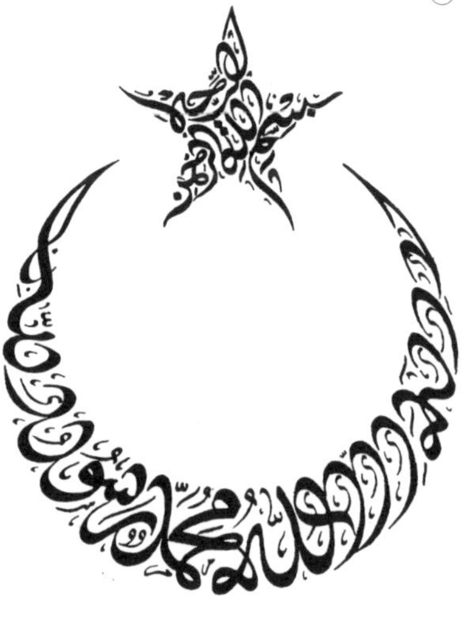

5

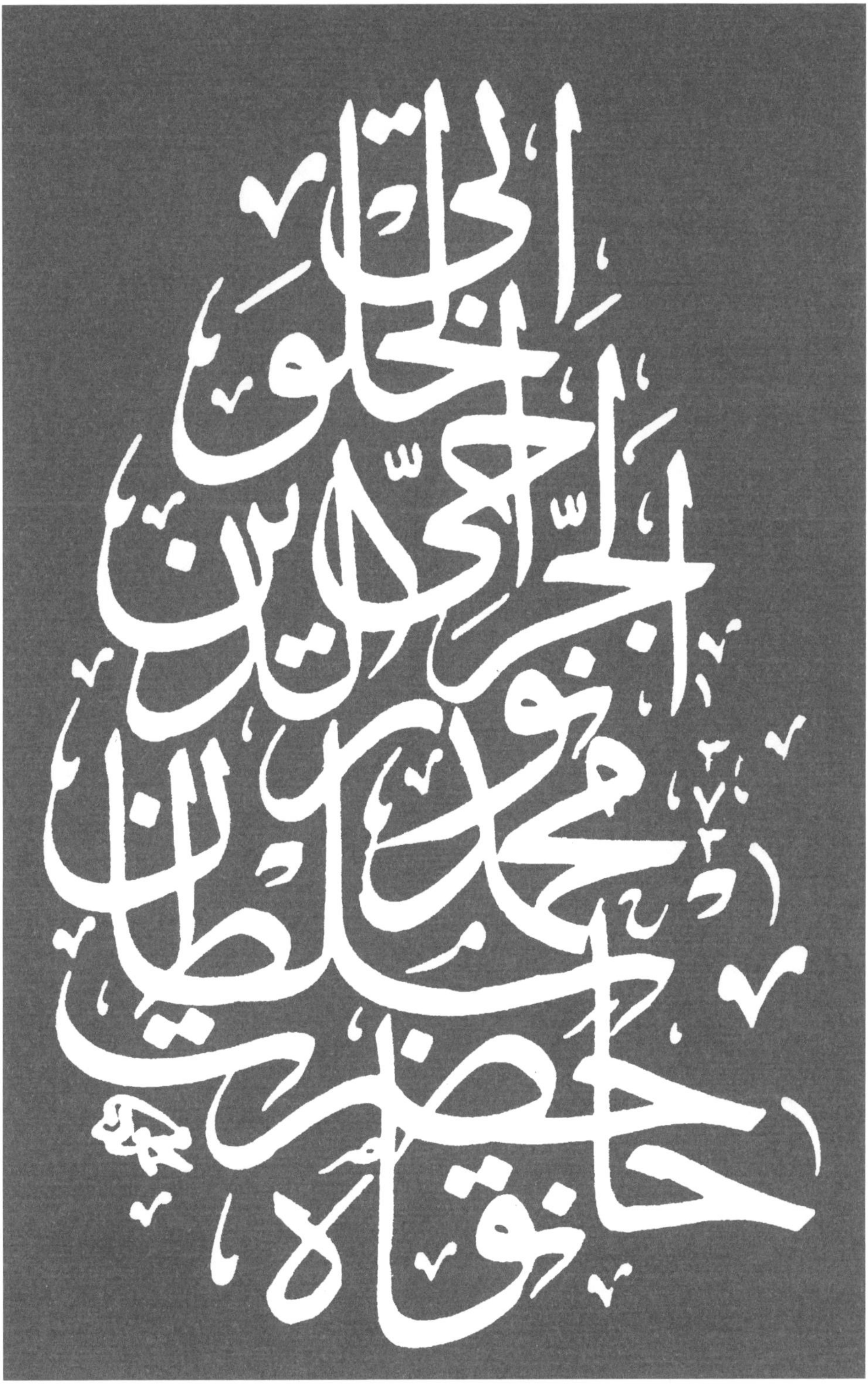

1

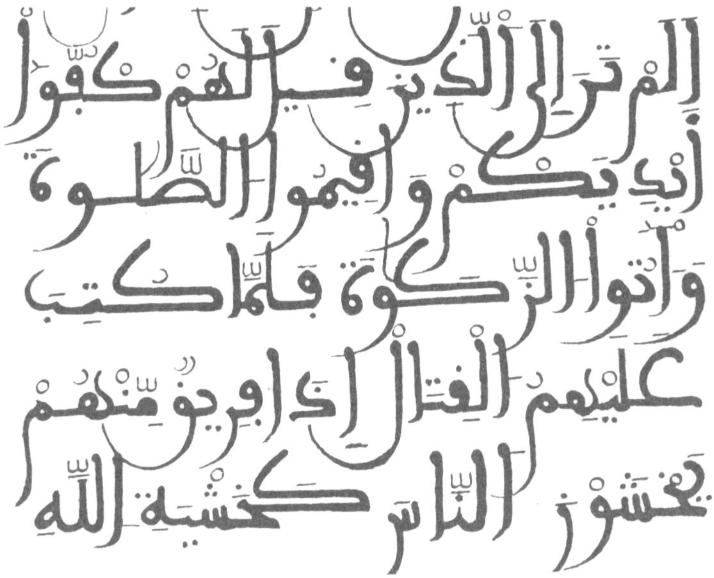

1. Detail from an Andalusian Qur'ān. Córdoba, fourteenth century.

2. Two pages from a Maghreb (North African) Qur'ān, written in Kano. Nigeria.

2

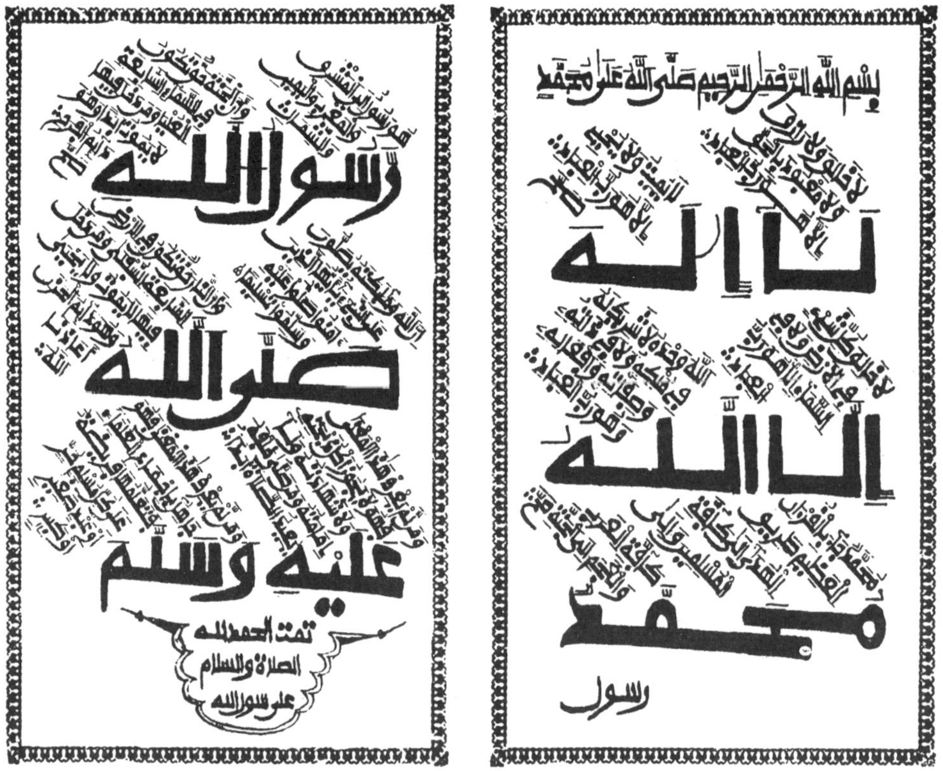

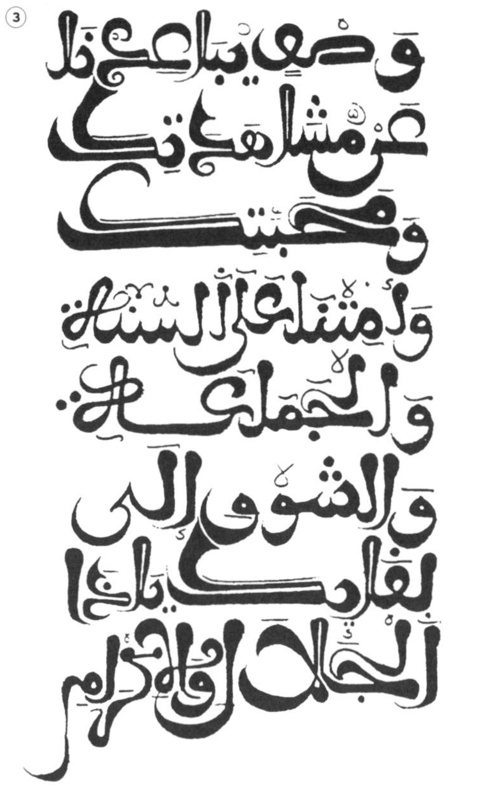

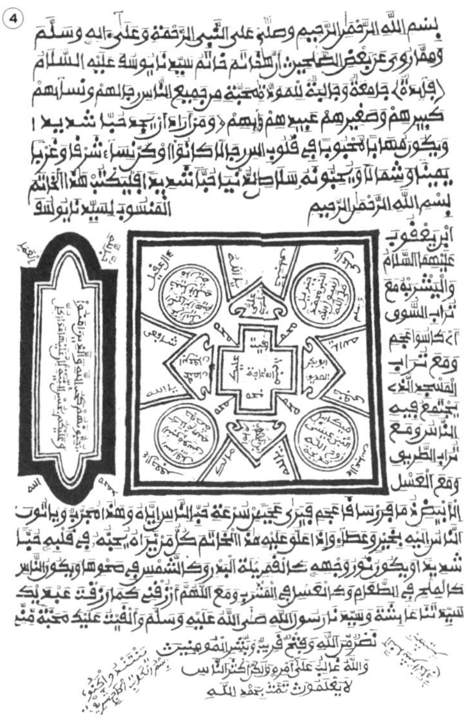

3. Page taken from a *maghribī*-style Qur'ān drawn by al-Qandusi.

4. Page from *Kitāb āl-Fawā'id āl-Ājīdā*, a book on magic by Ahmad al-Daraibi (d. 1738), in a Moroccan facsimile.

5. The name Muhammad drawn by al-Qandusi in the volume *Dalīl āl-Khayrāt* (Guide to the Celestial Gifts), 1850.

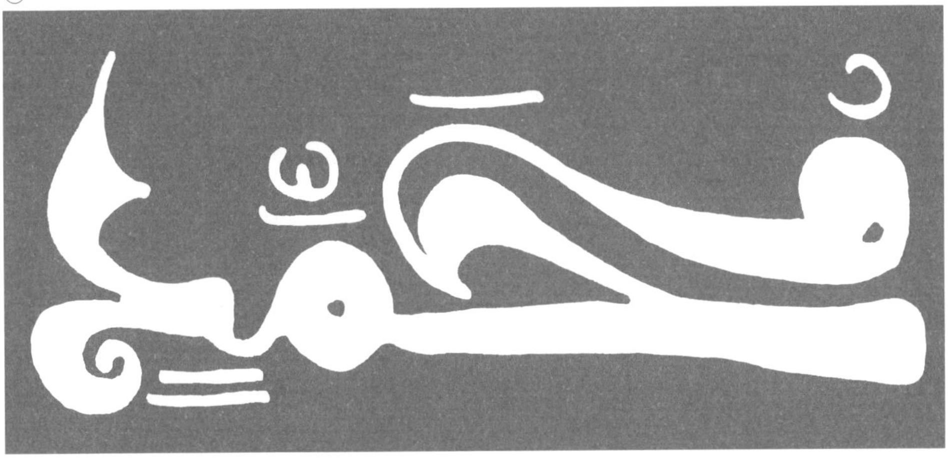

1

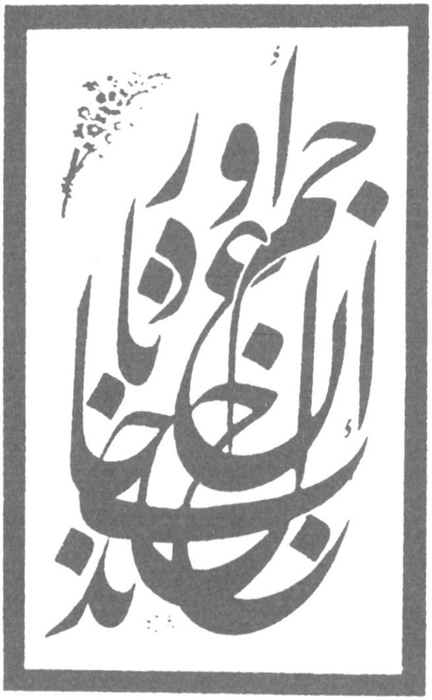

2

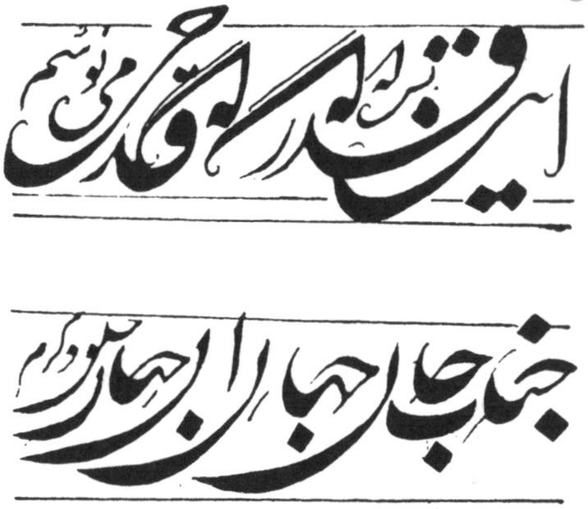

3

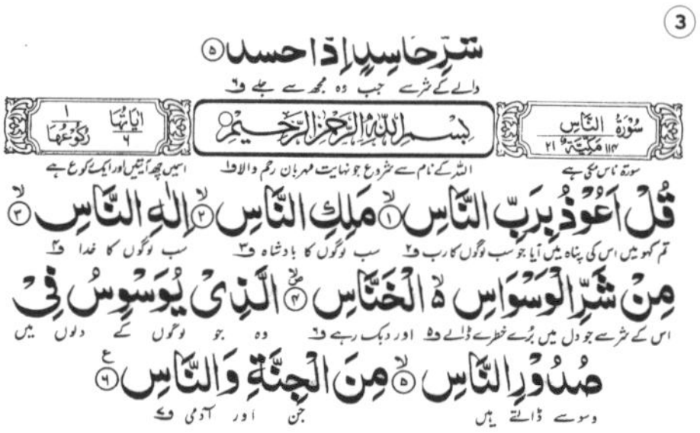
ومن شر حاسد إذا حسد ⑤
بسم الله الرحمن الرحيم
قل أعوذ برب الناس ① ملك الناس ② إله الناس ③
من شر الوسواس الخناس ④ الذي يوسوس في
صدور الناس ⑤ من الجنة والناس ⑥

1. Page drawn in Indian Farsi style.

2. *Zulf-i 'arūs* calligraphy, c. 1820, India.

3. The last sura of a Pakistani Qur'ān printed in Karachi, 1976.

4. Makhrafat Qur'ān, 1842, Delhi.

4

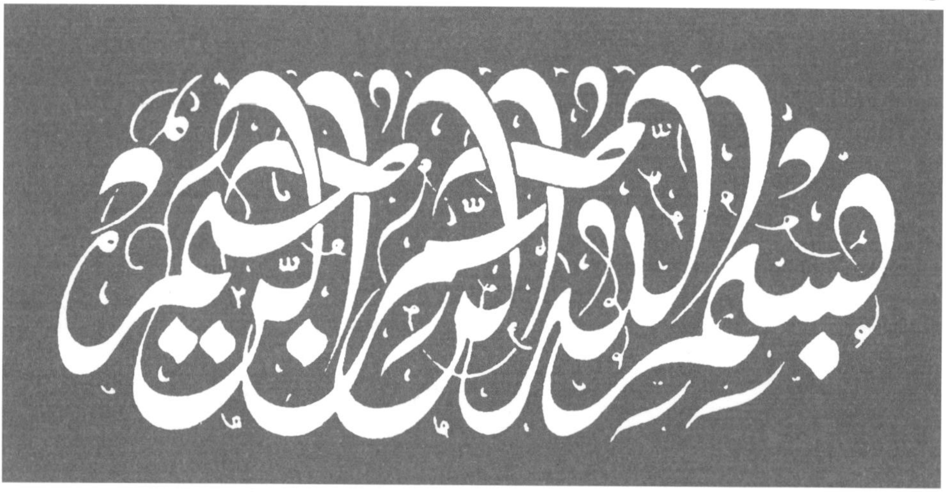

INTERLACINGS IN GULZAR STYLE

1. The phrase *āl-Ḥamdu, āl-Walī, āl-Ḥamdu* (God's attributes). *Musalsal* script done in *thuluth* characters using the *gulzar* style. Drawn by Ahmed Karahisari, 1547, Istanbul.

2. *Basmala* in *thuluth jalī* drawn by Ahmed Karahisari (1468–1556). Istanbul, Islamic and Turkish Museum.

(1)

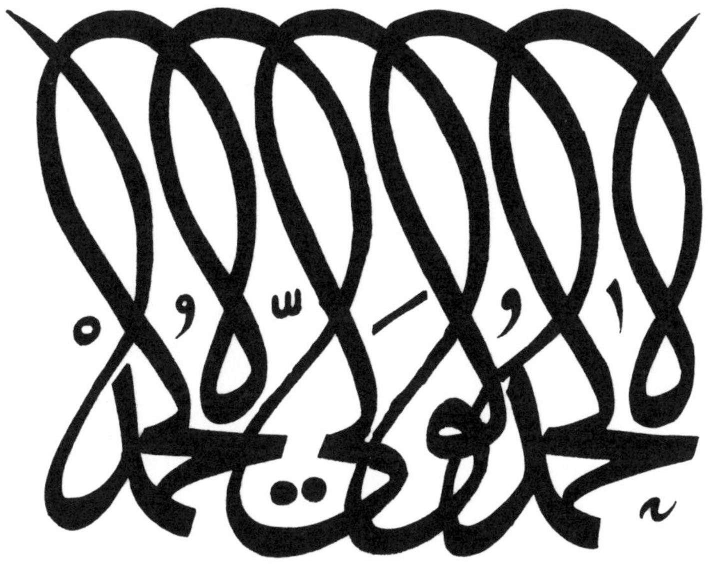

(2)

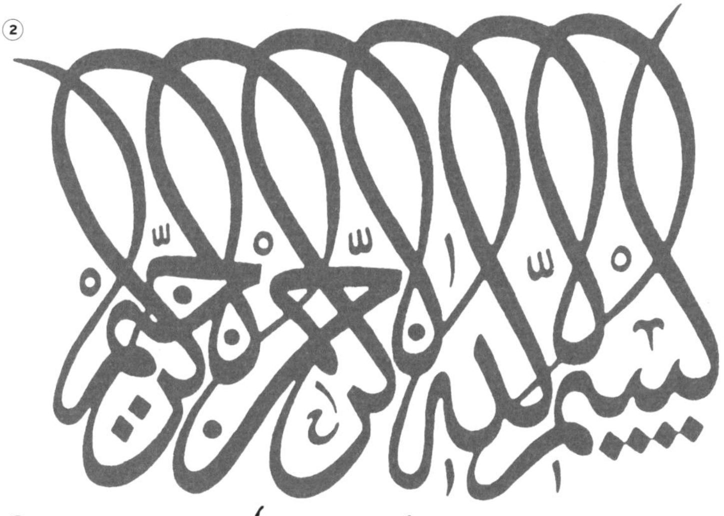

(3)

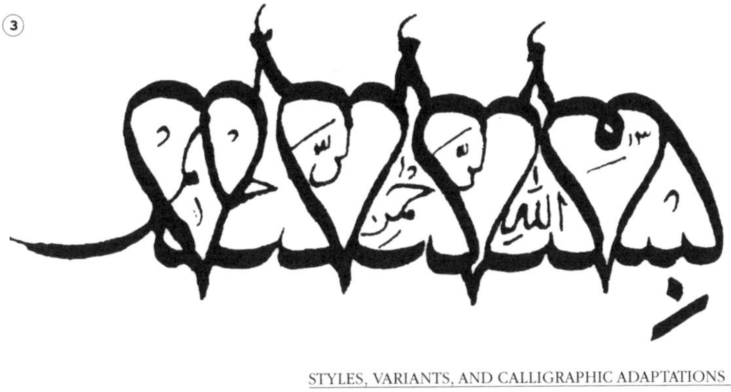

3. *Basmala* from a Qur'ān, Afghanistan, eighteenth century.

ARABIC CALLIGRAPHY IN CHINA

①

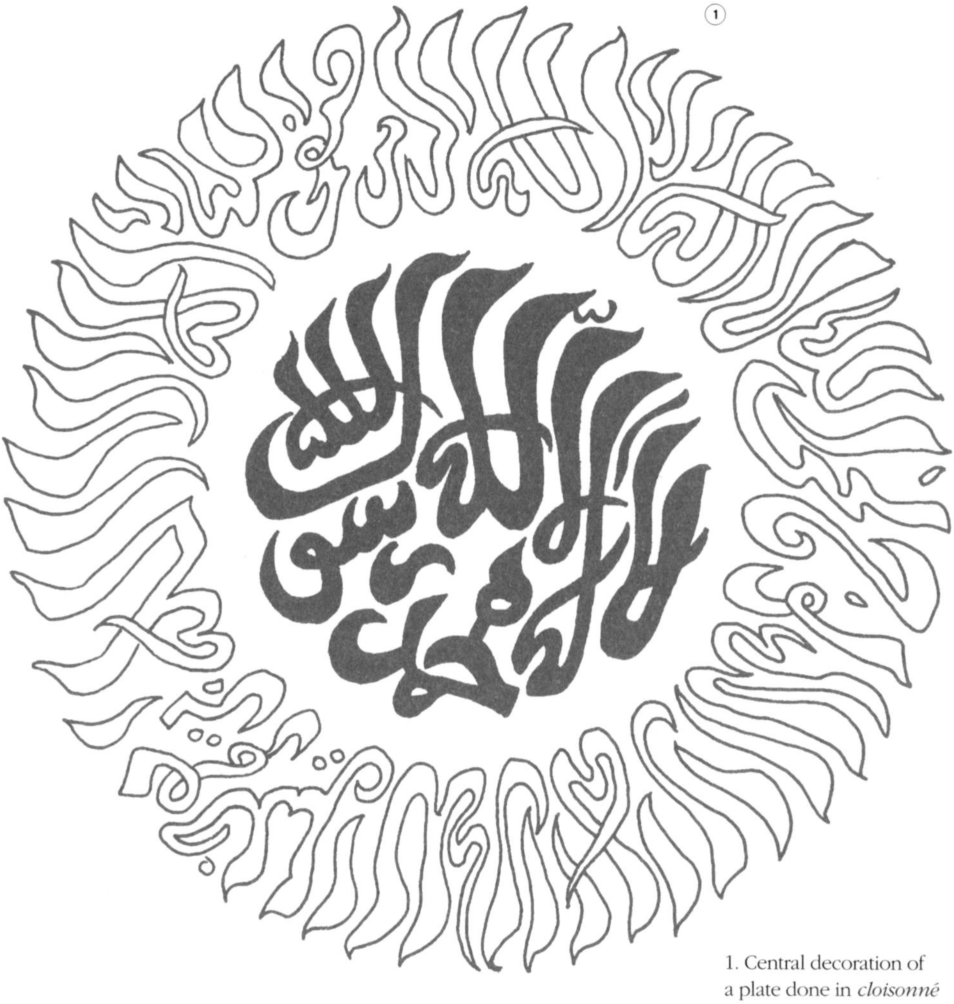

1. Central decoration of a plate done in *cloisonné* enamel from the twelfth or thirteenth century. Commissioned for an Ottoman Sultan in China. Istanbul, Topkapi Sarayë Museum.

②

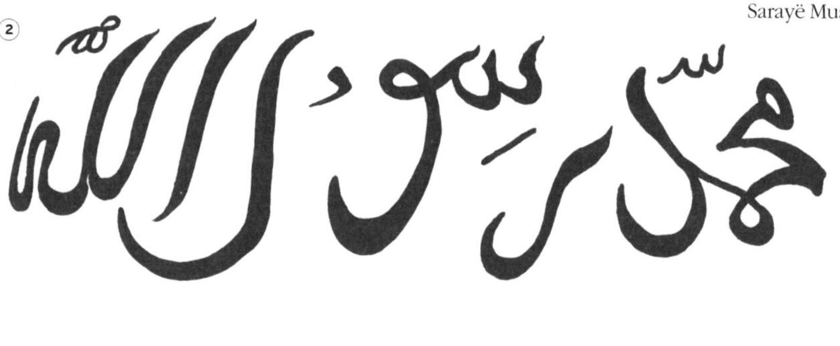

3

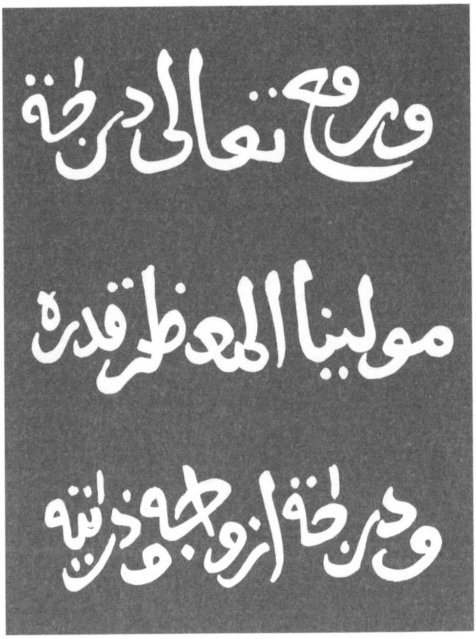

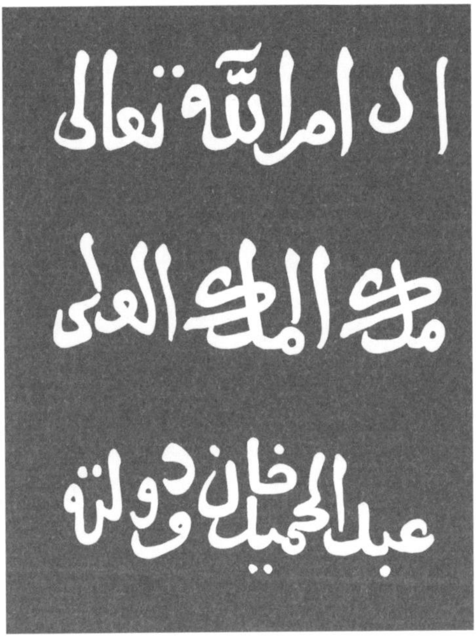

2. The second part of the *shahāda*, enamel on bronze, from the back of a vase. Istanbul, Topkapi Sarayë Museum.

3. Enamel on bronze decoration on a vase given by the Chinese Emperor Qianlong (1736–1796) to the Ottoman Sultan Selim III (1761–1808). Istanbul, Topkapi Sarayë Museum.

4. *Basmala* in *sīnī* characters.

5. A page from a Qur'ān written in Arabic and Chinese, 1892. Canton, China.

5

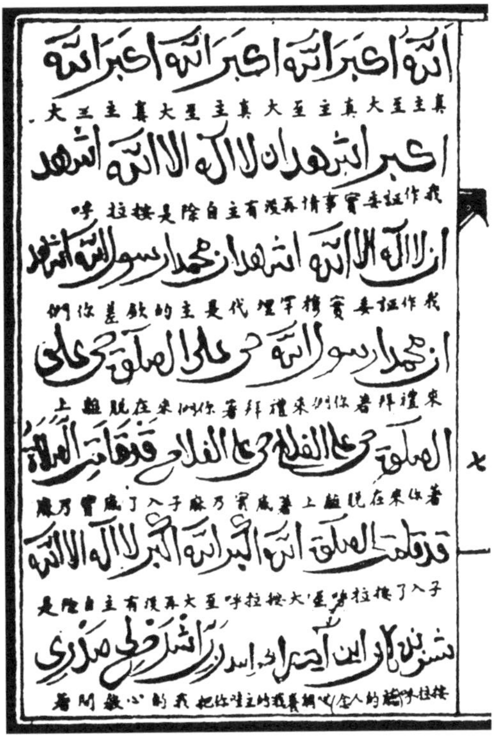

4

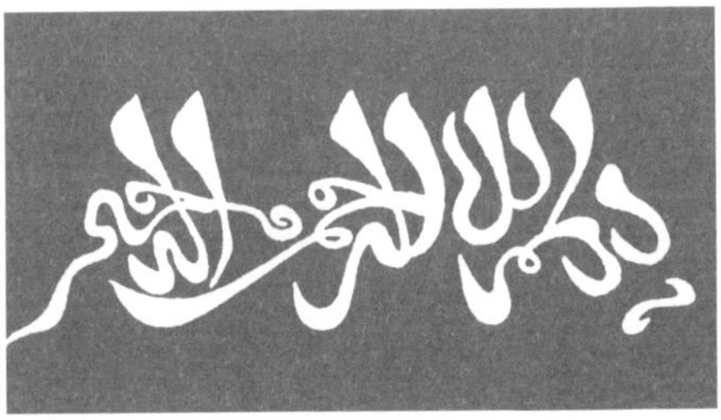

EXAMPLES OF OTTOMAN TUĞRA COMPOSITIONS

1

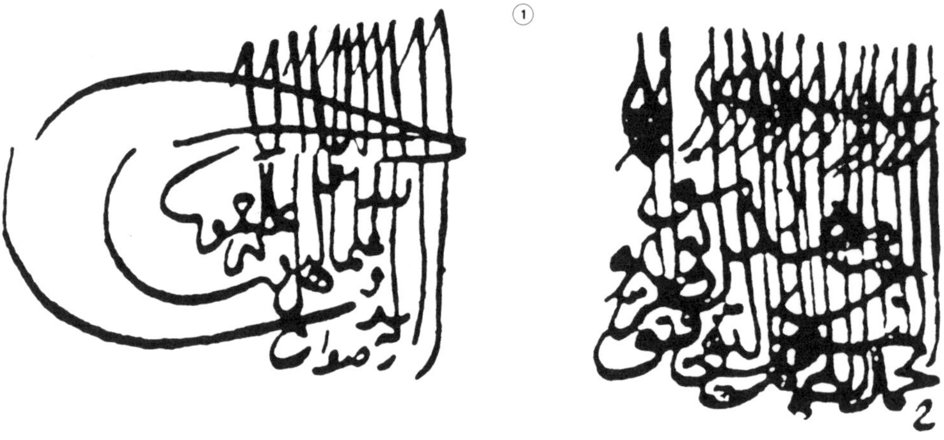

2

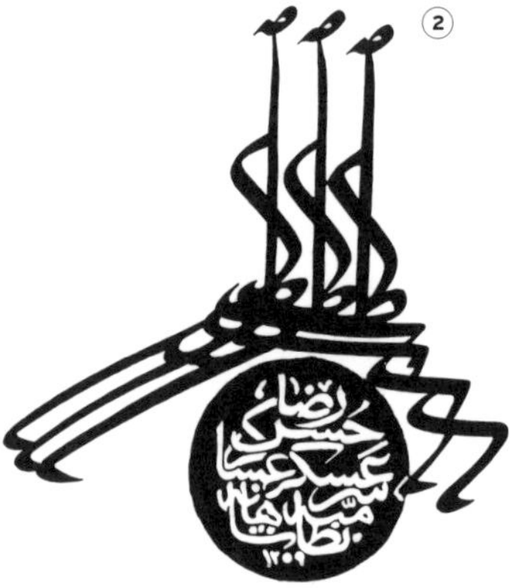

3

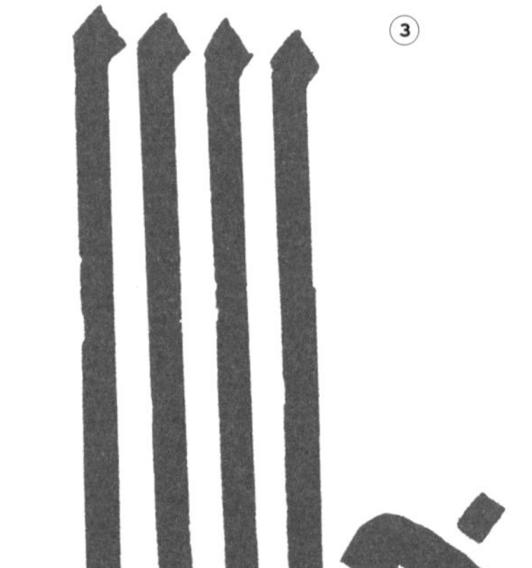
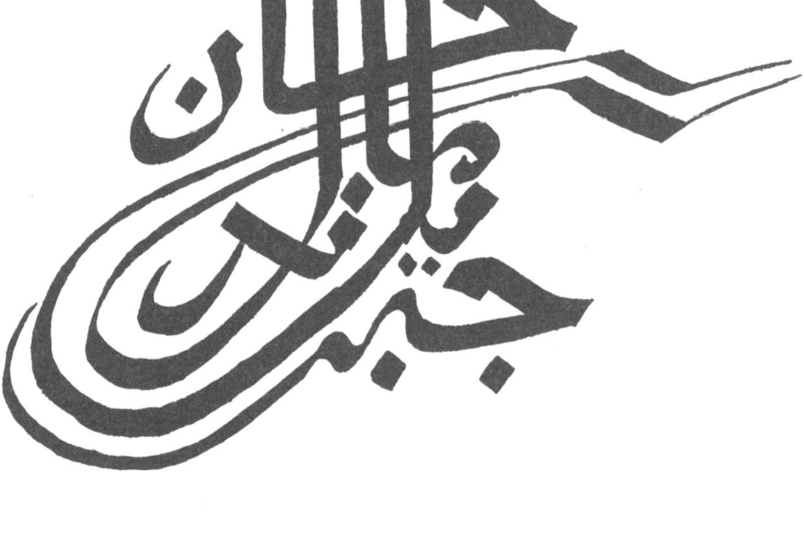

1. Signature of an Ottoman padisha. Turkey, eighteenth century.

2. Signature of the Ottoman military commander Hasan Razaku, 1843. Istanbul, Topkapi Sarayë Museum.

3. The name *Gibrail Mandel Khān* on a tomb of Buyuk Mazaristan, 1712. Uskudar, Turkey.

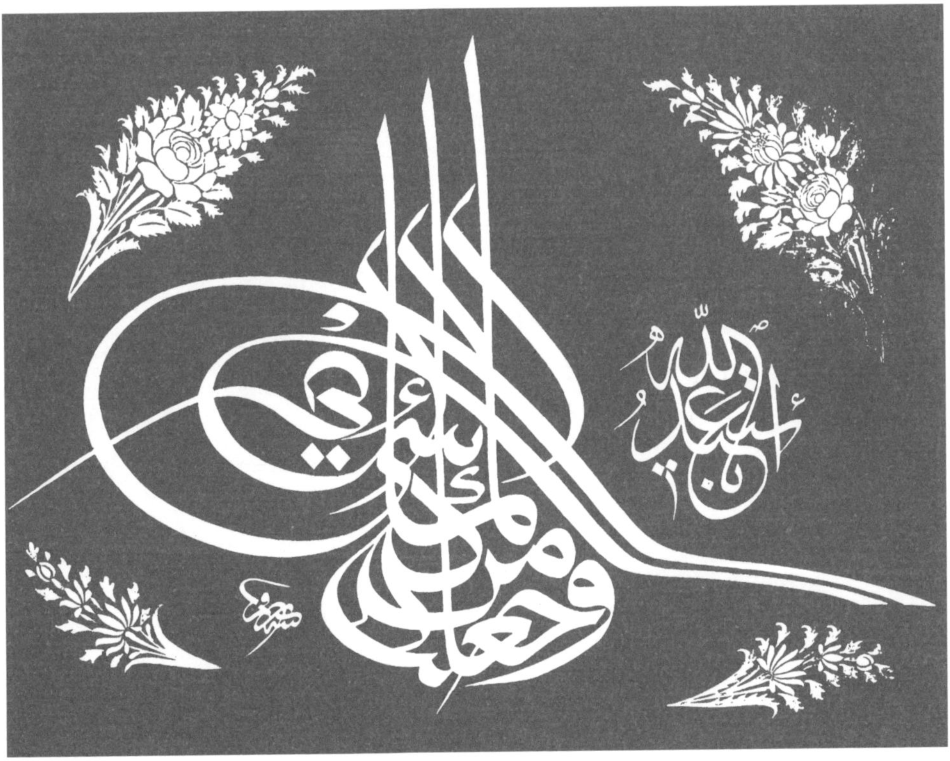

4

4. The phrase "I take shelter in God" drawn in *tuğra* form by Mustafa Rakim (d. 1767). Istanbul, Sabanci Hat Kollesiyonu.

5. The signature of Sultan Mahmūd Khān, drawn by Mustafa Rakim. Istanbul, Topkapi Sarayë Museum.

6. *Basmala* drawn in *tuğra* form by Hamad al-Madi.

6

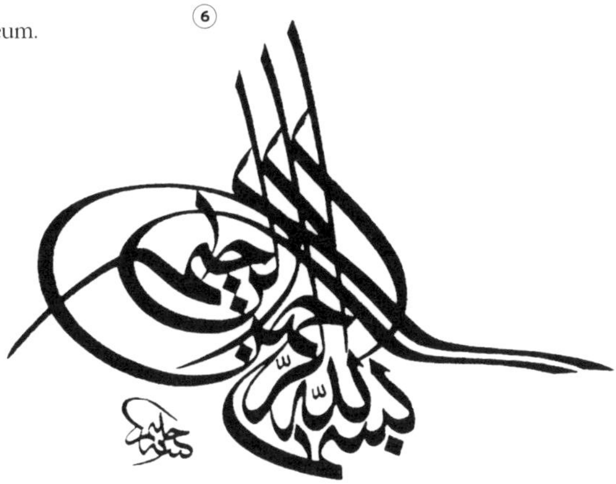

5

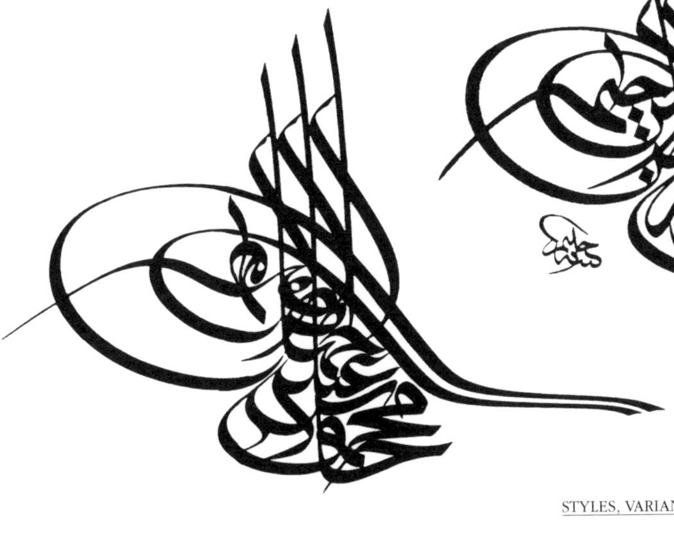

1

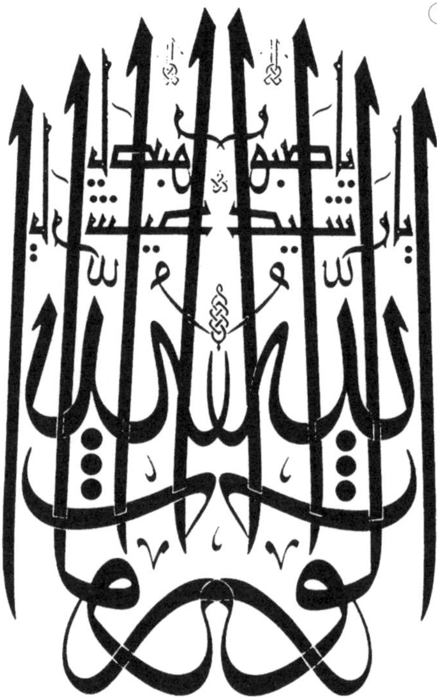

2

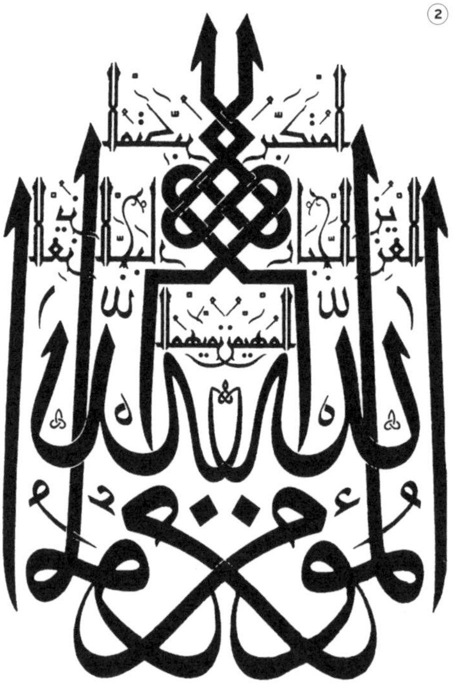

3

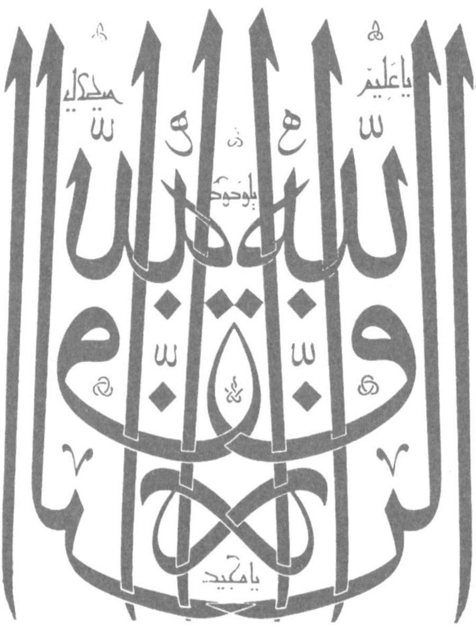

4

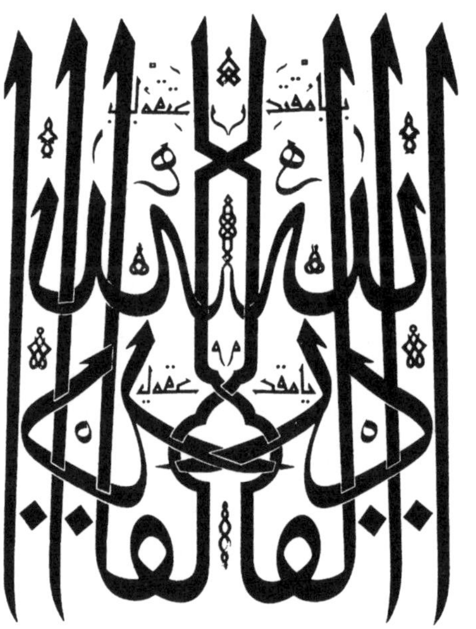

1–7. Decorations from the Ulu Jami' mosque of Bursa, Turkey, in specular style (*muthannā*). Bursa was the first capital of the Ottoman Empire. The Ulu Jami' was built between the years 1379 and 1421. Beginning in the eighteenth century, its walls were adorned by beautiful calligraphy, in paintings as well as frescoes, by masters such as Sadullah Efendi (1766–1843); Shevket Vahdeti (1833–1871); Mehmet Shefik Bey (1819–1879); Abdulfettah Efendi (1814–1896); Mehmet Nazif Bey (1846–1913); Aziz Efendi Rufai (1871–1934); and Refet Efendi (1873–1949).

5

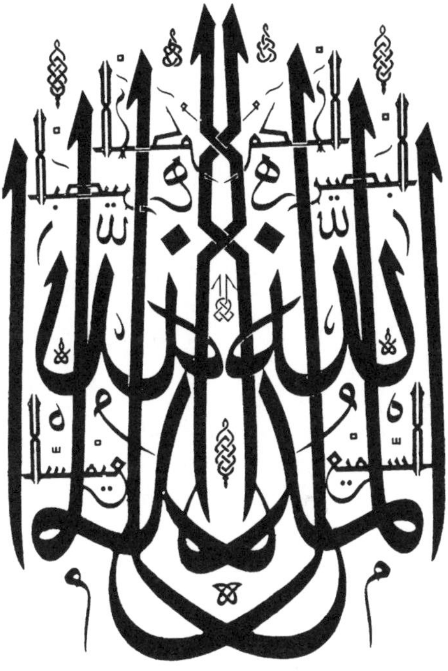

6

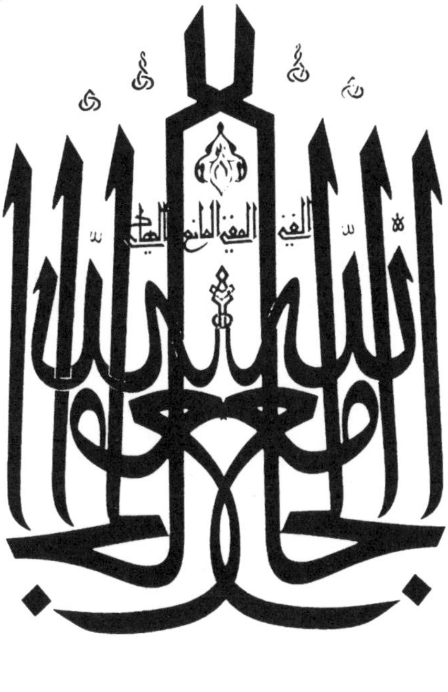

7

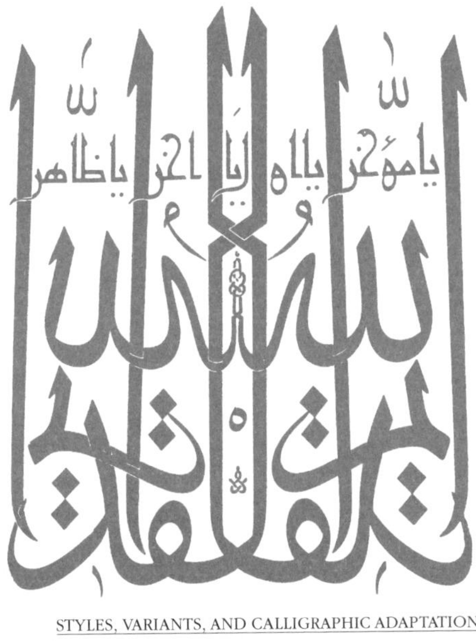

MUTANNĀZAR COMPOSITIONS

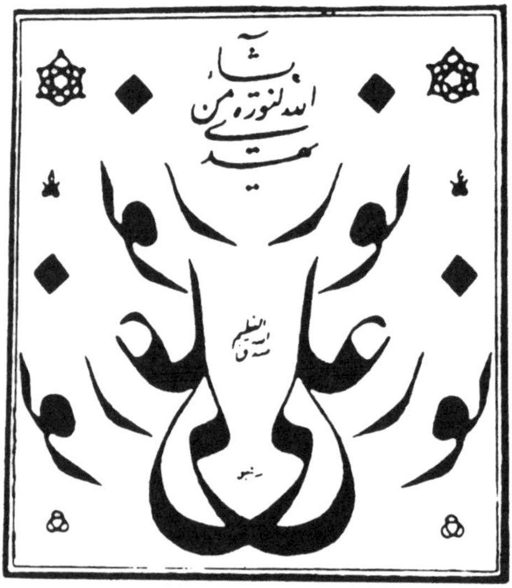

1

1. Specular calligraphy done in *ta'līq* style by the Turkish master Mehmet Shefik Bey (1819–1879).

2. *Mashāllāh* drawn by Emin Barin (1913–1996) of Bolu, Turkey. The calligraphic decorations in the Ataturk Mausoleum of Ankara, Turkey, and in the Grand Mosque of Karachi, Pakistan, are also his work.

3. *Basmala* in *thuluth* style by Muhammad Amin Sanat, 1920.

4. Specular calligraphy by the Turkish master Mehmet Shefik Bey (1819–1879).

2

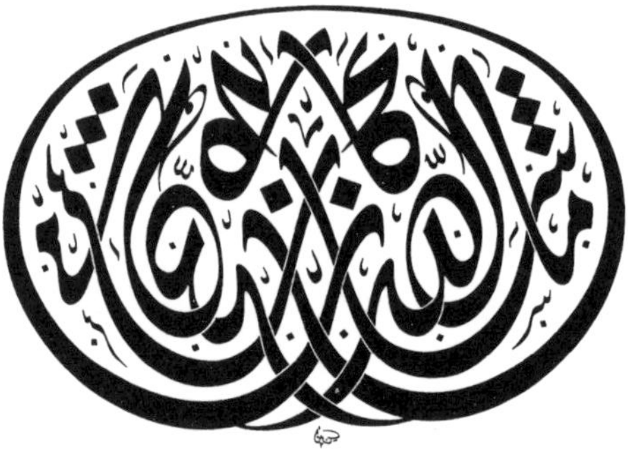

3

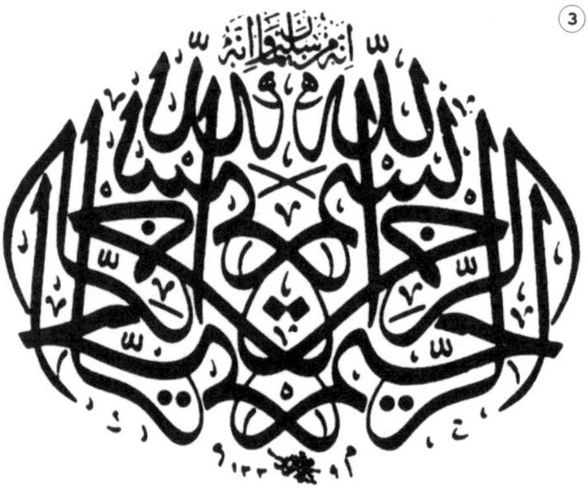

4

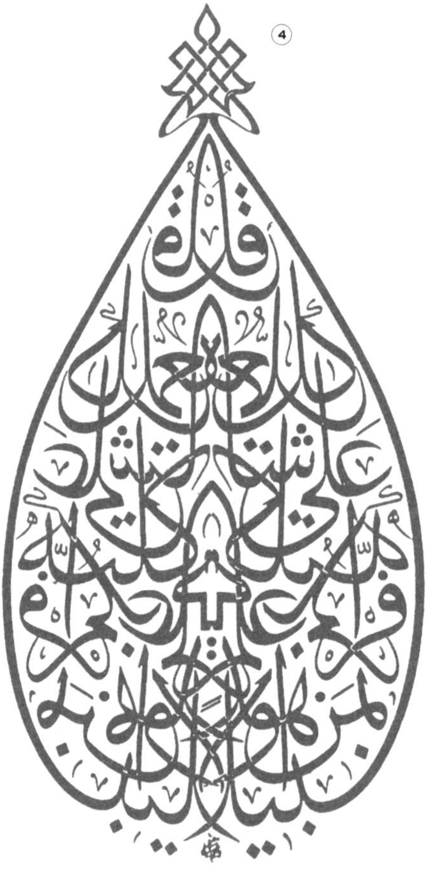

5. A *müsenna* composition, also called an *aynali*, from 1896. Drawn by Abdulfettah Efendi (1814–1896).

6. The phrase *Lā īlaha īllā Hū, Rabby āl-ālamīn* (No other God but him, the Lord of the worlds), drawn by Mehmet Shefik Bey (1819–1879).

7. The phrase *Ālḥamdu Lillāhi* (Glory to God), drawn in *thuluth* style by al-Muallef in 1978.

6

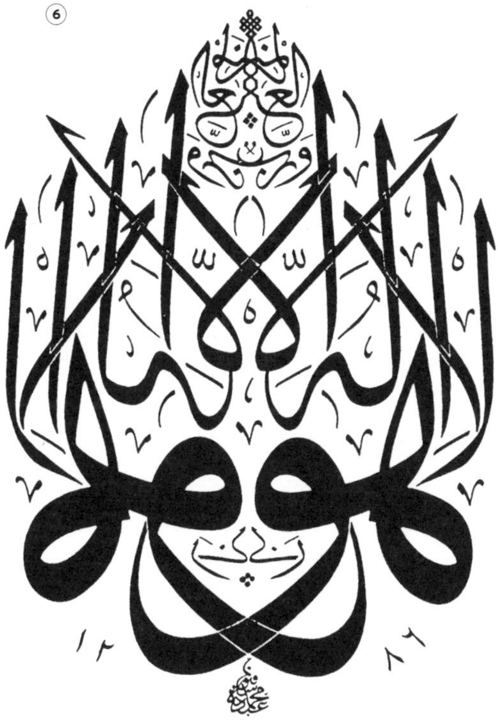

5

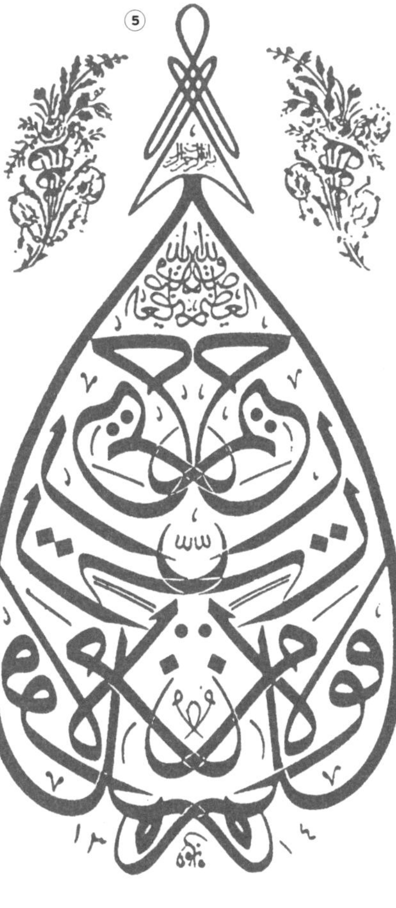

7

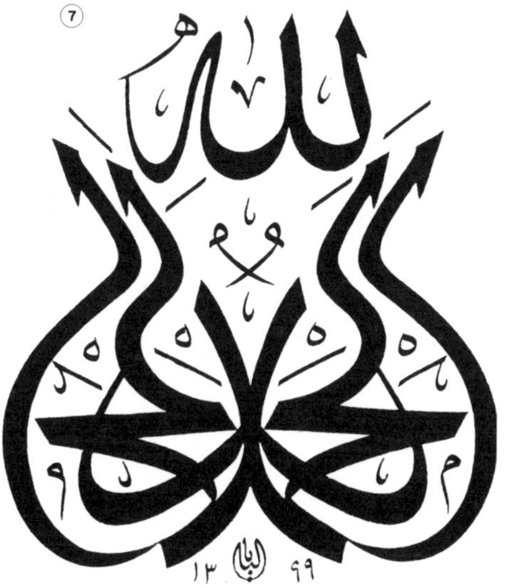

ARABIC SCRIPT IN SORCERY

1

[illegible]	[illegible]	[illegible]	#	IIII	[illegible]	[illegible]
ز	خ	ظ	ث	ش	ج	ف
زكي	خبير	ظهير	ثابت	شكور	جبار	فرد
كسفيايل	عنيايل	صرفيايل	ميكايل	سمسمايل	جبرايل	روفيايل
ميمون	ابيض	شهورش	برقان	احمر	مره	مذهب
السبت	الجمعة	الخميس	الاربعاء	الثلاثاء	الاثنين	الاحد
زحل	زهرة	مشتري	عطارد	مريخ	قمر	شمس

3

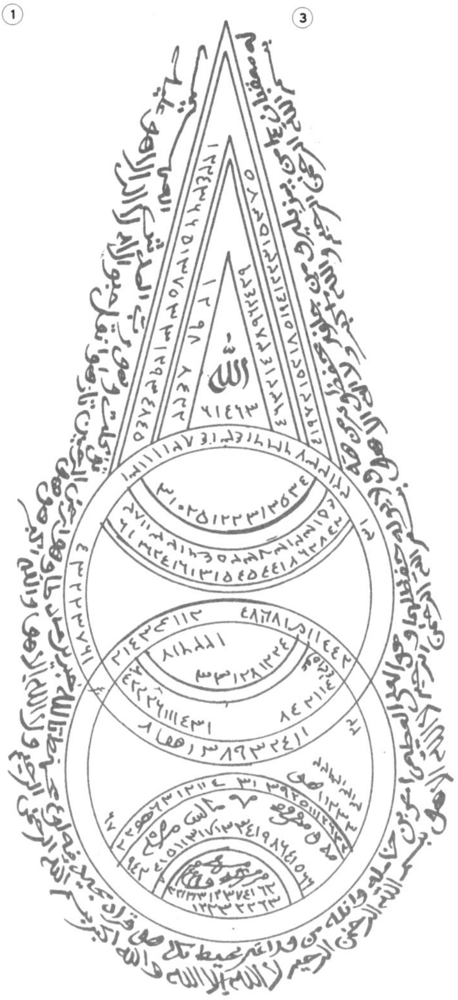

1. An amulet protecting against "the envy of the envious," with a portion of the second-to-last sura, the *āl-Falaq* (Dawn), Hermes Abu Thot's alphabet, as well as the names of demons. From the *Kitāb Shawq āl-Mustahām* by Ibn Wahshiyya, ninth or tenth century.

2. Magic square containing "The Throne Verse." Qur'ān, sura *Tawba*, verse 129.

2

العظيم	الله	لا اله	الاهو	عليه	توكلت	وهو	رب	العرش	العظيم
العرش	حسبي	بالمؤمنين	رؤف	رحيم	فان	تولوا	فقل	حسبي	الله
رب	فقل	عليكم	عزيز	عليه	ماعنتم	حريص	عليكم	بالمؤمنين	لا اله
وهو	تولوا	حريص	أنفسكم	رسول	من	أنفسكم	رحيم	رؤف	الاهو
تولوا	فان	ماعنتم	من	لقدجاءكم	لقدجاءكم	من	ماعنتم	فان	توكلت
عليه	رحيم	عليه	رسول	لقدجاءكم	لقدجاءكم	رسول	عليه	رحيم	عليه
الاهو	رؤف	عزيز	أنفسكم	من	رسول	أنفسكم	حريص	تولوا	وهو
لا اله	بالمؤمنين	عليكم	حريص	ماعنتم	عليه	عزيز	عليكم	فقل	رب
الله	حسبي	فقل	تولوا	فان	رحيم	رؤف	بالمؤمنين	حسبي	العرش
العظيم	العرش	رب	وهو	توكلت	عليكم	الاهو	لا اله	الله	العظيم

3. Amulet suggested in the *Ghāyat āl-Ḥakīm fī āl-Siḥr* (The Purpose of a Treatise on Magic) by Maslama al-Majriti (d. 1007), which the author believed had been "engraved on Moses' staff."

4. Talisman with verses fifty-one and fifty-two of the *āl-Qalam* sura (The Pen). India, eighteenth century. Riyadh, Rifa'at Shaikh al-Ard Collection.

5. The āl-Durr āl-Munazzam (string of pearls) amulet, described in the *Kitāb Shams āl-Ma'ārif* by Abu al'Abbas al-Buni (d. 1225).

6. An al-Buni talisman with the tetrad of magic names and the names of the kings of jinns.

7. Talisman in the form of a magic square, still in use today in North Africa as a counter spell. It is used to fight impotence and to favor mating.

5

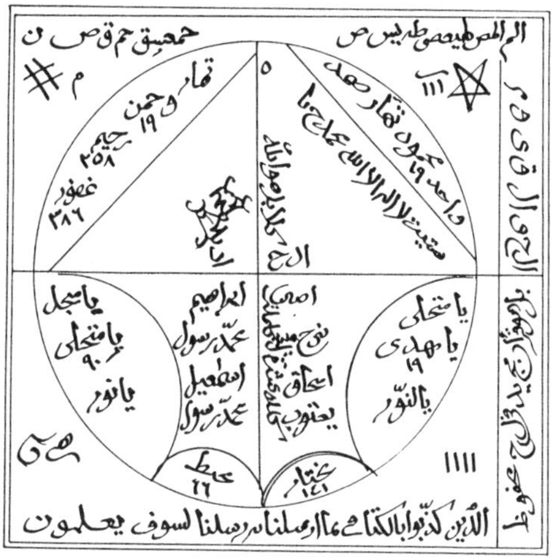

6

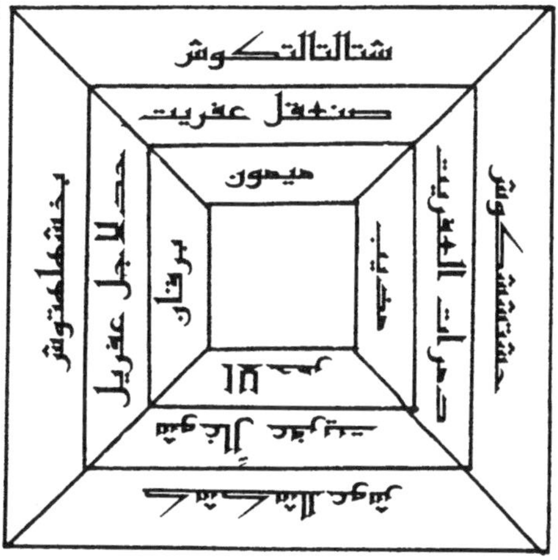

4

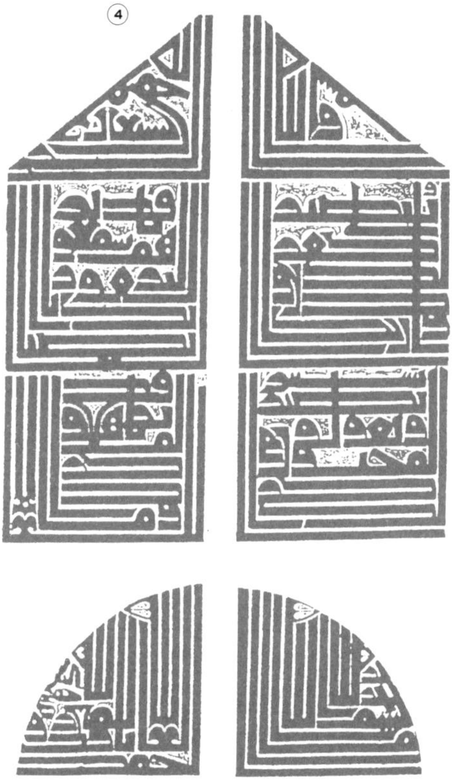

7

ا	ز	ج	ط	ه
ز	ح	ط	ه	ا
ج	ط	ه	ا	ز
ط	ه	ا	ز	ج
ه	ا	ز	ج	ط

EXAMPLES FROM SCIENTIFIC TREATISES

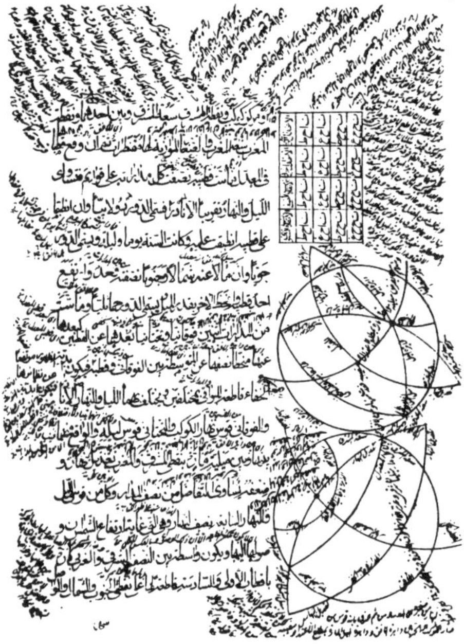

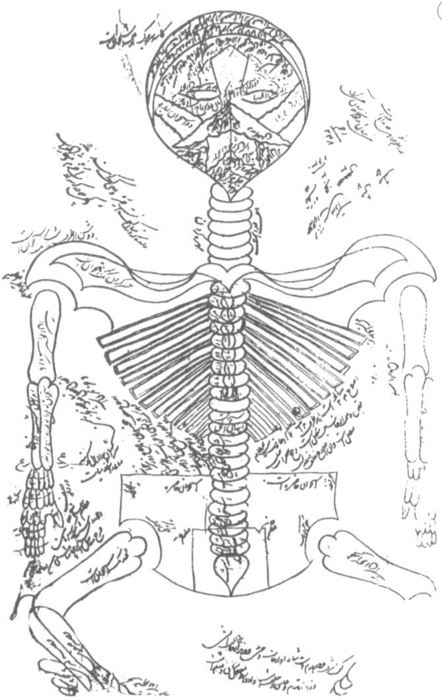

1. Page from a "Cosmogony" drawn in Iraq. Baghdad, Qahtane al-Madfa'i Library.

2. Table from the *Canon*—a fourteen-volume treatise by the Turkish Ibn Sina, better known in the West as Avicenna (c. 980–1037). London, Wellcome Institute for the History of Medicine.

3. Quadrature of the star Sirius, from a sketch by Nur al-Din al-Bitruji of Córdoba, known in the West as Alpetragius (d. 1204).

4. Astrological chart drawn in *zūlf āl-Ārus* (the style known as "the bride's curls"). Tunisia, eighteenth century.

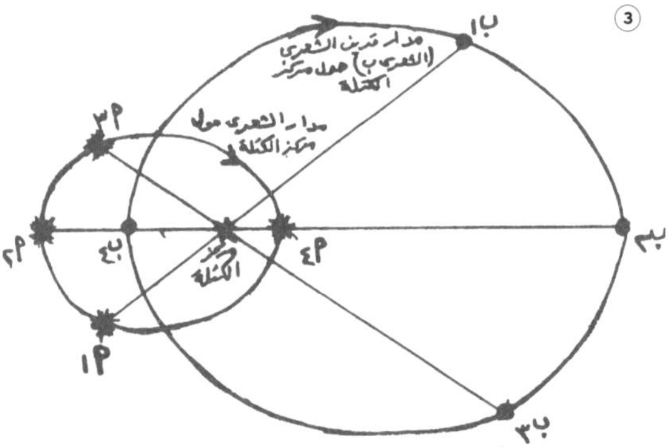

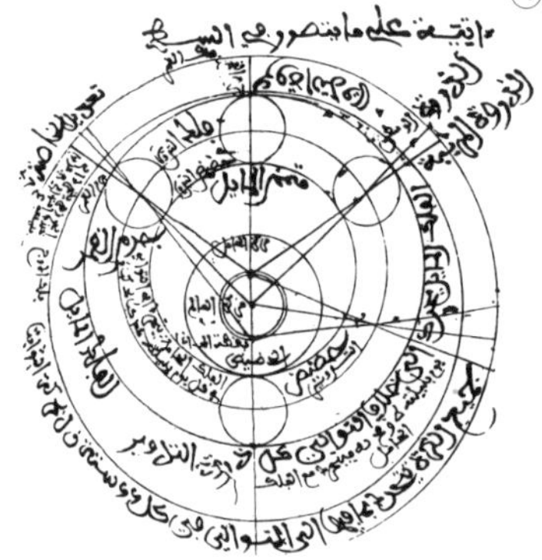

5
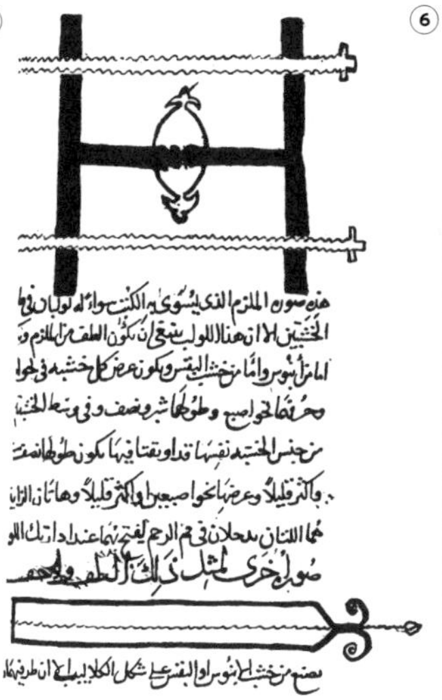

6
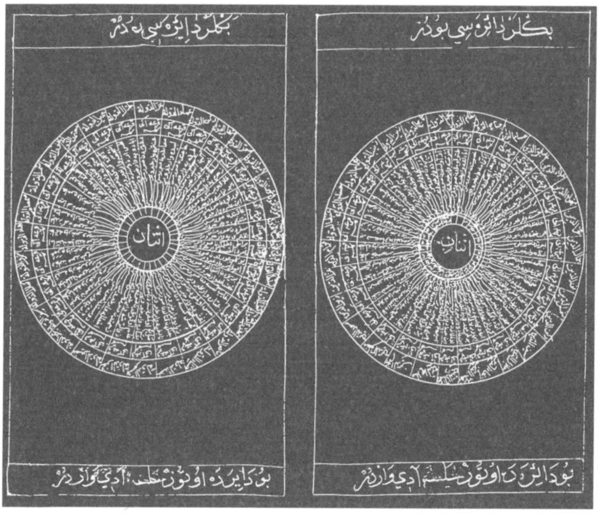

5. A page from *āl-Taṣrīf liman 'ajaz 'an āl-Ta'alif* (Manual of Surgery) by Abu al-Qasim al-Zahrawi (d. c. 1013; known in Europe as Abulcasis). London, Ms. Hunt, f. 85r.

6. Two pages from the "Treatise on the psychiatry of spirits" by Sultan Mughi al-Din. Turkey, eighteenth century.

7. A page from the "Treatise on the brightest stars for use in constructing mechanical clocks" by Taqi al-Din (1565).

8. A table taken from the "Treatise for the identification of psychological truths" by the Sufi physician Abu Abdallah al-Jazuli (d. c. 1470).

7
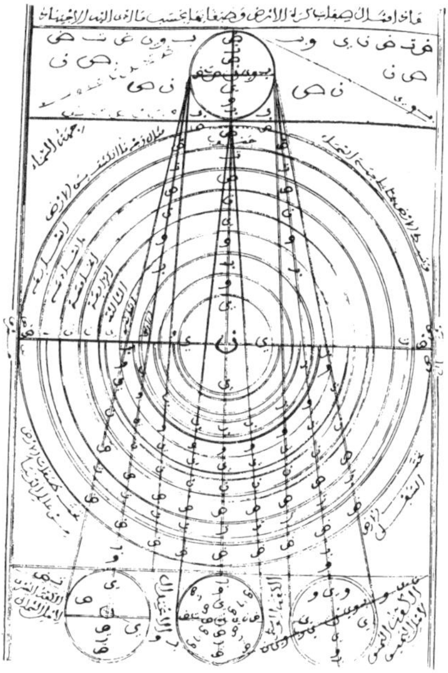

8
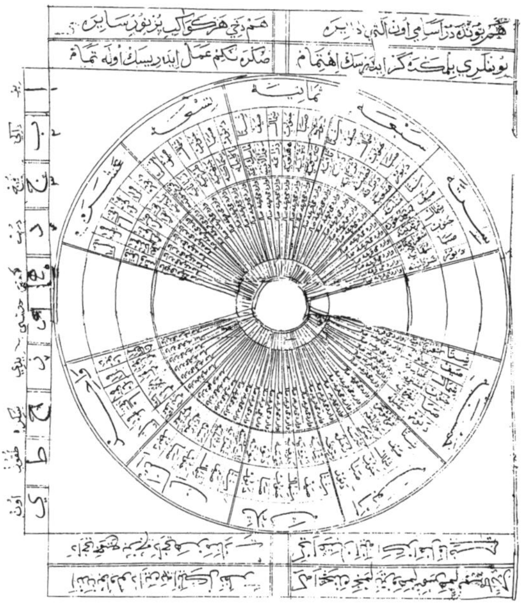

1, 2. Frontispiece and two pages of the *Kitāb ālī-Istilāḥat āl-Ṣūfīya* (Sufi Terminology) by the Sufi master Kamal al-Din al-Qashani of Samarkand, Uzbekistan. It gives the esoteric and mystical values of the letters of the Arabic alphabet.

3. Four pages from the "Code of Calligraphy" by Abu Ali Muhammad ibn Muqla (d. 940) taken from the 1663 facsimile composed by Muhammad al-Shafa'i. Cairo, National Library.

1

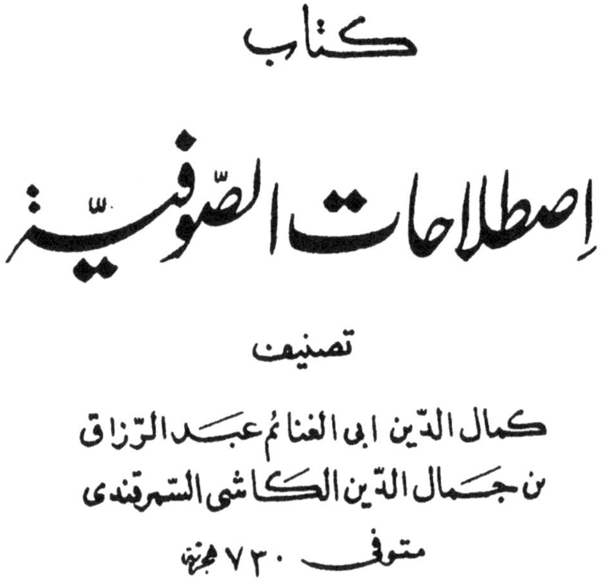

كتاب

اصطلاحات الصوفية

تصنيف

كمال الدين ابى الغنائم عبد الرزاق

بن جمال الدين الكاشى السمرقندى

متوفى ٧٣٠ هجرية

2

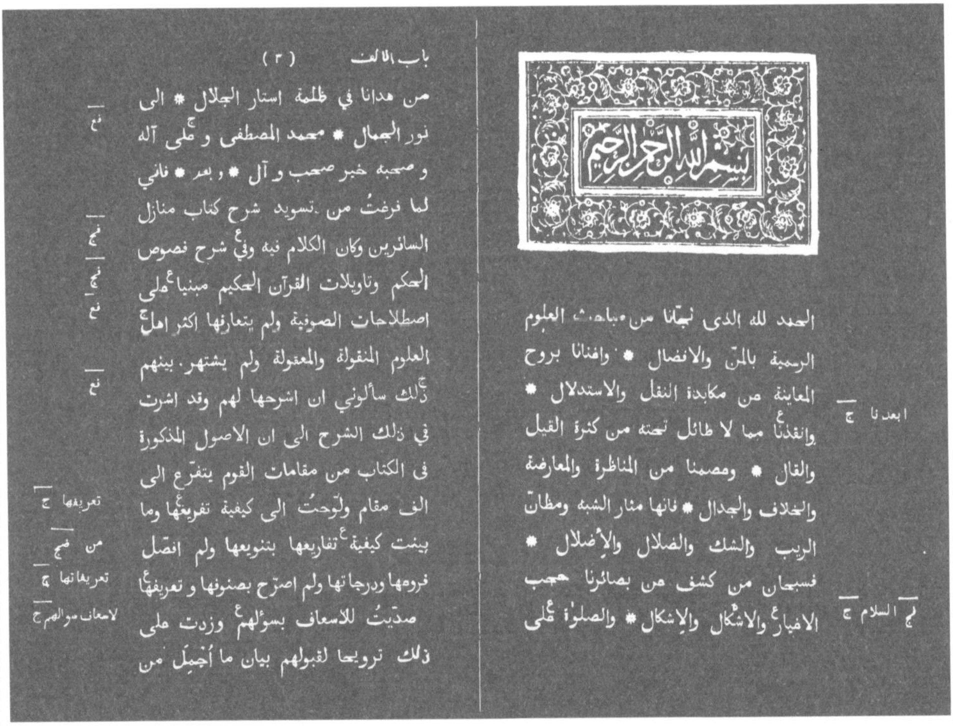

بسم الله الرحمن الرحيم

الحمد لله الذى نجانا من مباحث العلوم
الرسمية بالمنّ والانفضال * وافنانا بروح
المعاينة من مكابدة النقل والاستدلال *
وانقذنا مما لا طائل تحته من كثرة القيل
والقال * وعصمنا من المناظرة والمعارضة
والخلاف والجدال * فانها مثار الشبه ومظانّ
الريب والشك والضلال والإضلال *
فسبحان من كشف عن بصائرنا حجب
الاغيار والاشكال والإشكال * والصلوة على

ابعدنا ح
لم السلام ح

باب الالف (٣)

من هدانا في ظلمة استار الجلال * الى
نور الجمال * محمد المصطفى و على آله
وصحبه خير صحب و آل * وبعد * فاني
لما فرغت من تسويد شرح كتاب منازل
السائرين وكان الكلام فيه وفي شرح فصوص
الحكم وتاويلات القرآن الحكيم مبنيا على
اصطلاحات الصوفية ولم يتعارفها اكثر اهل
العلوم المنقولة والمعقولة ولم يشتهر بينهم
ذلك سألوني ان اشرحها لهم وقد اشرت
في ذلك الشرح الى ان الاصول المذكورة
فى الكتاب من مقامات القوم يتفرع الى
الف مقام ولوّحت الى كيفية تفريعها وما
بينت كيفية تفاريعها بتنويعها ولم افصّل
فروعها ودرجاتها ولم اصرّح بصنوفها و تعريفها
صدّيت للاسعاف بسؤلهم وزدت على
ذلك ترويحا لقبولهم بيان ما أجمل من

نع
فم
نم
نع
نع
تعريفها ح
من صح
تعريفاتها ح
لاسعاف سؤالهم ح

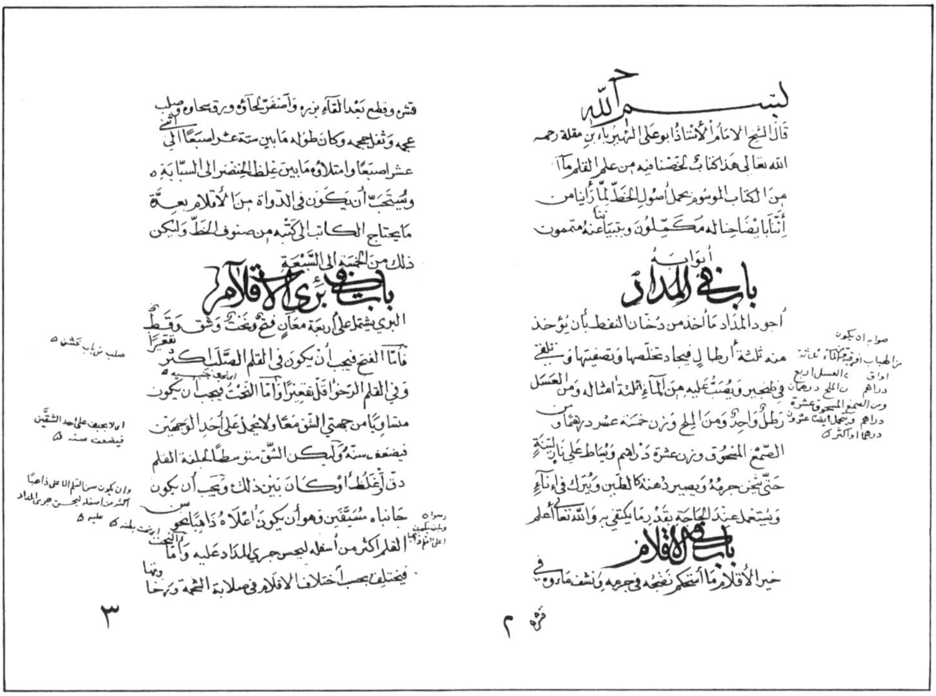

بسم الله

قال الشيخ الامام الاستاذ ابو علي الشهير بابن مقلة رحمه

الله تعالى هذا كتاب لخصنا فيه من علم القلم ما

باب في المداد

اجود المداد ما اخذ من دخان النفط بان يؤخذ

باب في الاقلام

خير الاقلام ما استحكم نضجه في جرمه ونشف ماؤه في

٢

باب في بري الاقلام

البري يشتمل على اربعة معان فتح ونحت وشق وقط

فاما الفتح فيجب ان يكون في القلم الصلب اكثر

٣

3

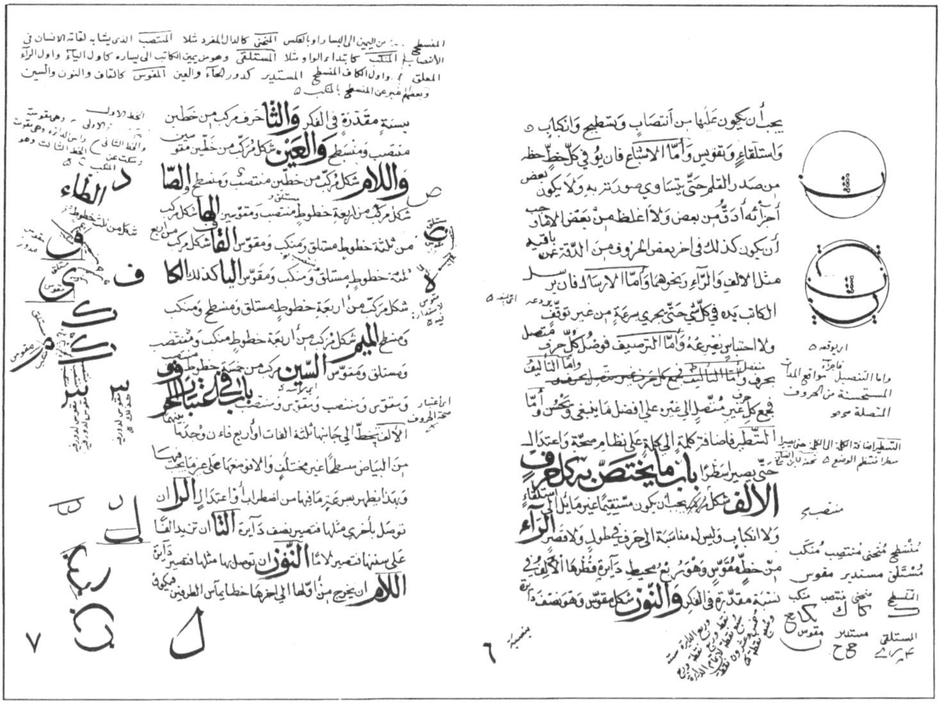

باب ما يختص بكل حرف

الالف

والراء

والنون

٦

والنون

واللام

باب في اعتبار الحروف

٧

EXAMPLES OF LAYOUT DESIGN AESTHETICS

1

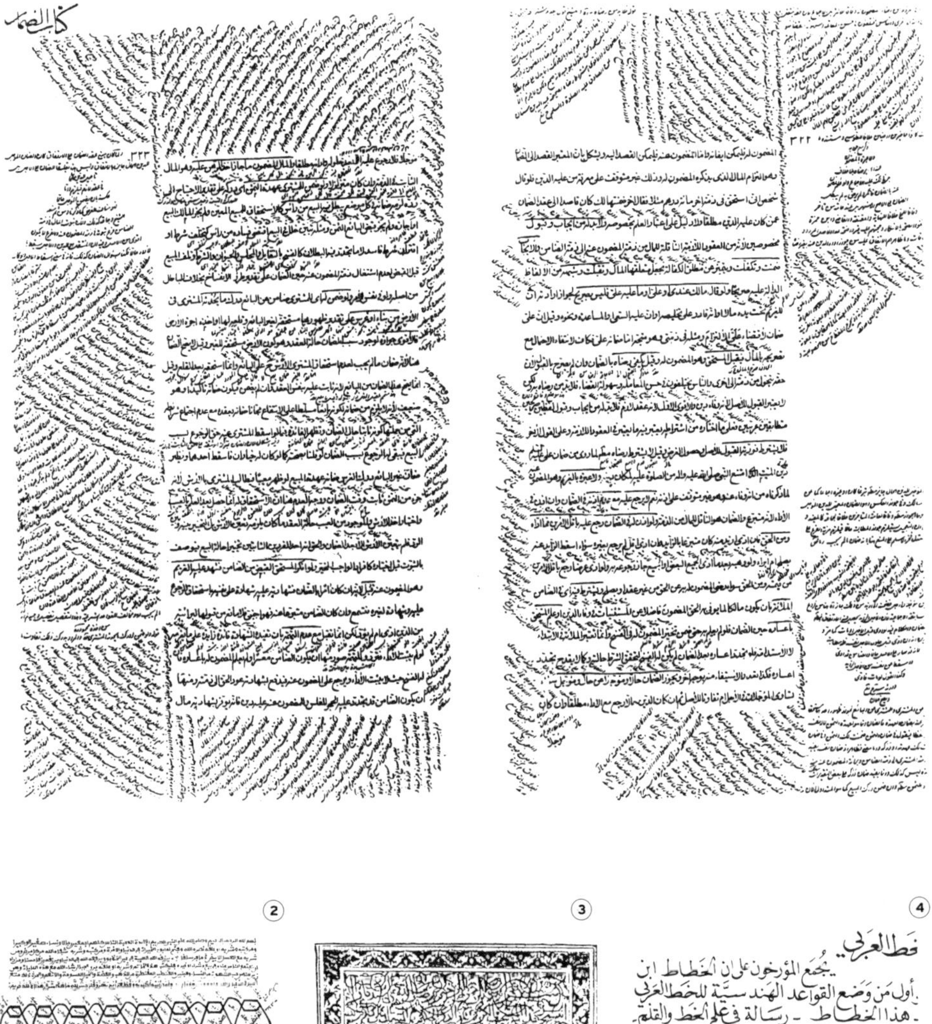

2

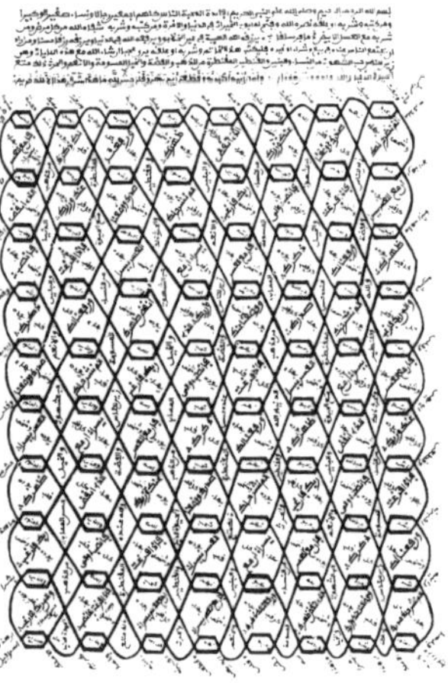

3

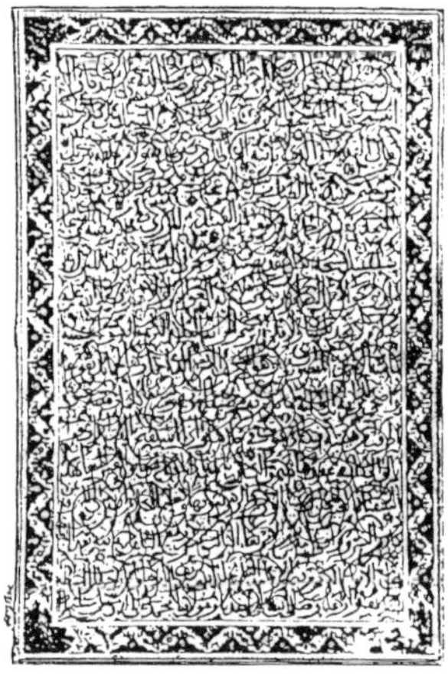

4

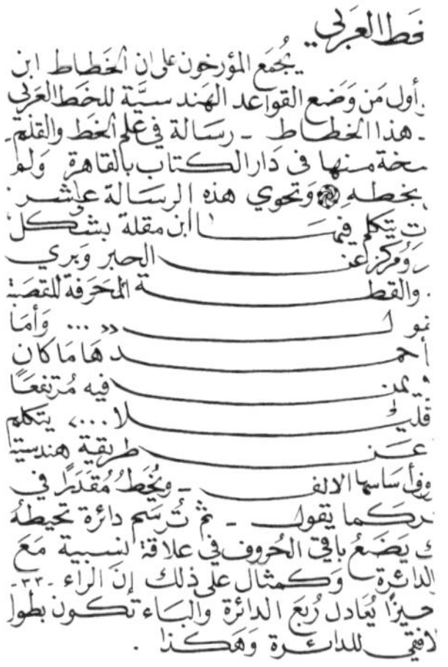

خط العربي

يجمع المؤرخون على أن الخطاط ابن
أول من وضع القواعد الهندسية للخط العربي
هذا الخطاط - رسالة في علم الخط والقلم
خة منها في دار الكتاب بالقاهرة ولم
بخطه وتحوي هذه الرسالة على عشر
ت يتكلم فيها ابن مقلة بشكل
ومركز عن الحبر وبري
والقطة المحرفة للتص
نو ل » ... وأما
أحمد ها ما كان
يمن فيه مرتفعا
قليلا ...» يتكلم
عن طريقة هندسية
وأساسها الالف - ويخط مقدرا في
كما يقول - ثم ترسم دائرة تحيطه
يضع باقي الحروف في علاقة نسبية مع
الدائرة وكمثال على ذلك إن الراء -٣٢-
جيزا يعادل ربع الدائرة والباء تكون بطول
أفقي للدائرة وهكذا .

1. Arab grammar written by Muhammad Tabizi in 1872: the text is in the center with notes and glosses in the margins. Marrakesh, Morocco, B. Wardi Library.

2. Introductory page from a Qur'ān drawn in Kano, Nigeria.

3. Page written in Andalusian script. Madrid, Escorial Museum.

4. Page containing text drawn by Hassan Massoudi, twentieth century.

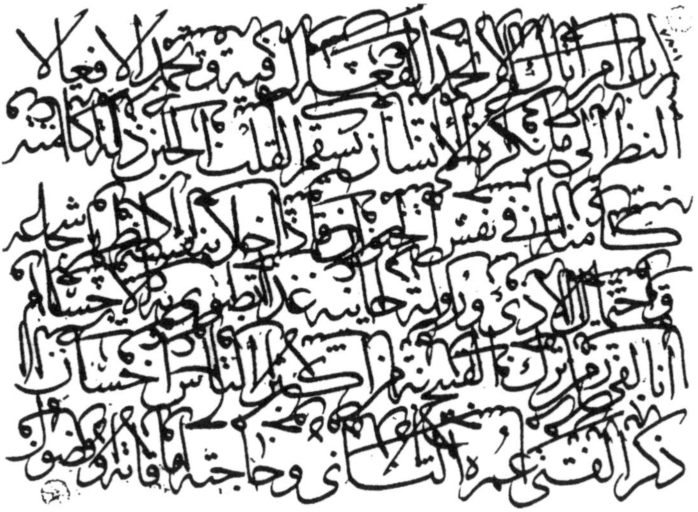

5

5. Calligraphic exercise of a text that can be read with double meanings, written in *thuluth* style by Mahmut Celaleddin Dagistani (d. 1829), Turkey.

6. Calligraphic exercise of a text that can be read with double meanings written in *thuluth* style by Sheikh Hamdullah (1436–1520), Turkey.

6

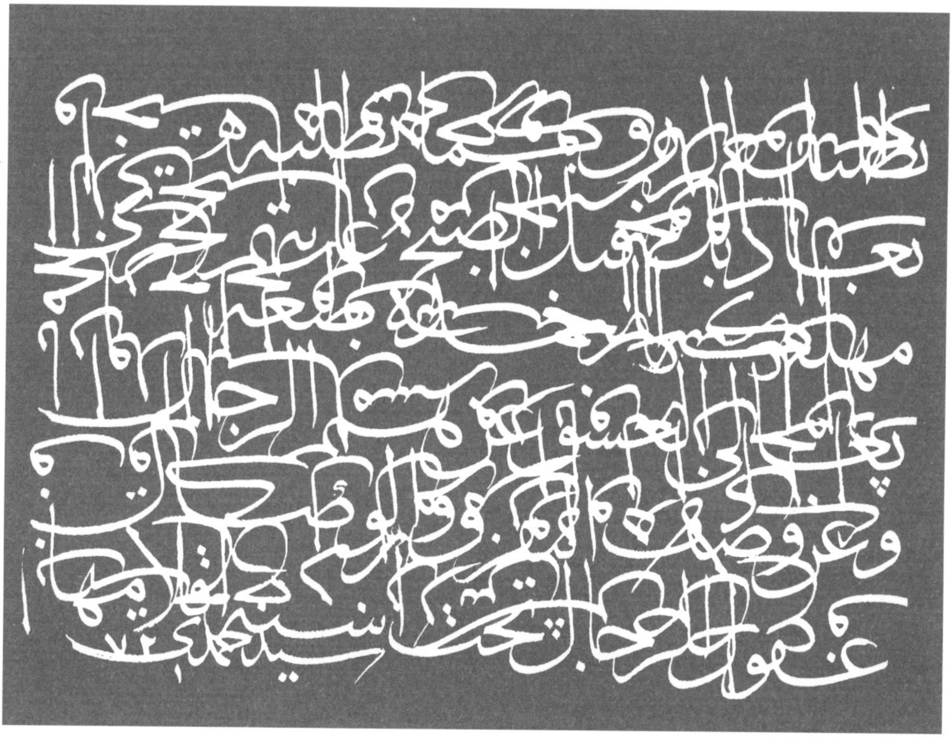

COMPOSITIONS AROUND A CENTRAL AXIS

1

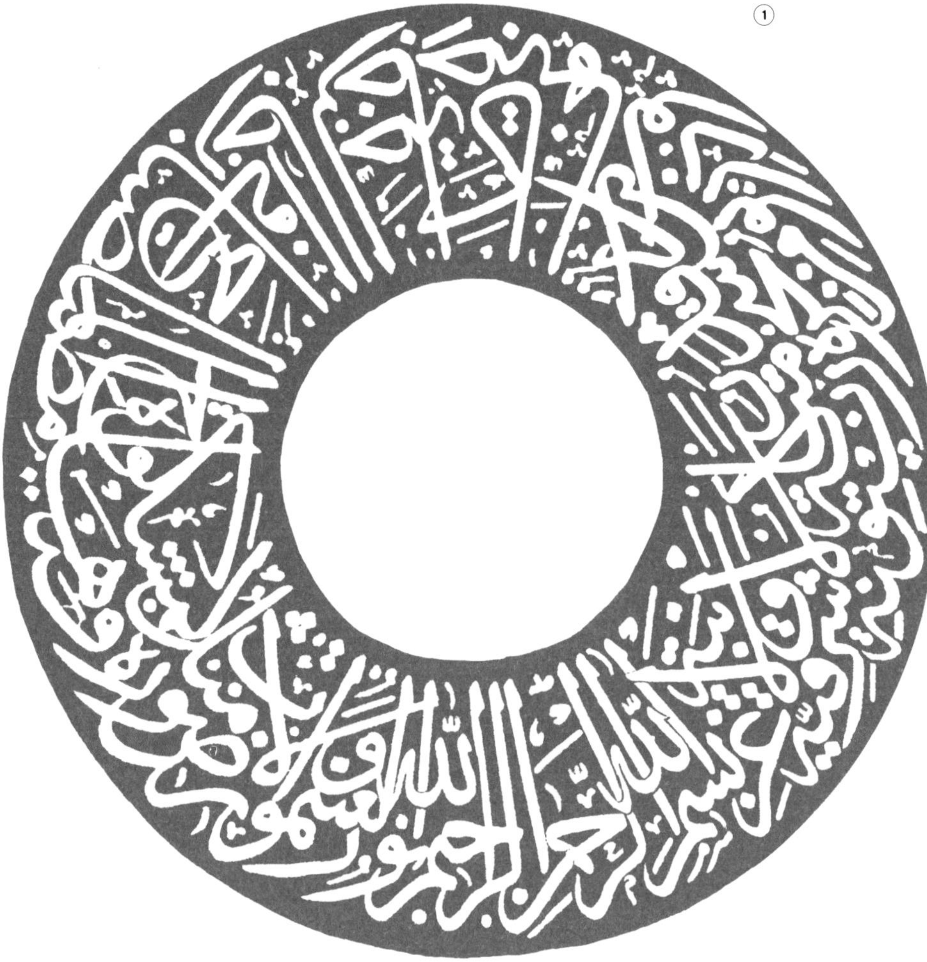

1. "The Light Verse" (Qur'ān, 24:35), sixteenth century, from the central cupola of Saint Sophia, Istanbul.

2. Central axis composition, in different characters, with emphasis on the letter *sin*, by Abd al-Kader, Tunisia, twentieth century.

3. Decoration of the cupola of the Selemiye mosque of Istanbul, drawn in *thuluth* by Hasan al-Tuzi.

4. Decorative composition, drawn in *thuluth* at the end of the sixteenth century, from the Sokollu Mehmet Pasha mosque in Istanbul.

2

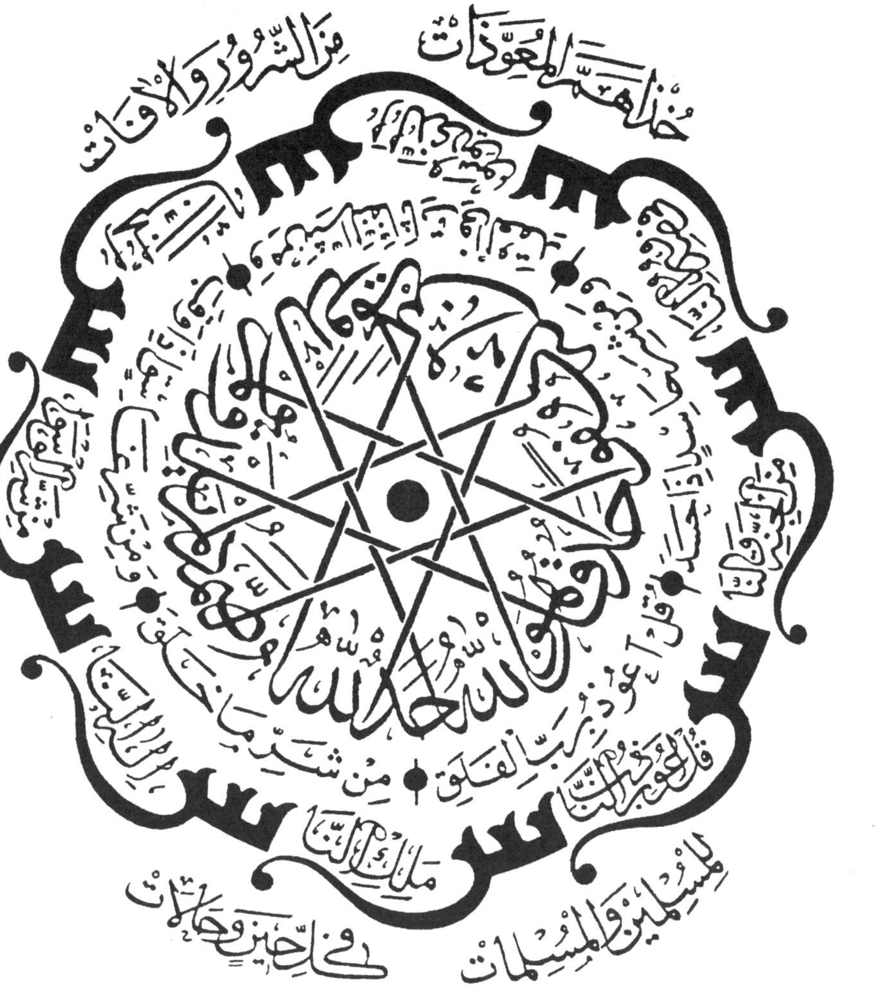

3

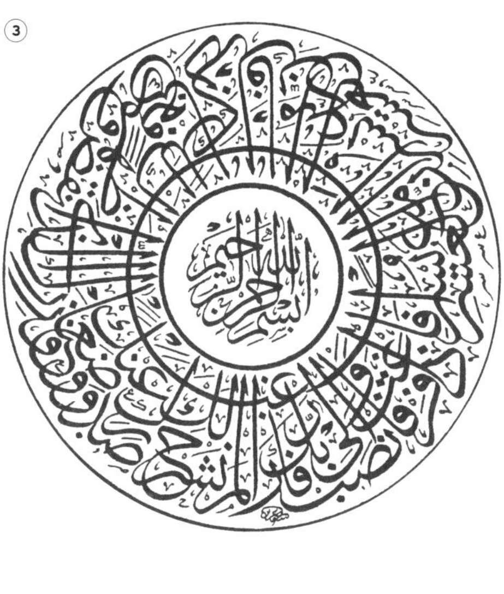

4

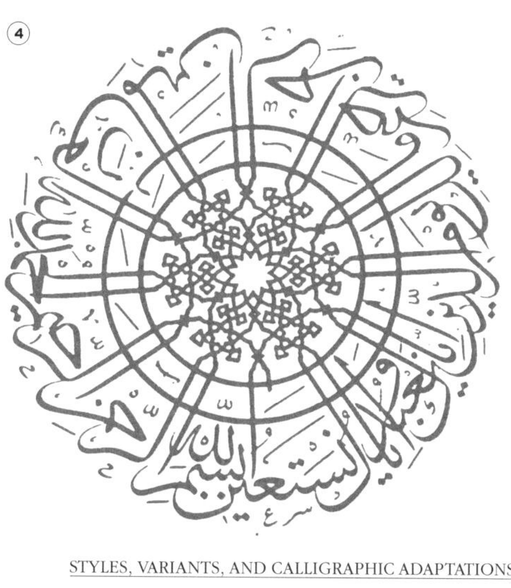

TILE COMPOSITIONS FOR MURAL DECORATIONS

1. Mural from the Grand Mosque of Isfahan, Iran. It reads: *Muḥammad rasūl Āllāh, āl-Ṣādiq āl-Āmīn.*

2. Mural from the Shahid Mathara *madrasa* of Tehran, Iran: *Īā Muḥammad.*

3. Mural from the Grand Mosque of Isfahan, Iran: *Bir zadū mubīrān 'amal sanjīdad.*

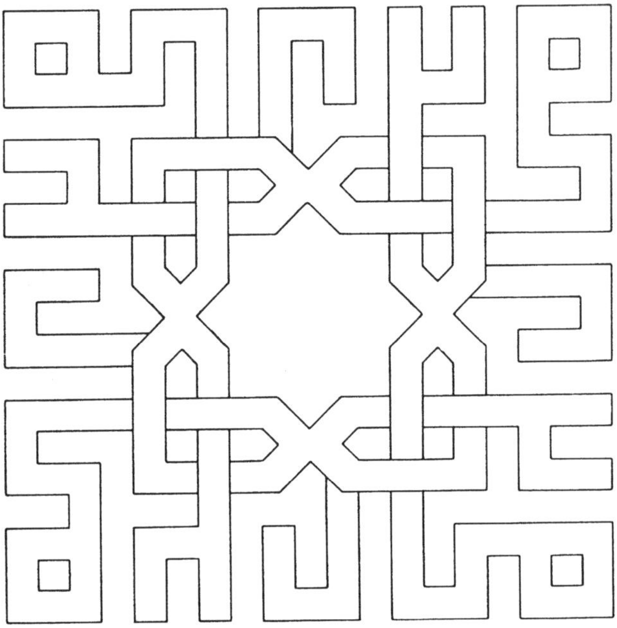

(2)

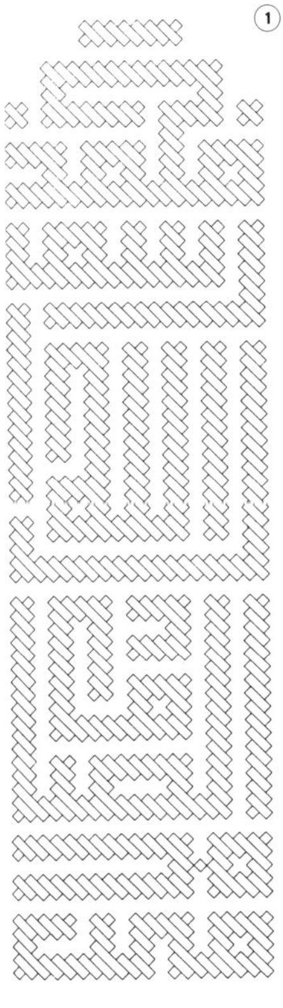

(1)

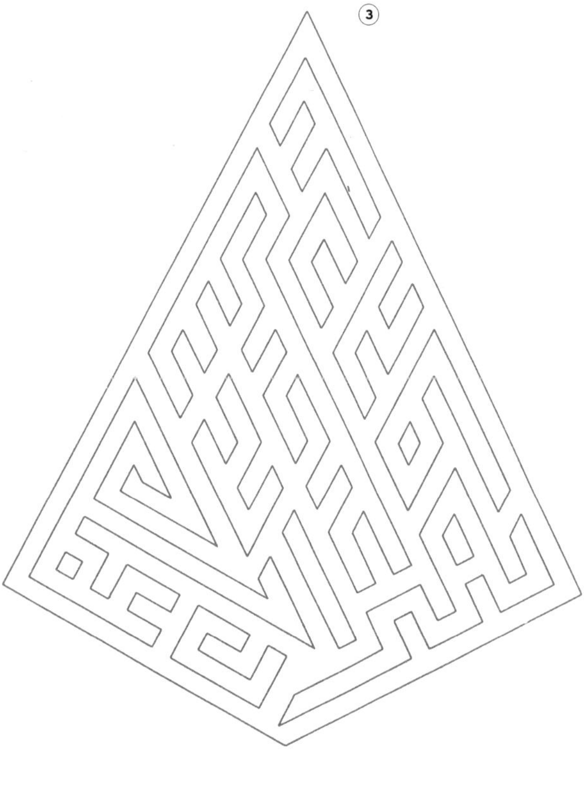

(3)

4

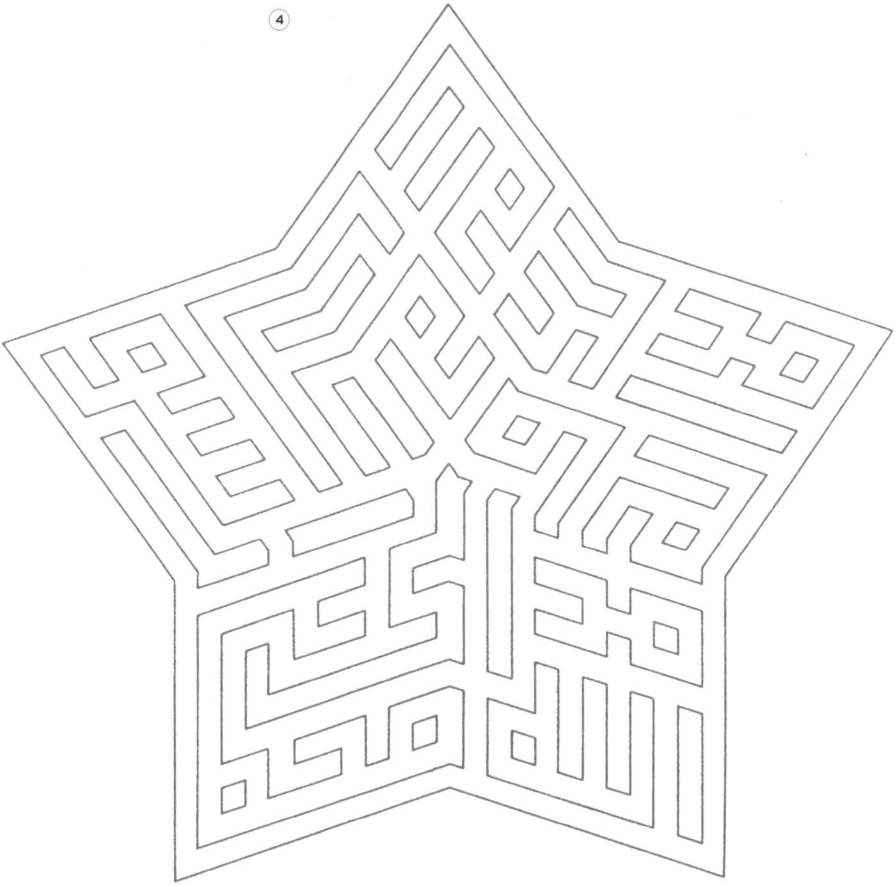

4. The *shahāda*, a mural from the Aliqula aqa mosque of Isfahan, Iran.

5. Mural from the Grand Mosque of Izd, Iran: *Ālqūt Īllāh*.

6. Mural from the Kasah Gran madrasa of Isfahan, Iran: *Āllāhu Ākbar*.

5

6

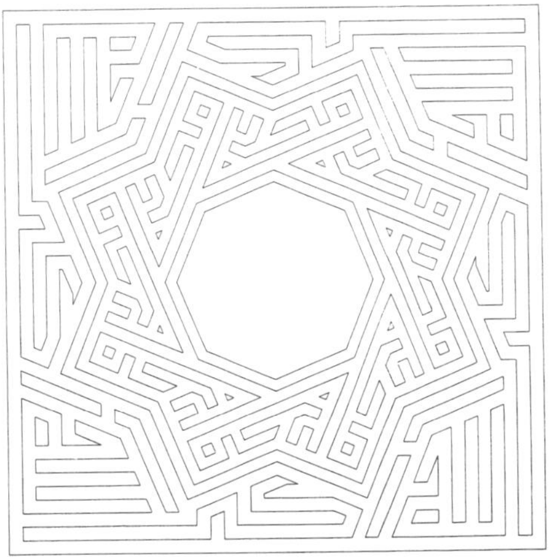

COMPOSITIONS IN CHINESE LABYRINTH STYLE

1

2

3

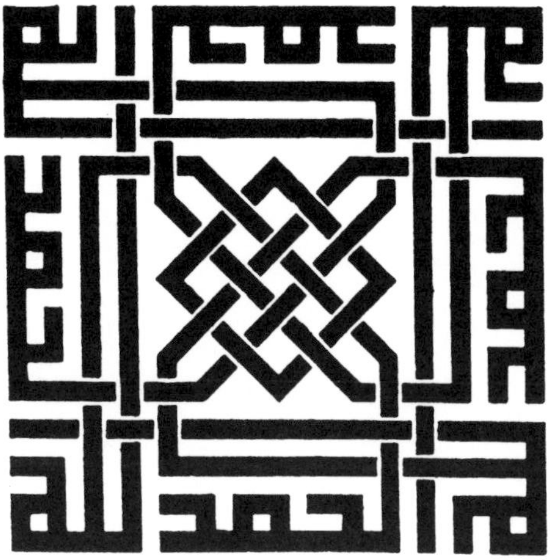

4

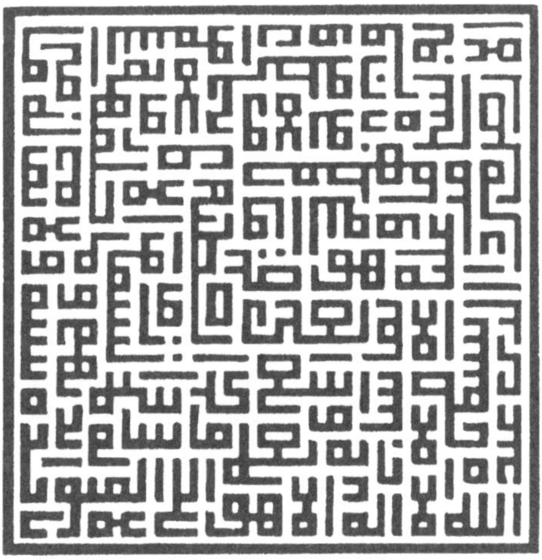

1. Koranic sura no. 112: *āl-Īkhlāṣ* (Pure Faith), drawn by Ahmed Karahisari (Turkish, 1468–1556).

2. *Shahāda* done in a geometric composition often used in mural decorations.

3. The phrase *Ālḥamdu Lillāhi* (Glory to God) in a geometric composition.

4. Mural composition found in the Sultan Muayiad mosque of Cairo, containing the koranic verse 2:255: *Āllāh, lā īlāha īllā hw*. . . (God, no other God but Him . . .).

5. Compositon in geometric Kufic: *Āllāh-Hū* (God-Him).

6. Composition with the names: *Āllāh, Muḥammad, Ābu Bakr, Umar, Uthmān, Alī, Talḥa, Zūbair, Saad, Said, Abd Allāh, Abd āl-Raḥmān.* Drawn by Ahmed Karahisari (Turkish, 1468–1556) for the Ahmed mosque of Istanbul, and replicated in the al-Bardini mosque of Cairo.

5

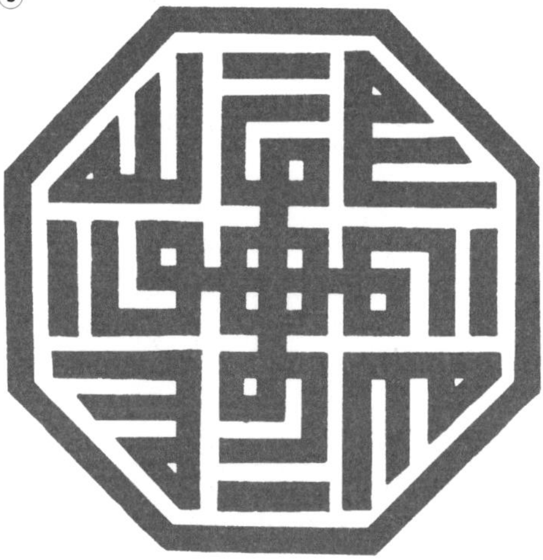

6

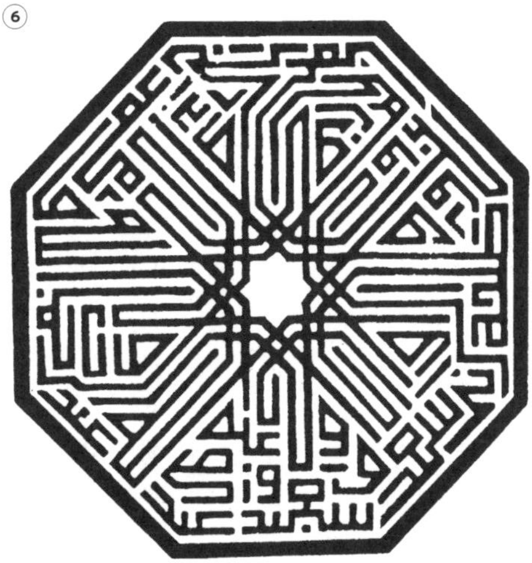

COMPOSITIONS IN THE SHAPE OF *SIKKÉ*

1

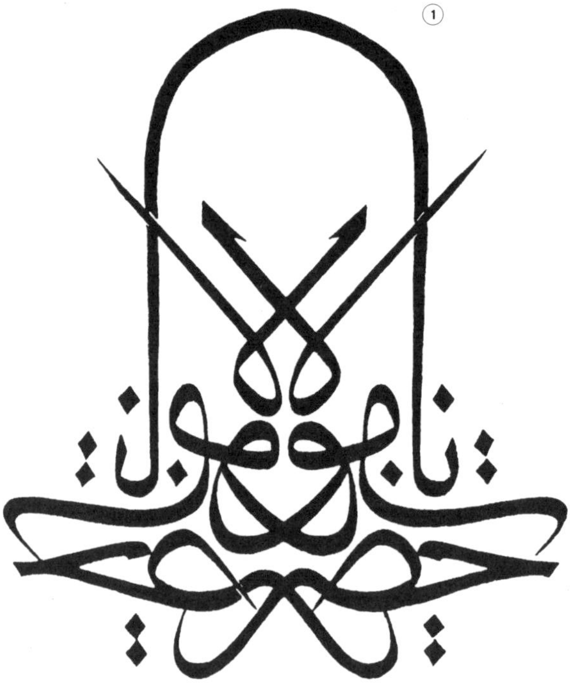

1. The phrase *Yā hazzeti Mevlāna* (O, our saintly Master), drawn by the Sufi *mevlevi* Mehmed Nazif Bey (1846–1913). Konya, Turkey, Museum of the Mevleviyya.

2. Calligraphy by Fevzi Gunuc, student of Huseyn Kurtlu, known as the Imam. Konya, Turkey, Seljuk University.

3. The two names of God: *Ḥayyu, Qayyūm* (the Living, the Subsisting), drawn in 1773 by the Sufi *qadiri* Haji Amin Siri.

2

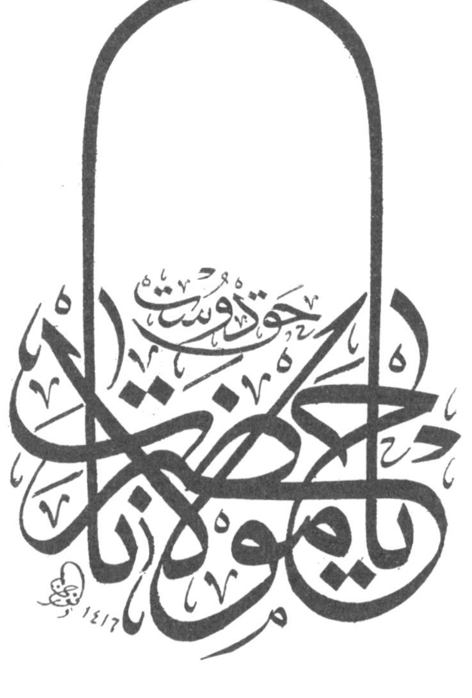

3

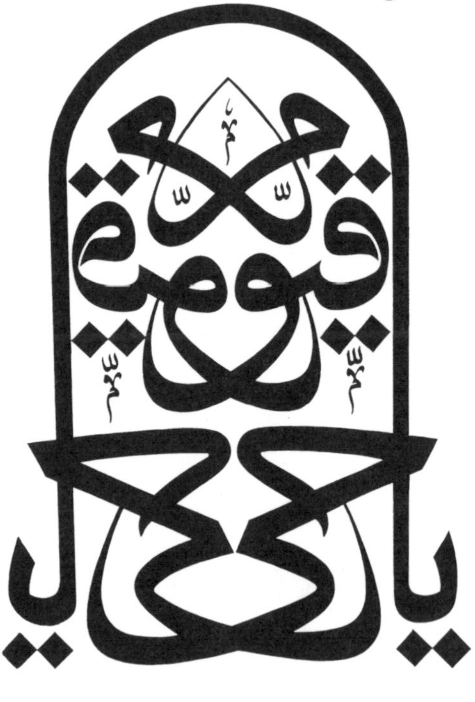

4. The phrase *Yā Hū* (O, Him), drawn in 1908 by Necmeddin Okyay (1883–1976).

5. The artist's own name, drawn by the Sufi *jerrahi-halveti* Jibrail Mandel Khan, 1984.

6. The phrase *Yā hasirat Mevlāna Muḥammad Jalāl āl-Dīn Rūmī* (O, our sweet Master Muhammad Jalāl āl-Din Rumi), drawn by Mehmet Emin Efendi, 1923.

5

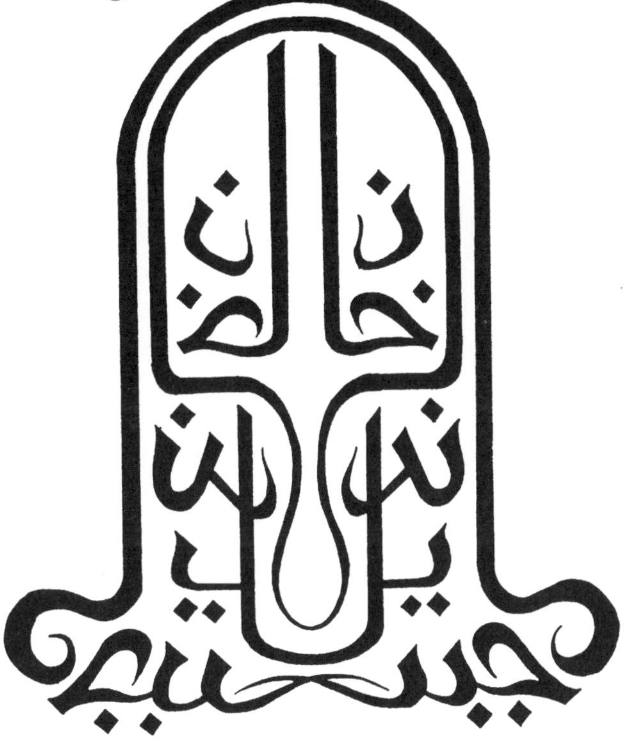

4

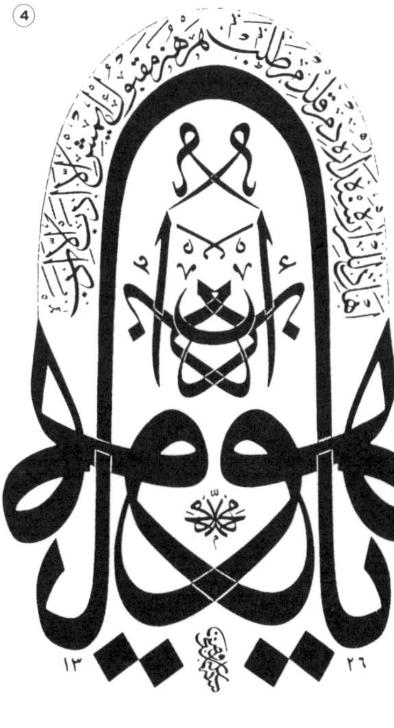

6

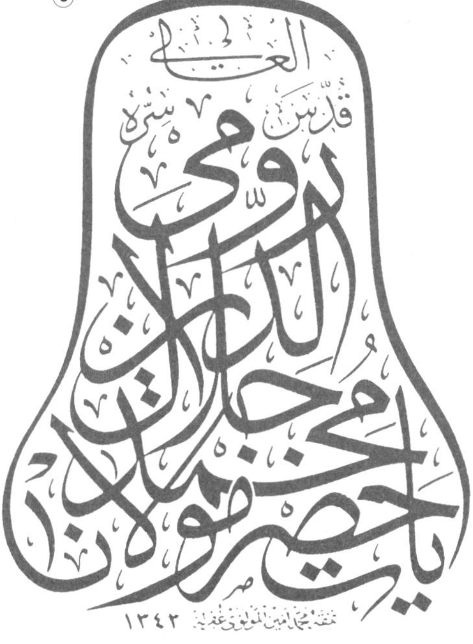

COMPOSITIONS IN THE SHAPES OF DIFFERENT OBJECTS

1

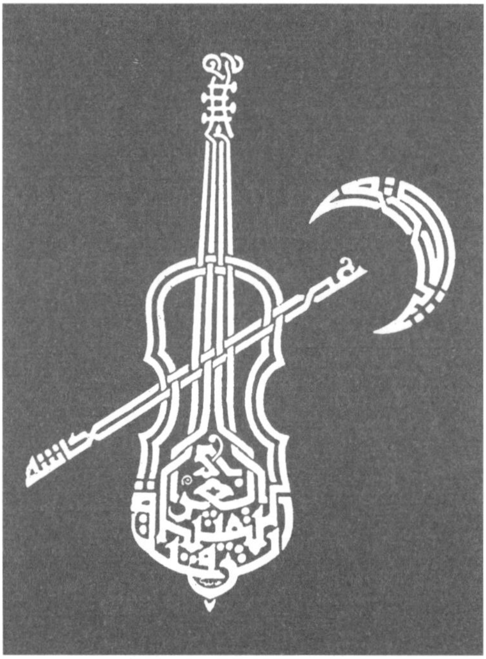

1. *One night, under the crescent moon . . .* Composition by Hamed the Egyptian, Cairo, twentieth century.

2. Amphora decorated with the invocation *Yā Fattāḥ, yā Karīm* (O Conqueror, O Generous One). Calligraphy by Basur Ibraya, Iraq, twentieth century.

3. Amphora decorated with specular calligraphy (*muthannā*), by Mazhar Shevket, Istanbul, twentieth century.

2

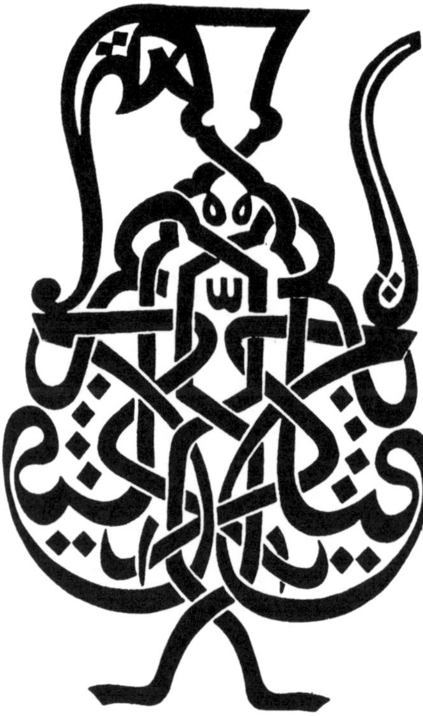

3

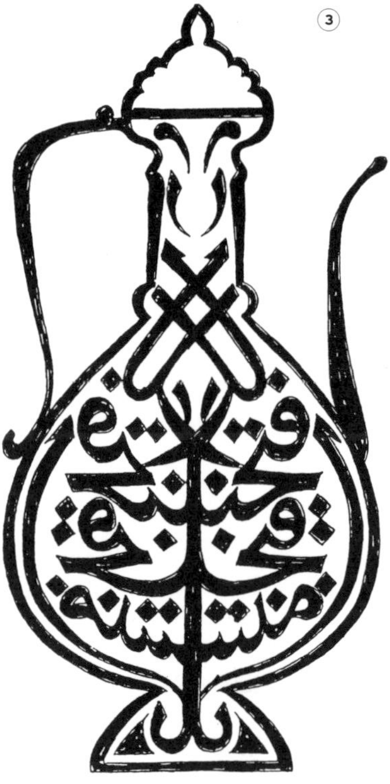

4. Amphora with two specular *waw* letters done in *gulzār* style, Turkey, eighteenth century.

5. Amphora decorated by Muhammad Izzat al-Karkuki (Istanbul, 1904–1986).

6. Amphora containing the phrase *Wa Hū, 'Alī, kul shaya qadīr*, drawn by Basur Ibraya.

5

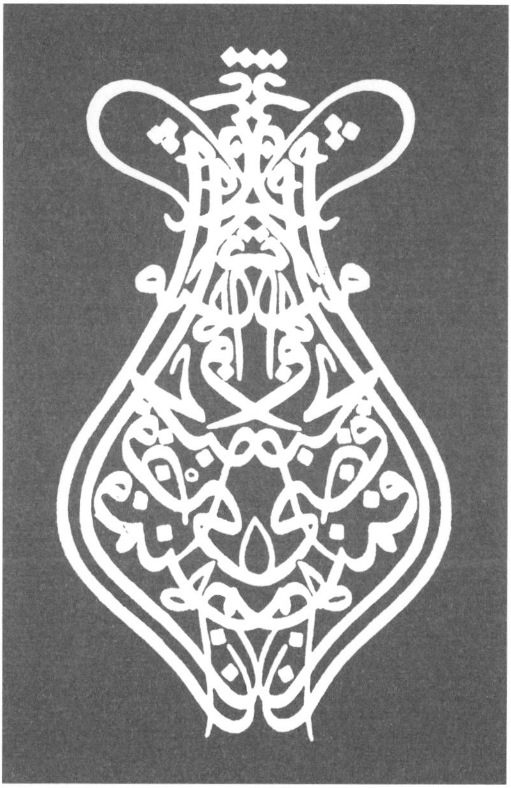

4

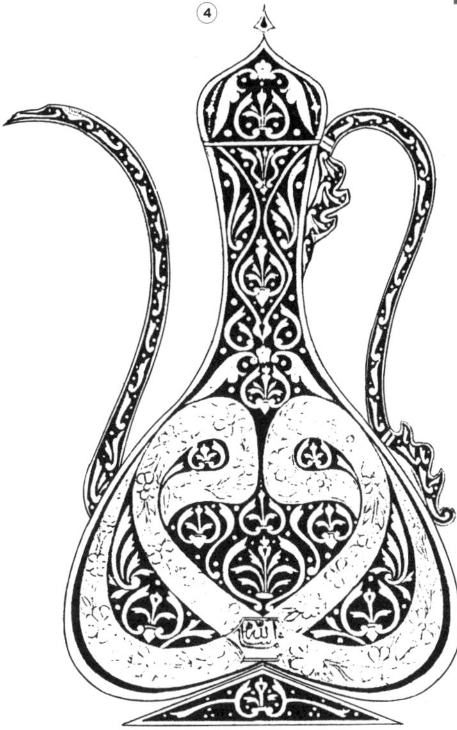

6

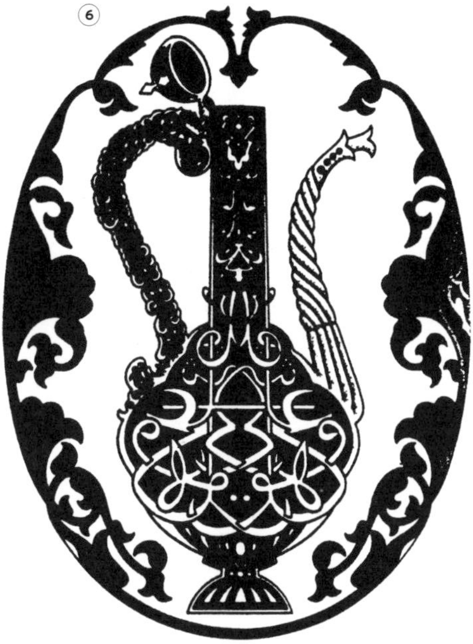

ZOOMORPHIC COMPOSITIONS

1

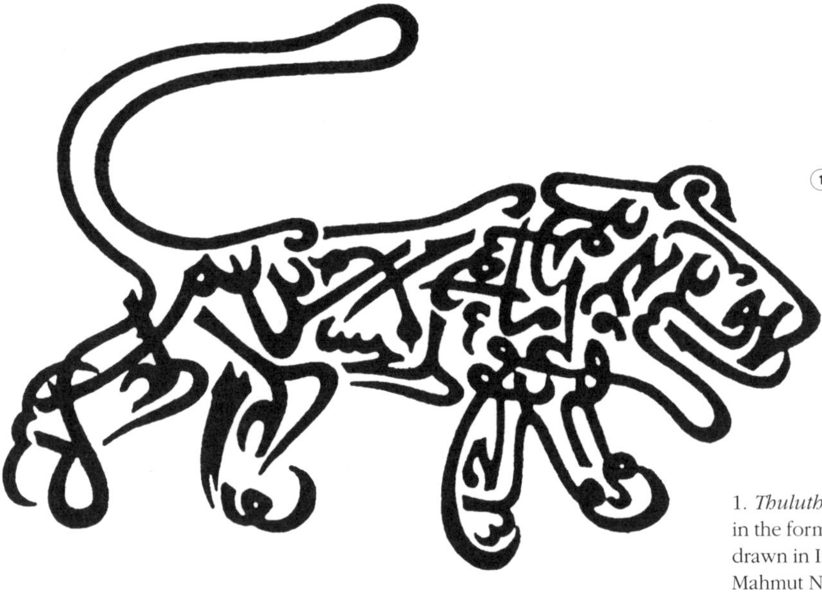

2

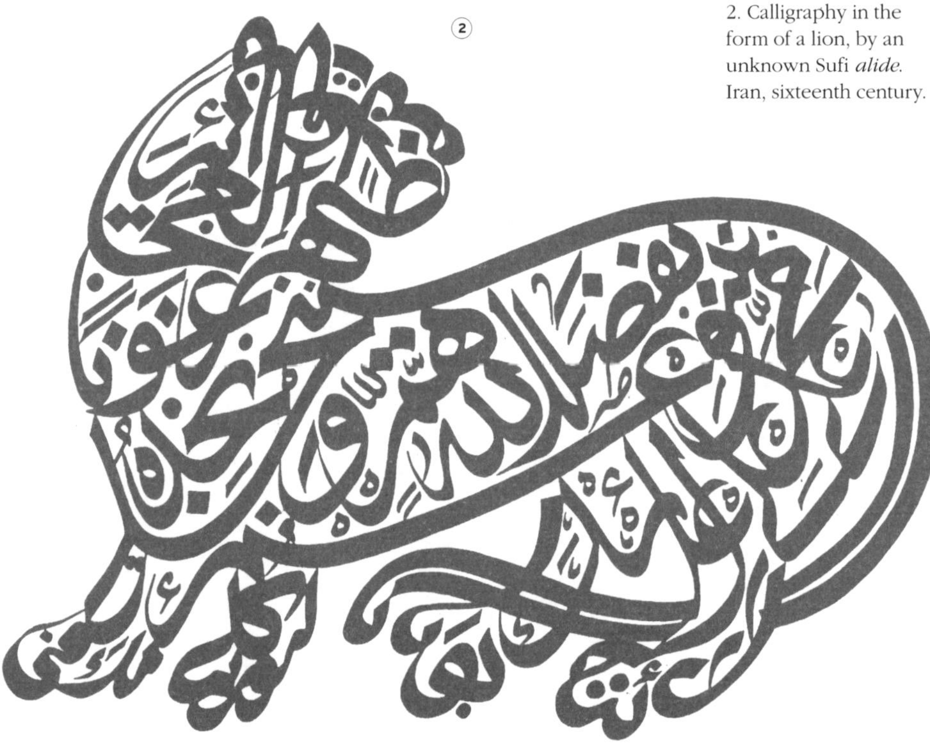

1. *Thuluth* calligraphy in the form of a lion, drawn in Iran by Shah Mahmut Nishaburi (d. 1495). Istanbul, University Library.

2. Calligraphy in the form of a lion, by an unknown Sufi *alide*. Iran, sixteenth century.

3

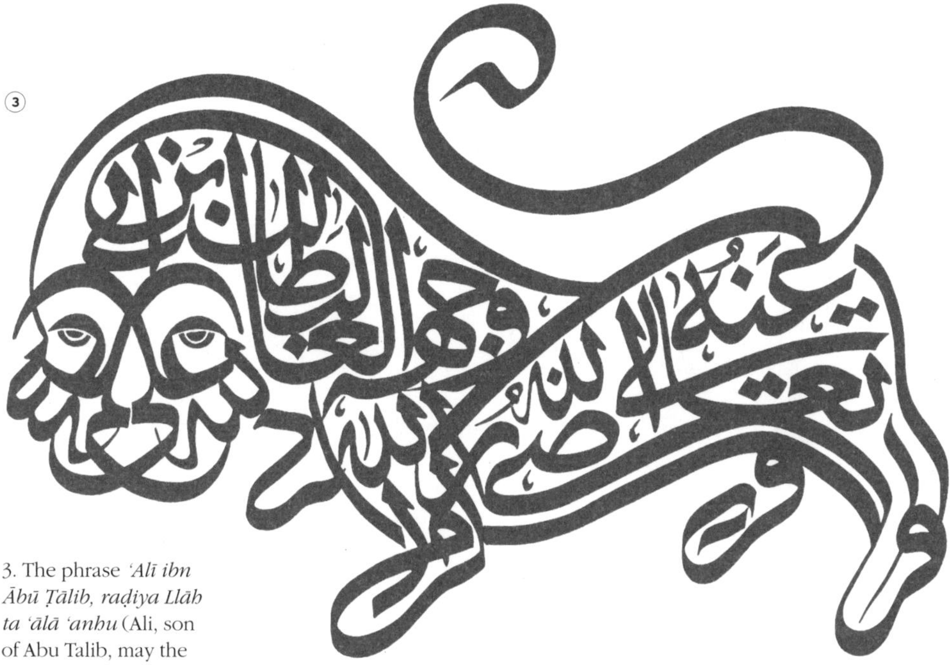

3. The phrase *'Alī ibn Ābū Ṭālib, raḍiya Llāh ta 'ālā 'anhu* (Ali, son of Abu Talib, may the all-powerful God be pleased with him). Iran, nineteenth century.

4. The *shahāda* drawn in the form of a fish by Gabriele Mandel Khān. Afghanistan, 1946.

4

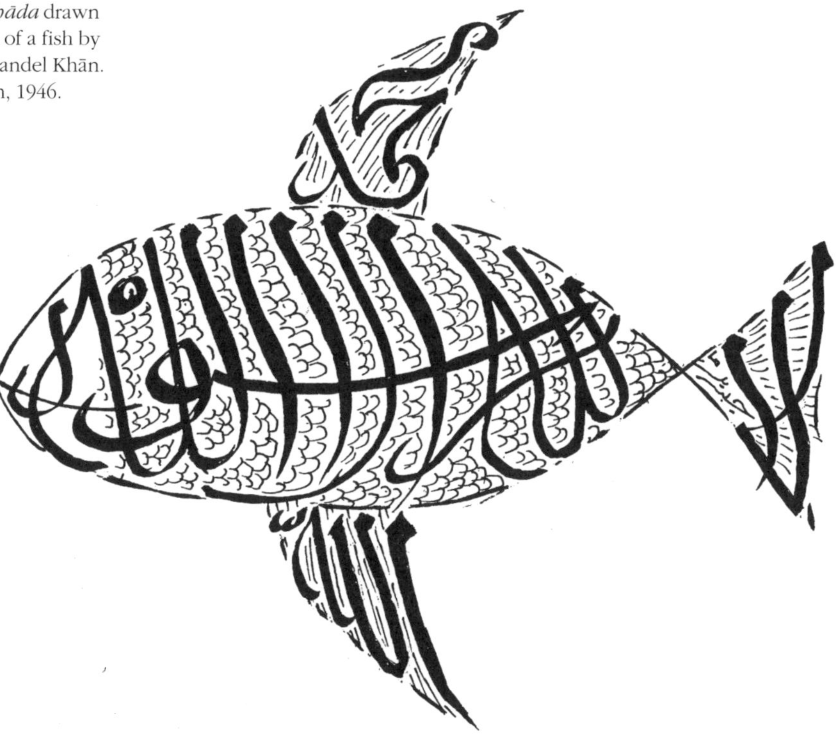

COMPOSITIONS IN THE SHAPES OF BIRDS

1

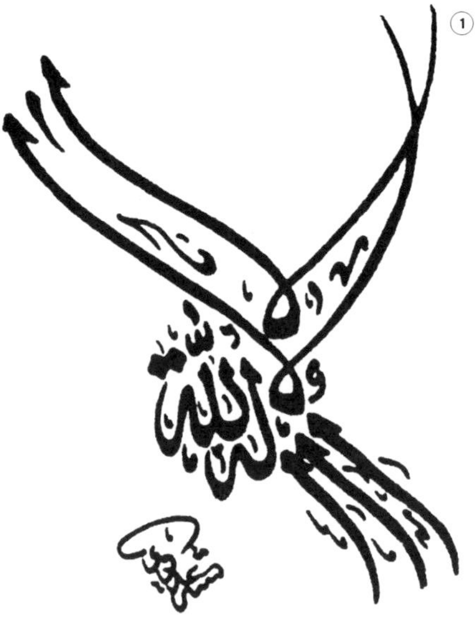

3

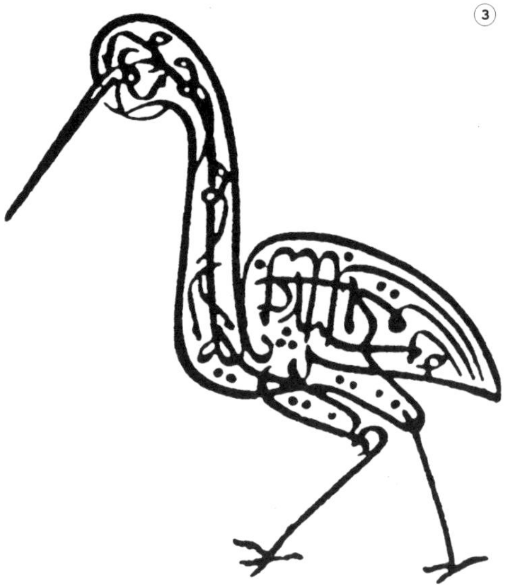

1. The phrase *Lā ilāha illā Āllāh* (There is no other God but God) in *dīwānī jalī* script by Yahya Zakariyya Adawi (b. 1962, Bethlehem).

2. Calligraphy in *thuluth musalsal*, with the name of the dissident separatist Bahaullah, drawn in 1889 by Mishkin Qalam.

3. Calligraphy in the form of a stork done by the Sufi *mevlevi* Hasan Leylek Dede (d. 1827, Konya, Turkey).

4. *Basmala* in the form of a stork drawn by Mustafa Rakim Tashmektepli (d. Istanbul, 1767). This is a facsimile drawn by his apprentice Isma'il Zuhdu Efendi (d. 1806).

2

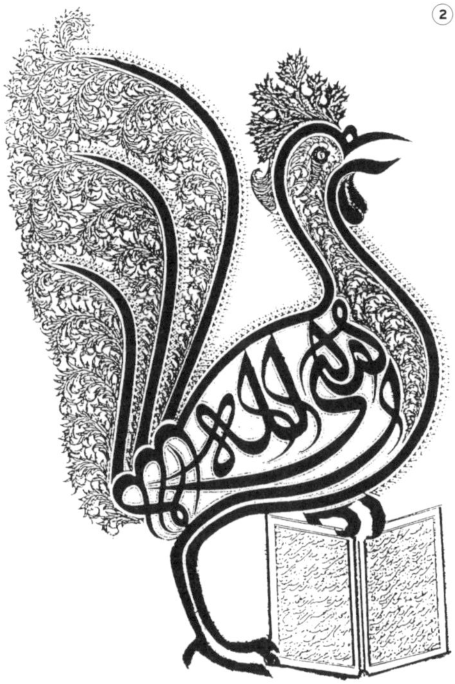

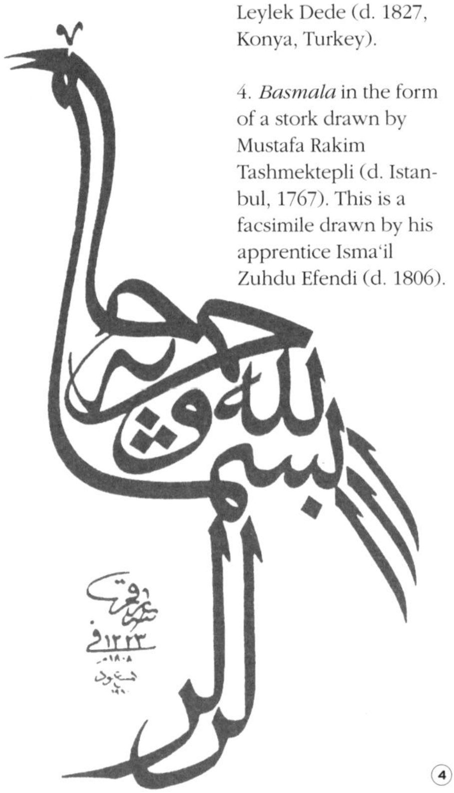

4

5

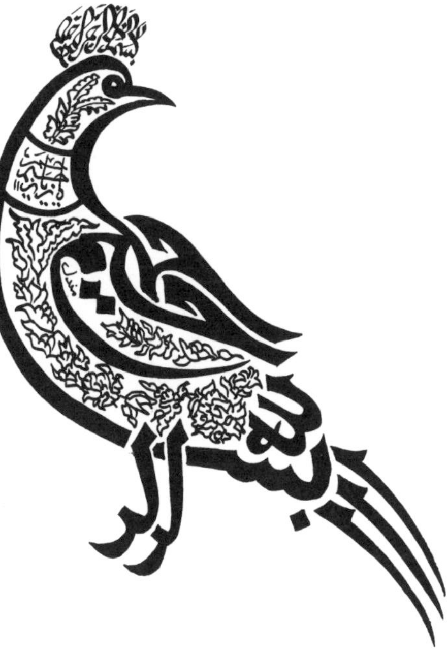

6

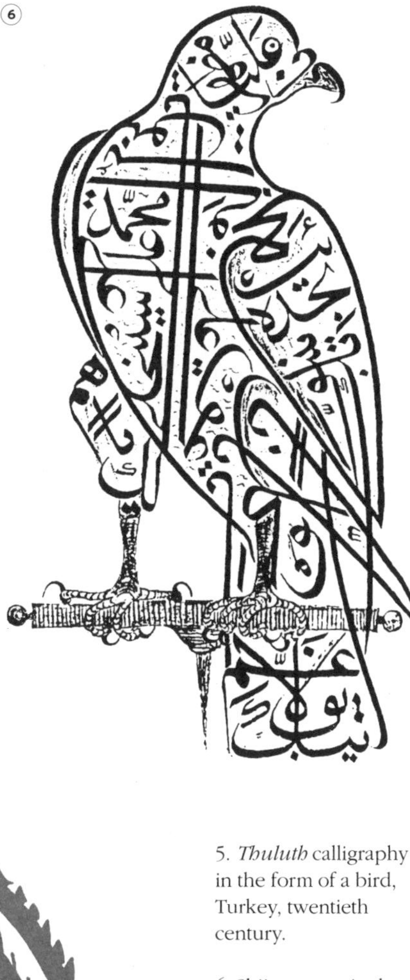

7

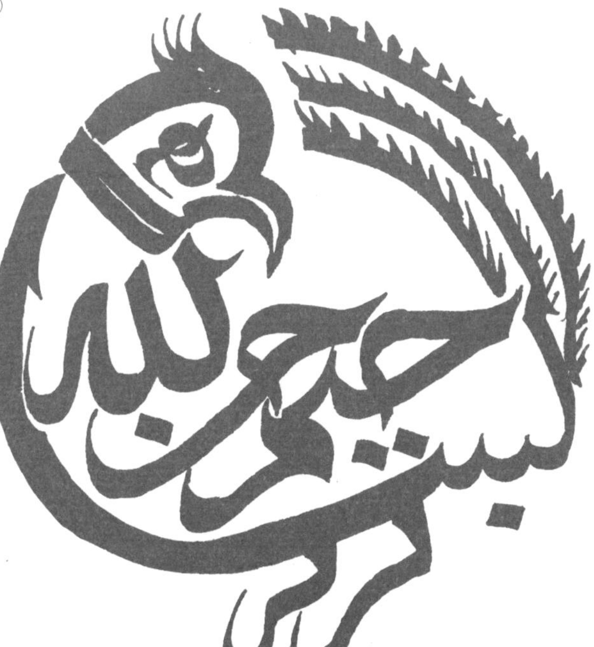

5. *Thuluth* calligraphy in the form of a bird, Turkey, twentieth century.

6. Shiite prayer in the form of a hawk, drawn in *thuluth* style by Muhammad Fathiyab, Iran, nineteenth century.

7. Talisman with the *basmala*, drawn in the form of a bird on faience. Iznil, Turkey, 1760.

ZOOMORPHIC AND ANTHROPOMORPHIC COMPOSITIONS

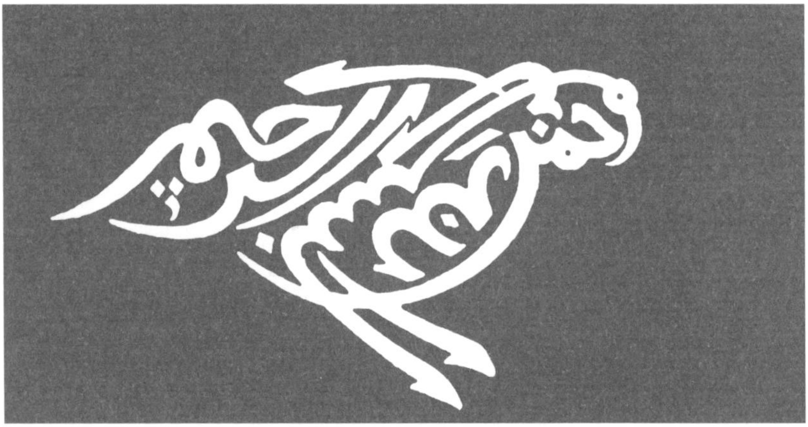

(1)

1. *Basmala* in the form of a bird, drawn by Ahmet Naili Galatali (d. 1813), Eyyub, Istanbul.

(2)

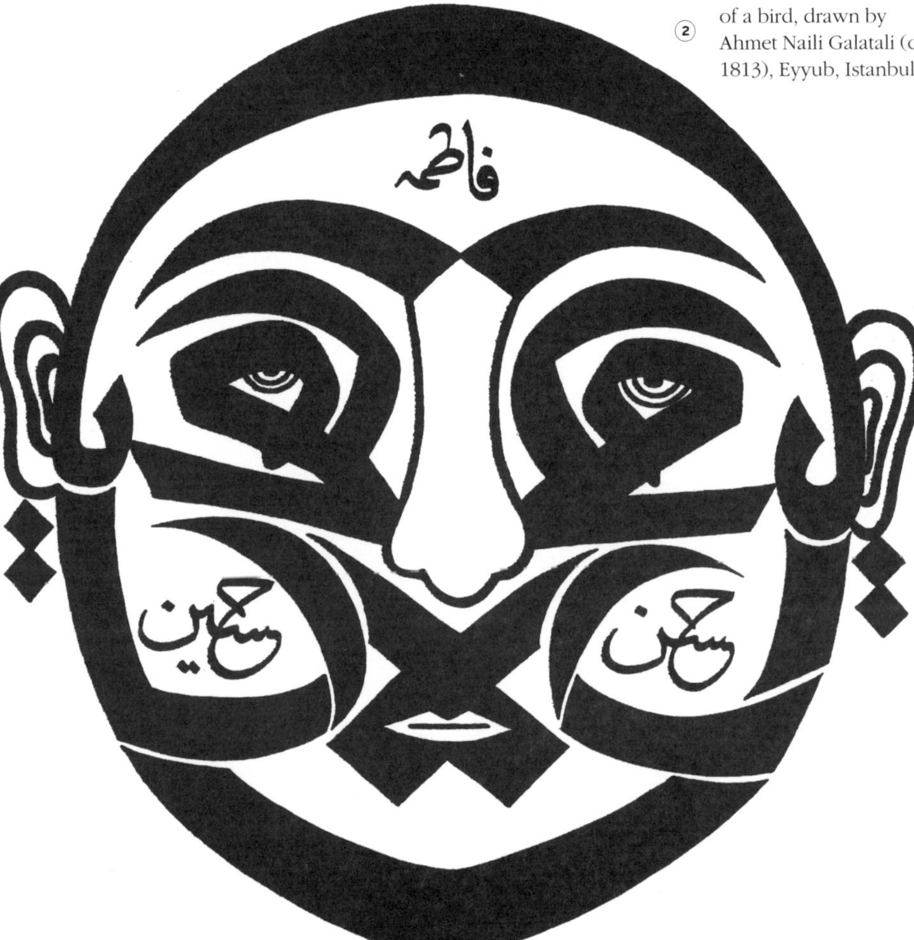

2. Composition containing the names *Muḥammad, 'Alī, Ḥassan, Ḥusaīn, Fāṭima*, Iran, nineteenth century. Tehran, *Dergah* of the Nimatallah.

3. Amulet protecting against "transgression of the interdict" with the names *Ḥasan, Muḥammad, Alī, Āllāh*. Drawn in the form of a human face by Mirza Zahde Isfahani. Iran, 1816.

4. Shiite prayer in *naskhī* style drawn in the shape of a horse by Sayyid Husain Ali. Iran, 1848.

③

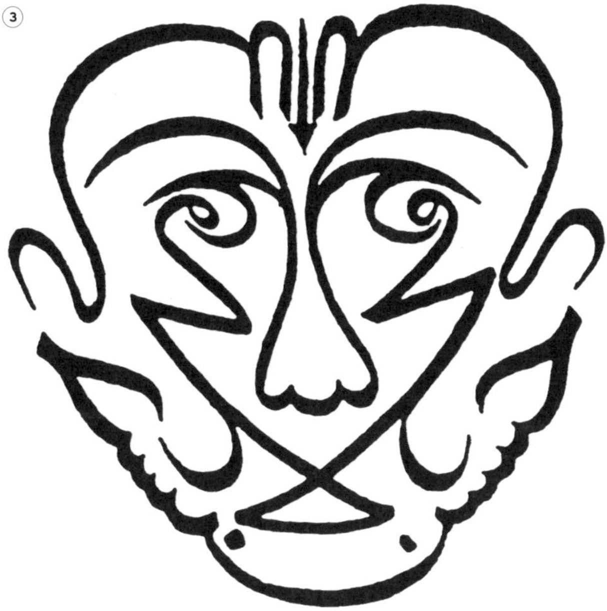

④

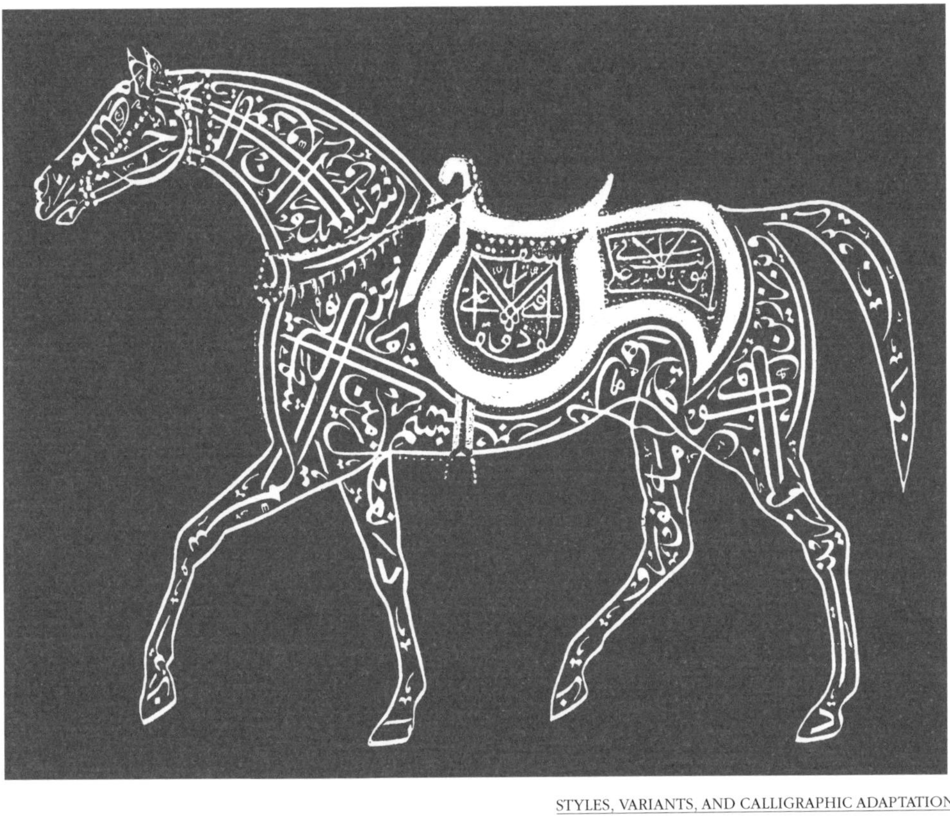

COMPOSITIONS IN THE SHAPES OF PLANTS AND FRUITS

1

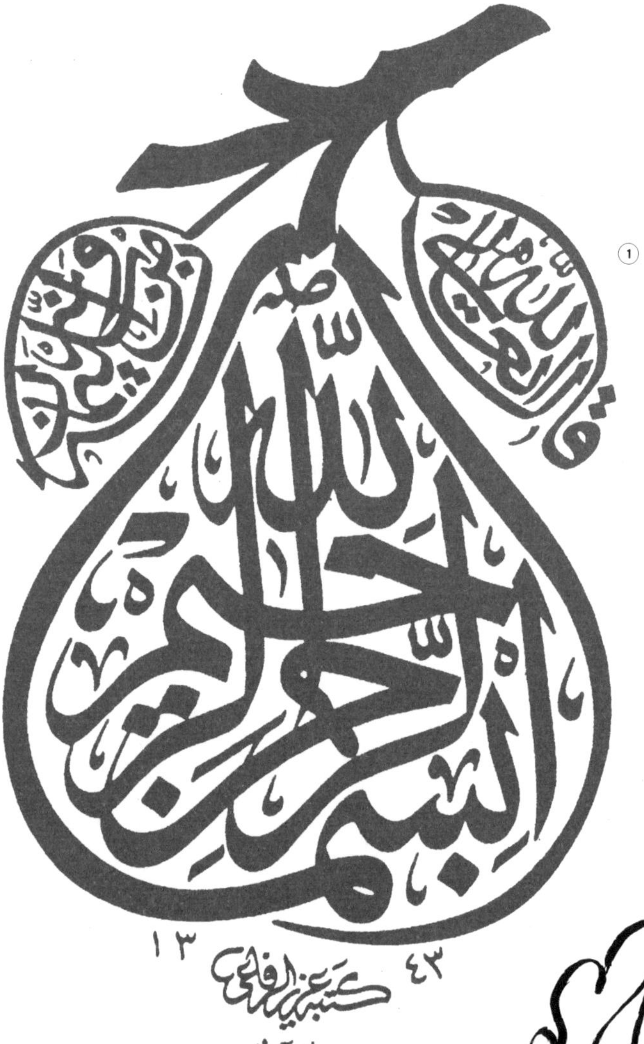

2

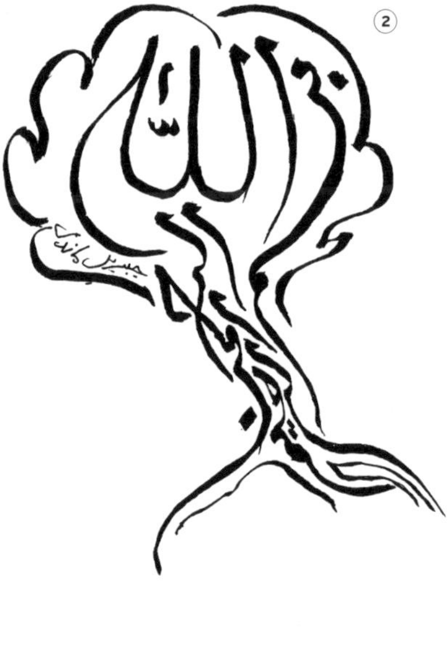

1. *Basmala* in a pear-shaped composition, drawn by Abdel Aziz al-Rifa'i, 1924.

2. *Basmala* in the shape of a tree, drawn by Gabriele Mandel. Kabul, Afghanistan, 1946.

3. The Tree of Life. Calligraphy by Izzet Efendi, Turkey, 1912.

4. A pear-shaped composition drawn by Mehmet Shefik Bey (1819–1879). Istanbul, Sabanci Hat Kollesiyonu.

4

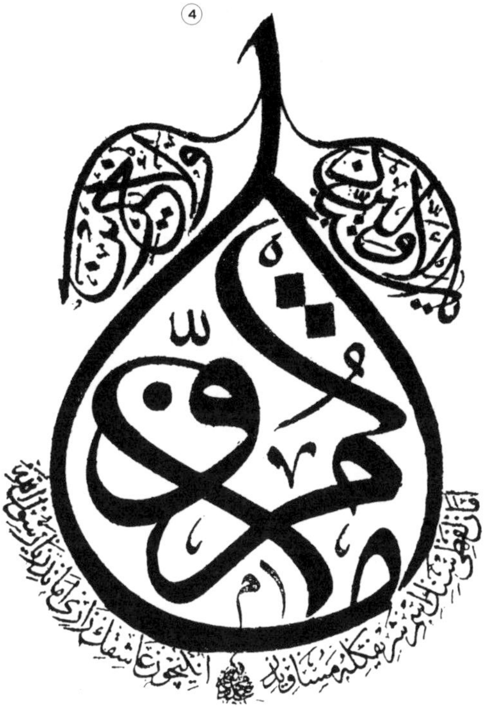

3

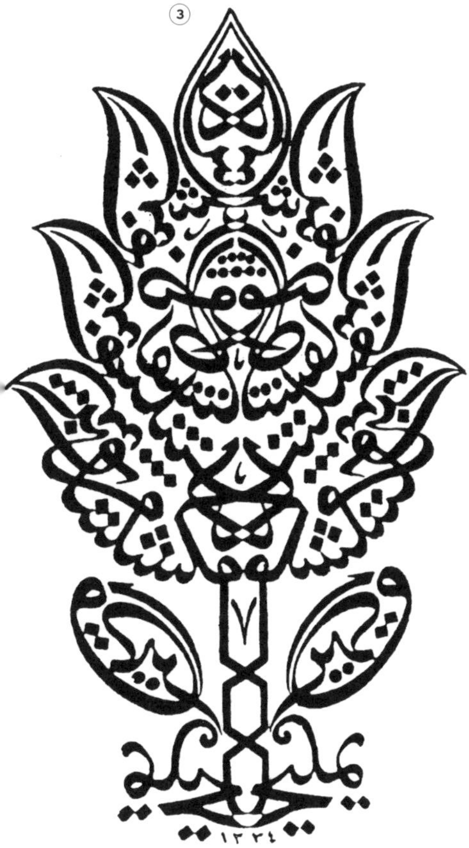

5. *Dīwānī* calligraphy in the form of a pear with the phrase: *Alḥamdu Lillāhi, Rabbi āl'ālamīn* (Glory to God, Lord of the Worlds), by Nasib Makarim. Lebanon.

5

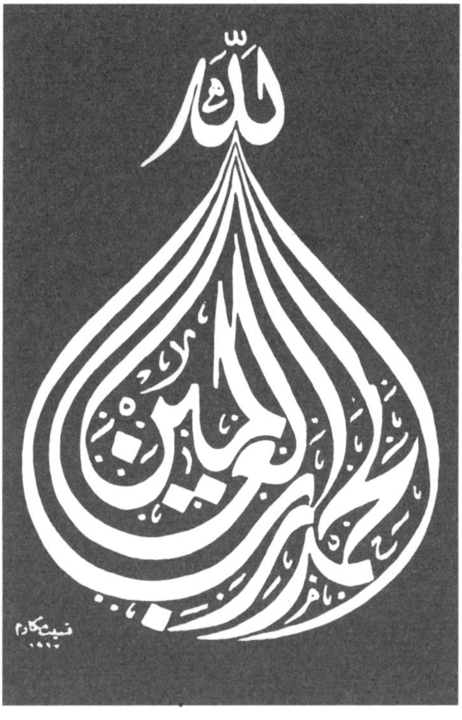

ARCHITECTURAL COMPOSITIONS

1

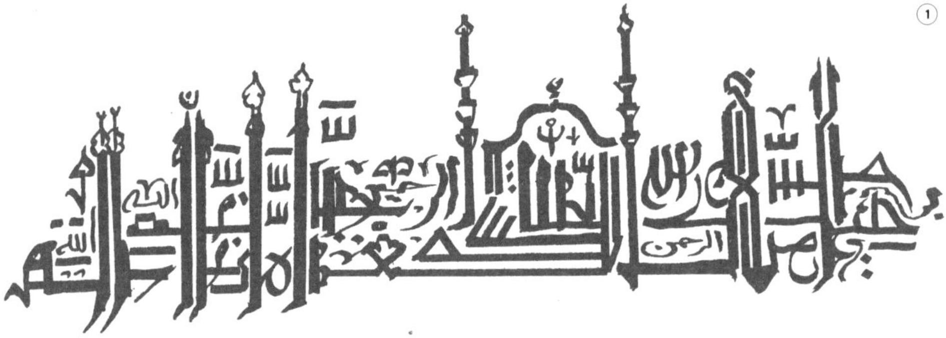

1, 2. The *shahāda* in geometric Kufic, Turkey, nineteenth century.

2

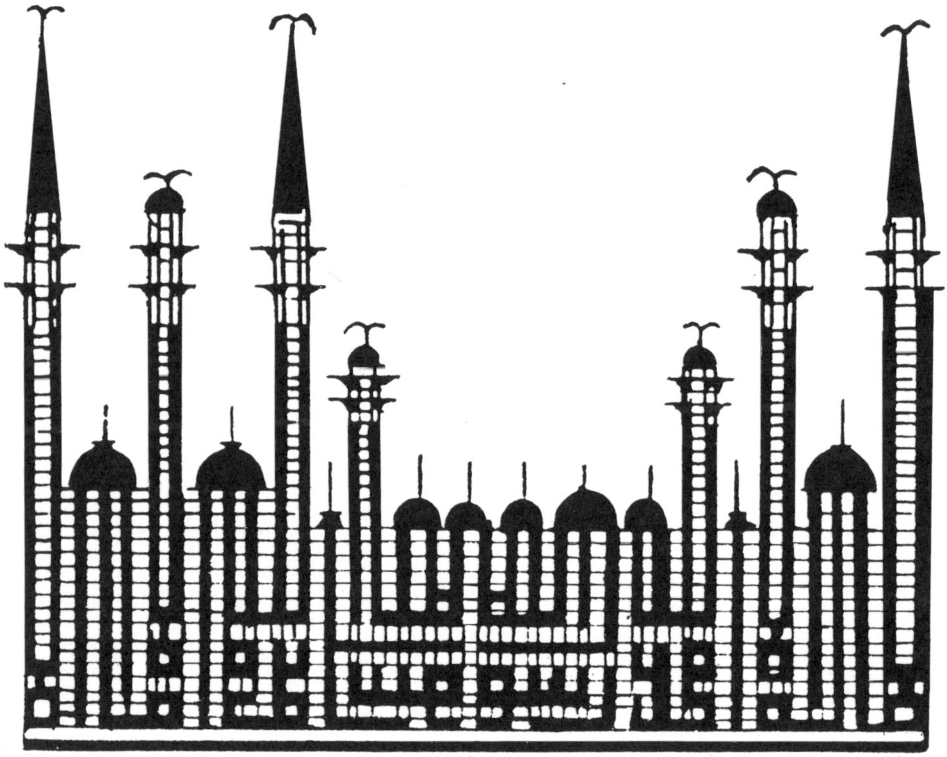

3

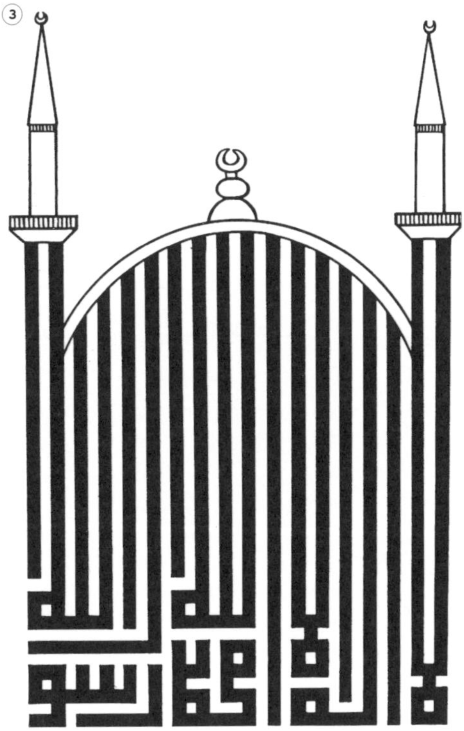

4

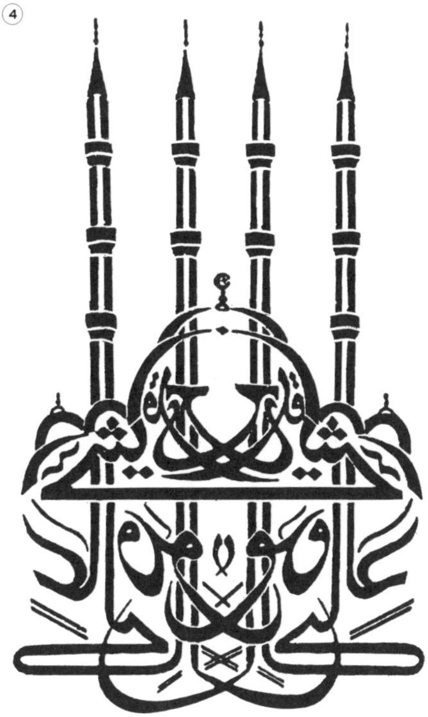

3. The *shahāda* in geometric Kufic, Turkey, nineteenth century.

4. The phrase *Wa Hū, 'ala kul shaya qadīr,* drawn in *thuluth* script, Turkey, nineteenth century.

5. The *basmala* in geometric Kufic, Turkey, nineteenth century.

5

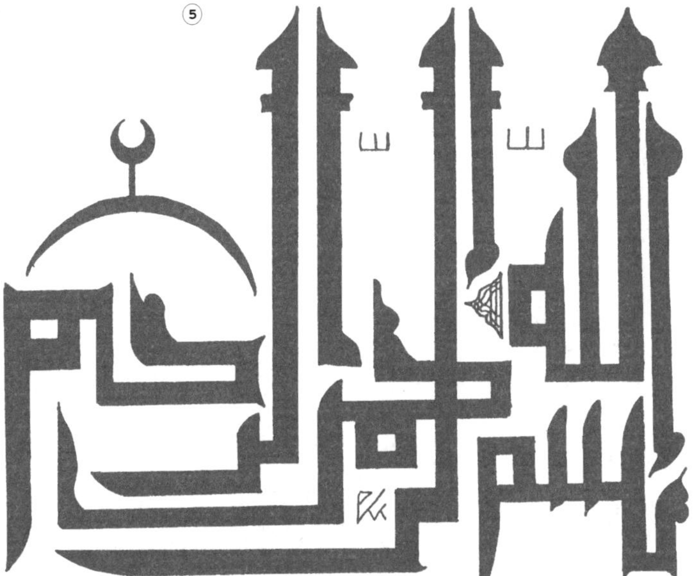

EXAMPLES OF CALLIGRAPHY ON FAIENCE PLATES

1

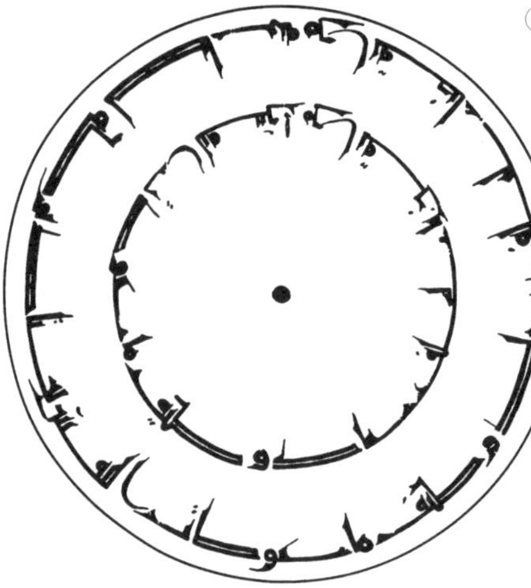

3

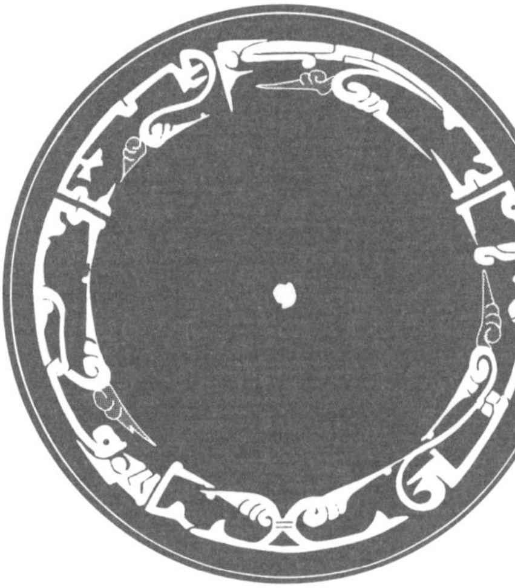

1. Calligraphic decoration on a faience from Afrasiab (today Samarkand, Uzbekistan), tenth century.

2. Calligraphic decoration on a faience from Nishapur, Iran, tenth century.

4

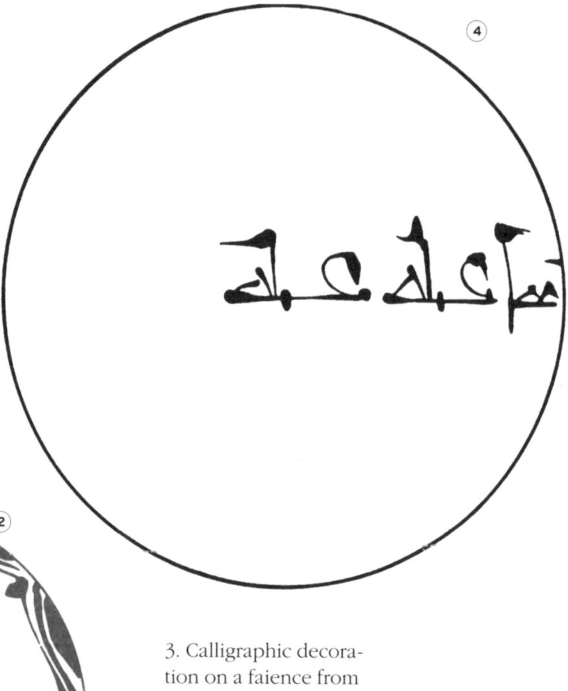

2

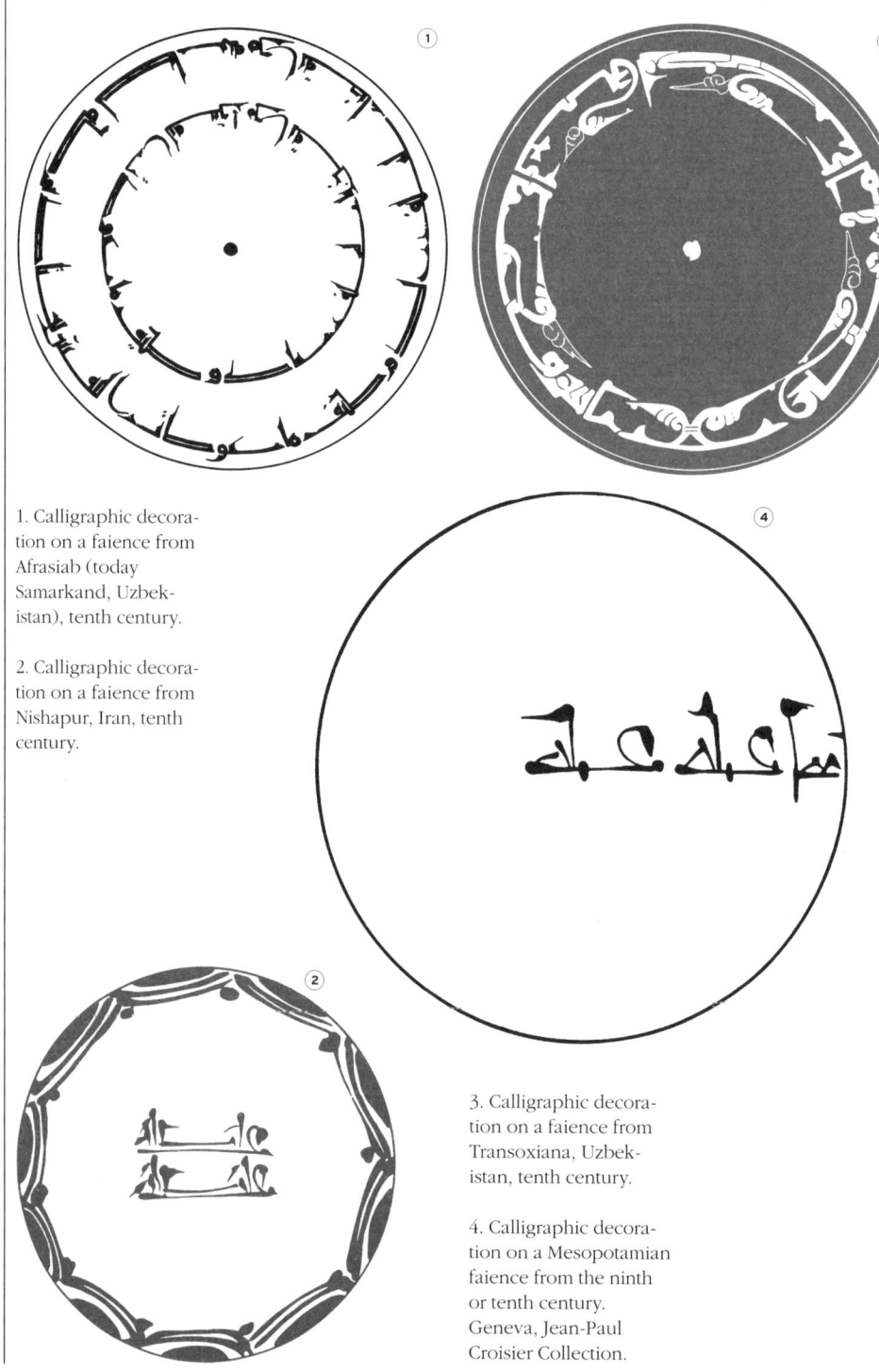

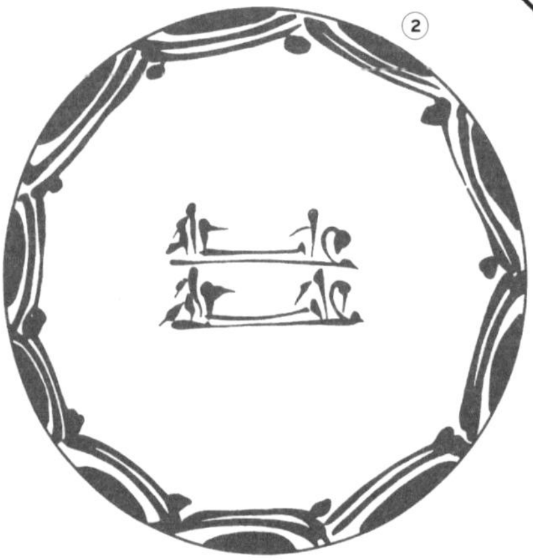

3. Calligraphic decoration on a faience from Transoxiana, Uzbekistan, tenth century.

4. Calligraphic decoration on a Mesopotamian faience from the ninth or tenth century. Geneva, Jean-Paul Croisier Collection.

5

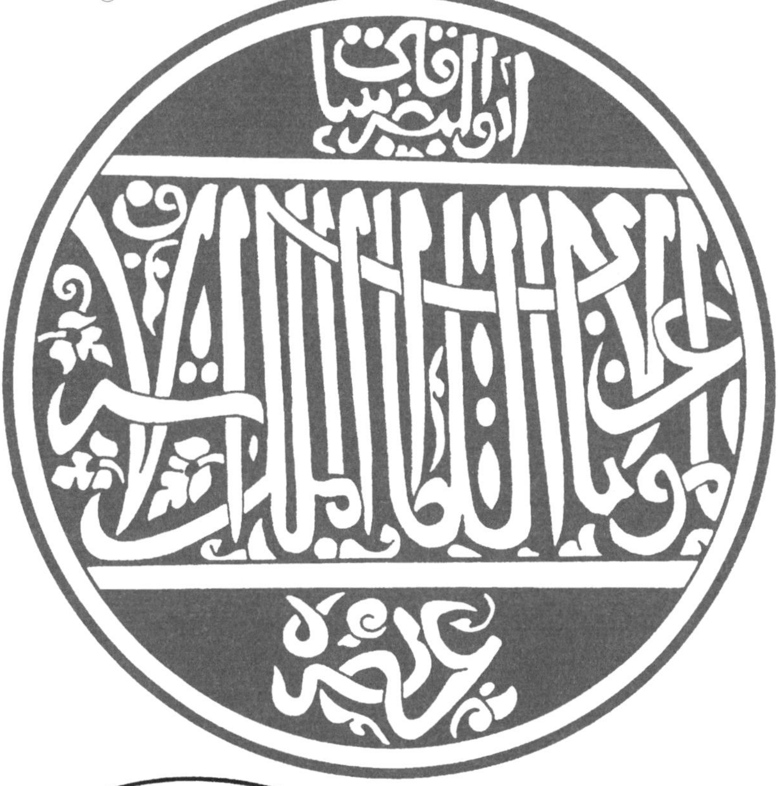

6

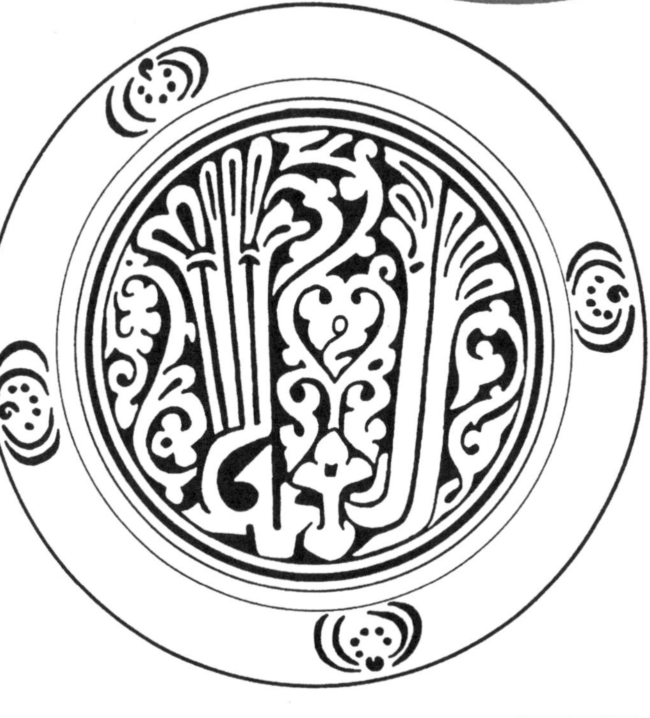

5. Calligraphic decoration from an Andalusian faience, eighth century. The motif is taken from a mural found in the Alhambra of Granada, Spain.

6. Contemporary calligraphic decoration in a traditional motif, drawn on faience by Gabriele Mandel. Museum of Art, São Paulo, Brazil.

CALLIGRAPHY AND OPENWORK METALS

1. Openwork iron design for use in the gold-leaf printing of a leather case, created by special order of Shah Sulayman I in 1693. We can read in *thuluth* characters: *Na'am: Īnnahu min Sulaymān wa īnnahu Bismi Llāhi āl-Raḥmani āl-Raḥimi* (Yes, he comes from Solomon, and in truth here he is: in the name of God, the Mercy-giving, the Merciful).

2. The names *Āllāh, Muḥammad, Alī* done in openwork metal embroidery on an Ottoman banner decoration, Turkey, seventeenth century. Istanbul, Topkapi Sarayë Museum.

(1)

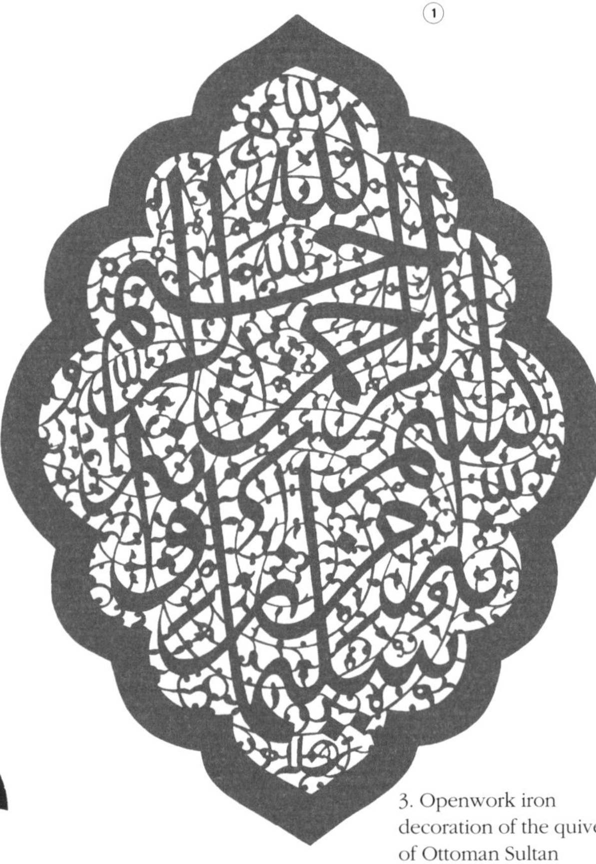

(2)

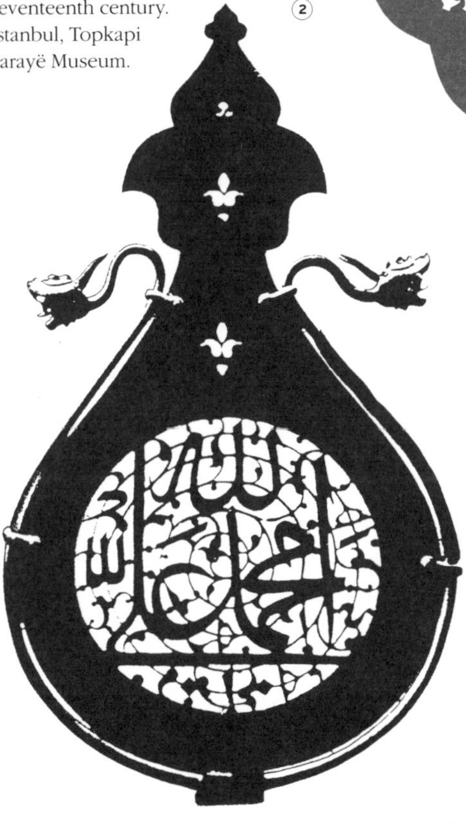

3. Openwork iron decoration of the quiver of Ottoman Sultan Ahmed III (1673–1736). Designed by Hafiz Osman (1642–1698). Istanbul, Topkapi Sarayë Museum.

(3)

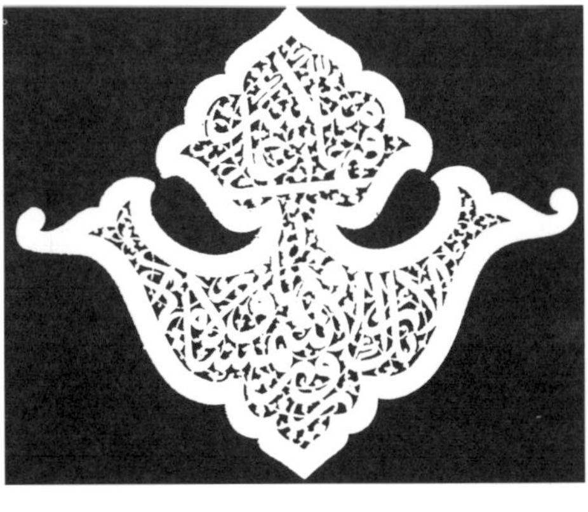

4

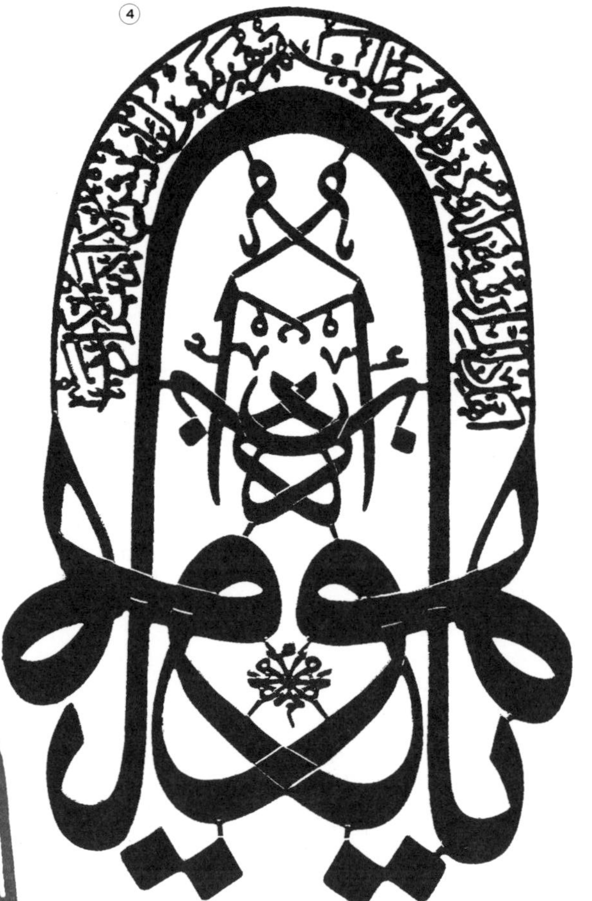

4. Openwork design on gold foil by Necmeddin Okyay (1883–1976), done by Mehmet Koseoglu, Konya, Turkey.

5

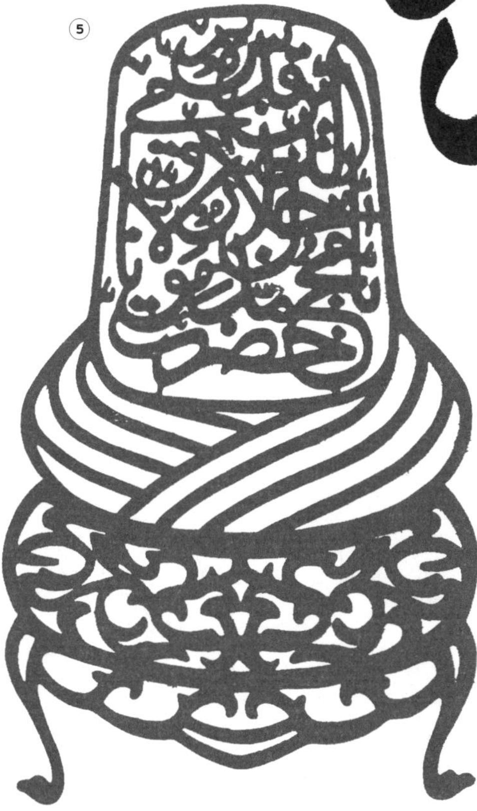

5. Openwork decoration on gold foil done by Oglu Rahim, representing a *sikké* (the hat worn by the Sufi *mevlevi*) placed on a throne. It contains the name of Jalal al-Din Rumi. The original sixteenth-century design is in the Mevleviyya Museum of Konya, Turkey.

(1)

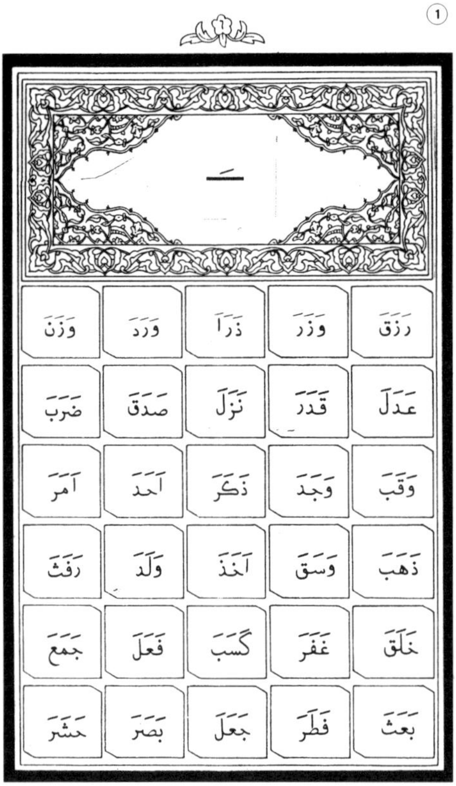

(3)

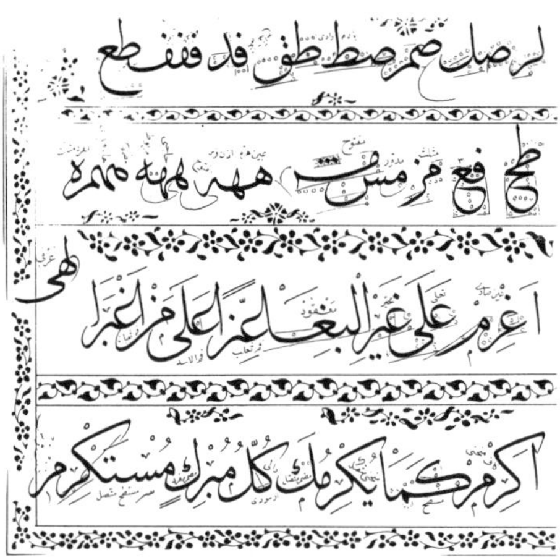

(4)

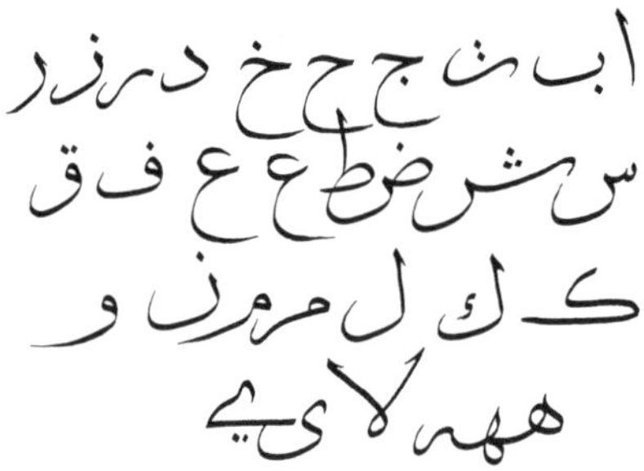

1. A page from the book of exercises *Her Hakki mahfuz dur,* published by the Hayrat Vakfi Neshriyati. Istanbul, 1983.

2. A page from the book of calligraphy exercises *Khudāmūz khūshnūysā* by Ismail Qujani. Iran, Capdaham, 1955.

(2)

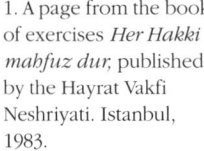

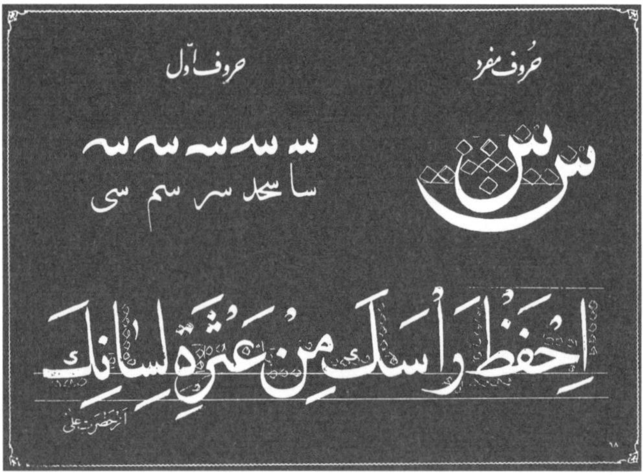

3. A page from the famous treatise *Mizānü al-Hatt* (A Measure of Calligraphy) by Hakkak-zade Mustafa Hilmi Efendi (Istanbul, 1763–1852), great-uncle of the author of this book and professor of calligraphy at the Validesultan Nakshidil School.

4. A page of *thuluth* calligraphy, by Muhammad Sijelmassi and Abdelkebir Khatibi.

5

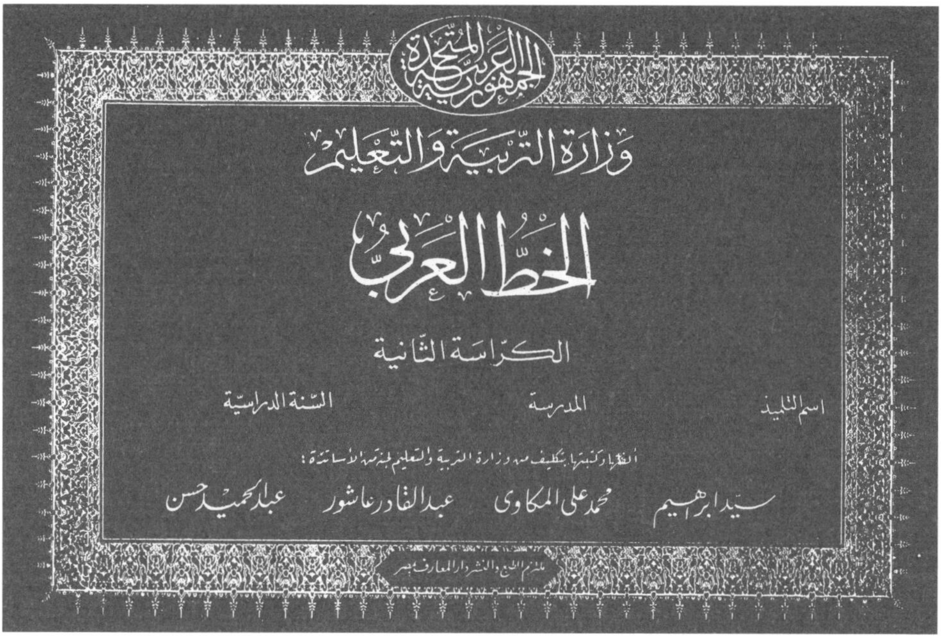

5, 6. Frontispiece and page from the *ālkhatt ā'arabiyya* calligraphy notebook by Muhammad al-Makawi, et al.

6

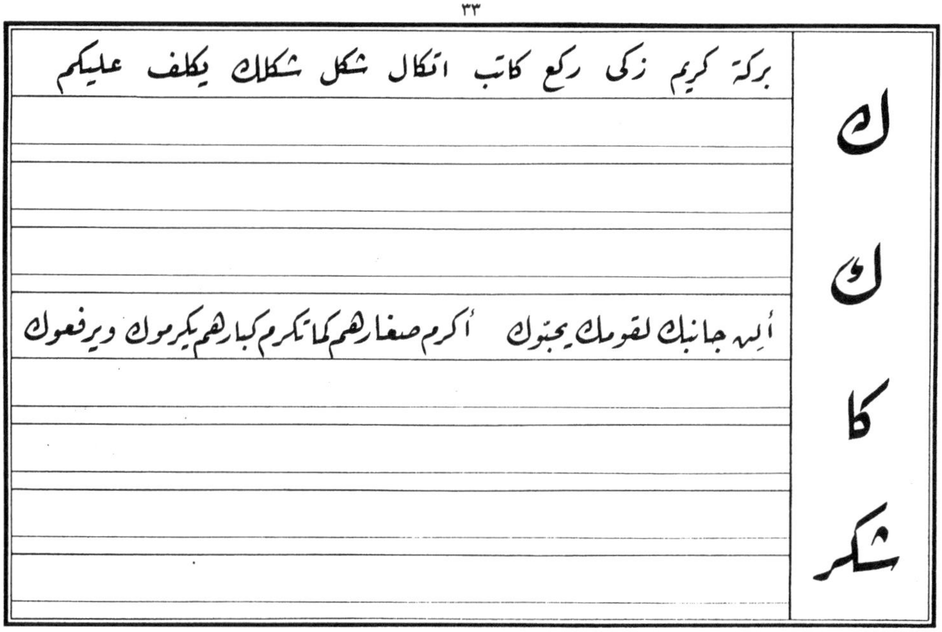

Wood engravings by Gabriele Mandel:

1–3. *Basmala* for use in four-color lithographic prints.

1

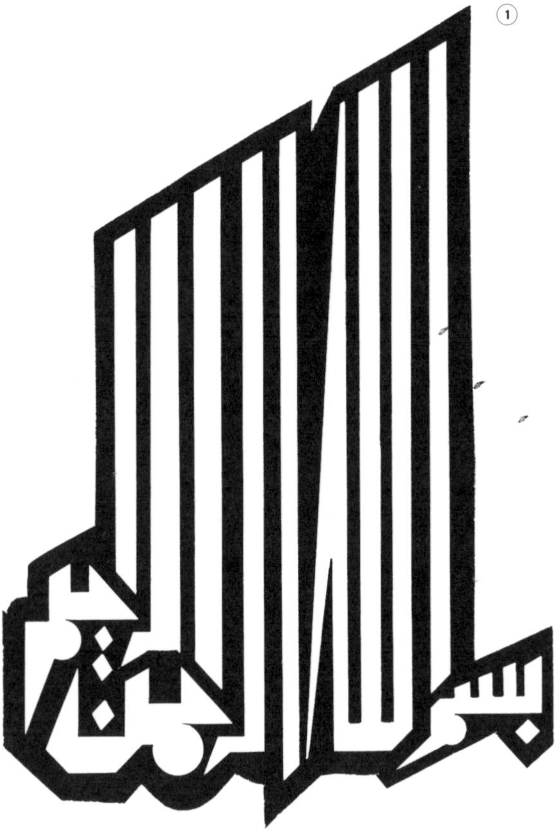

3

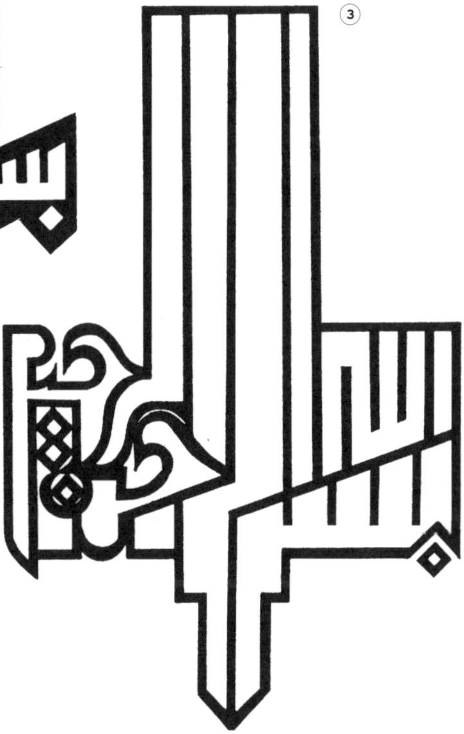

2

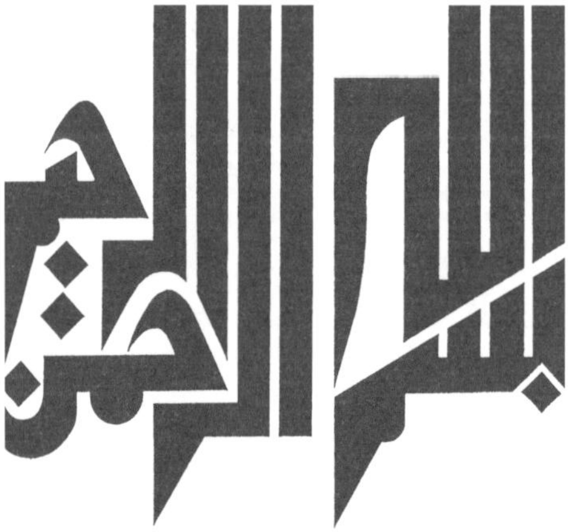

4. Turkish proverb: "Patience is the key to serenity."

5. Emblem of the Islamic Cultural Center and Mosque of Milan.

6. Title of the book *Arabic Homilies on the Nativity*, edited by the Bishop of Jerusalem and published by Pier Francesco Fumagalli for the 2000 Jubilee. Calligraphy and decoration are done in the classic Kufic tradition.

4

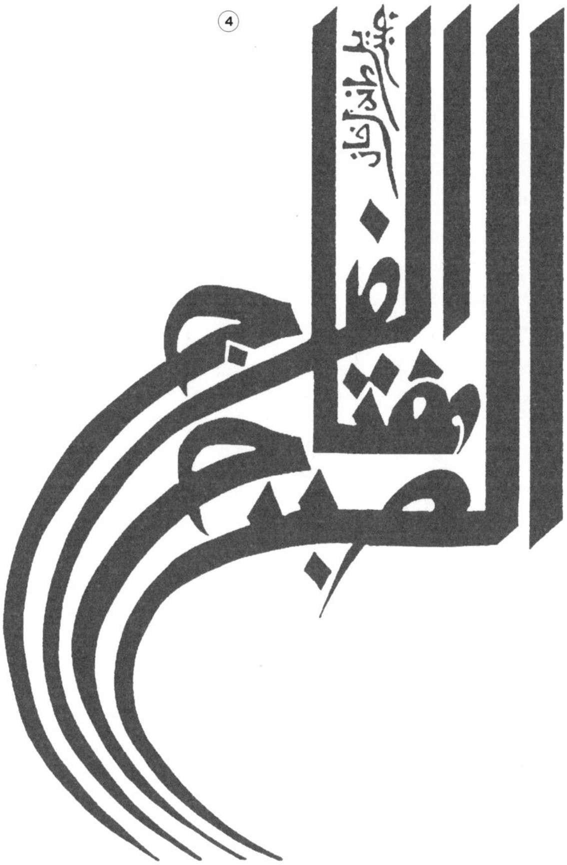

5

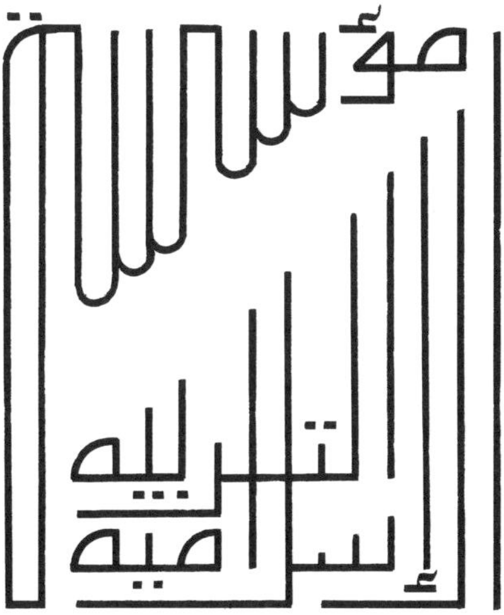

6

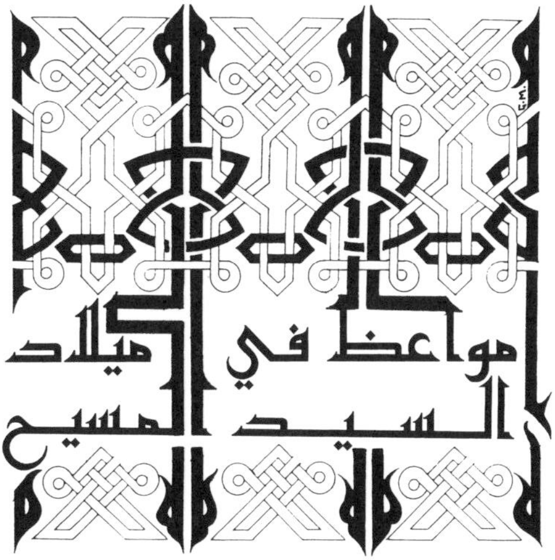

CONTEMPORARY CALLIGRAPHY

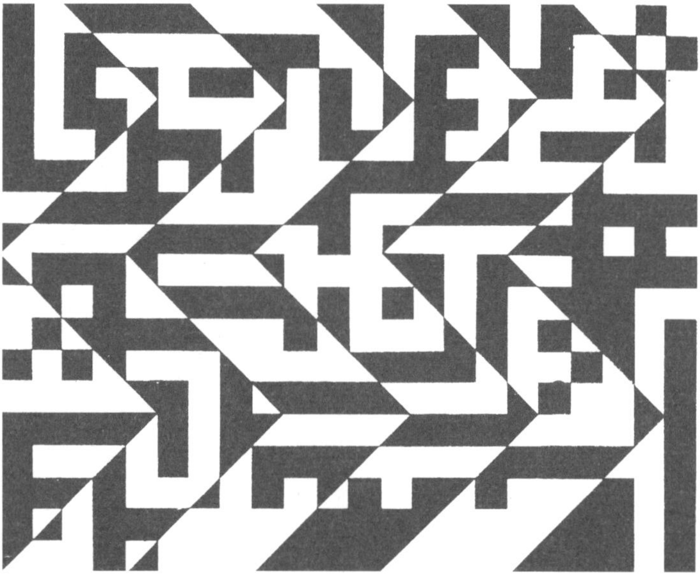

1

4. Calligraphy consisting of the repeated word *āl-Ḥurriyya* (Liberty). Work of Hassan Massoudi, b. Nejef, Iraq.

5. Modern calligraphy containing the phrase *Lā ilāha illā Āllāh* (There is no other God but God). Calligraphy by Emin Barin (1913–1996), Bolu, Turkey.

1. Modern calligraphy by Muhammad Meleti, Morocco.

2. Modern calligraphy by Muhammad Meleti, Morocco.

3. Modern calligraphy (the word *Āllāh* repeated ten times) by Emin Barin (1913–1996), Bolu, Turkey.

6. Modern calligraphy (the word *Āllāh* repeated eight times) by Emin Barin (1913–1996), Bolu, Turkey.

2

3

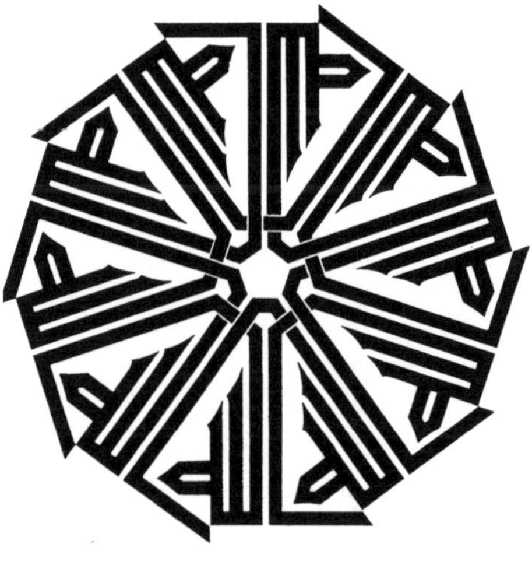

4

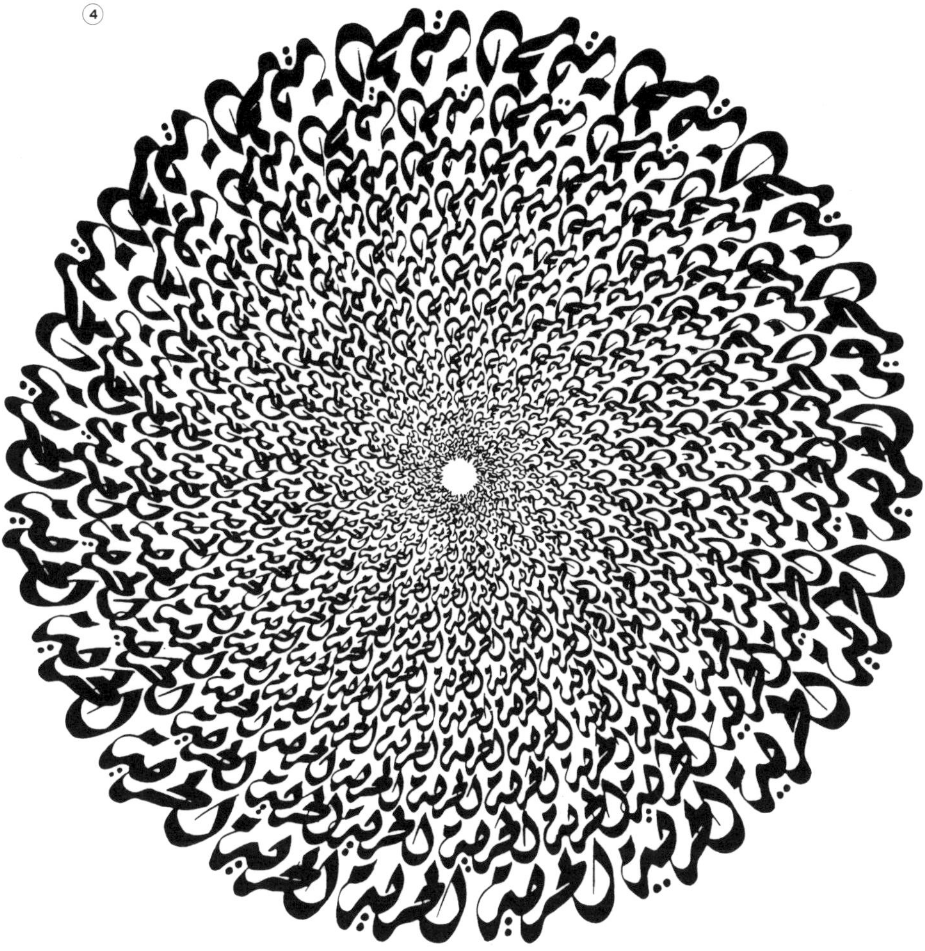

5

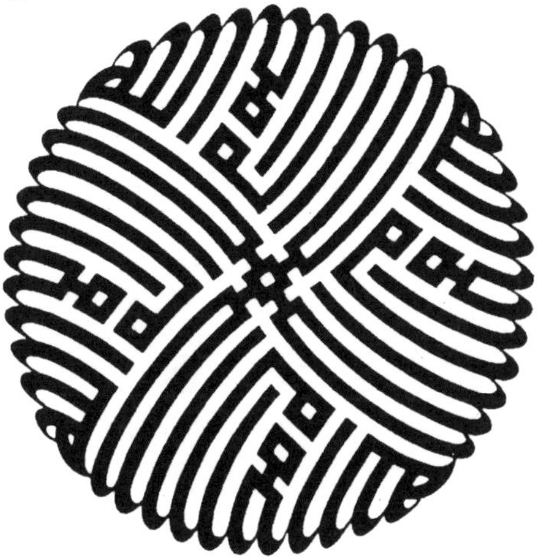

6

1

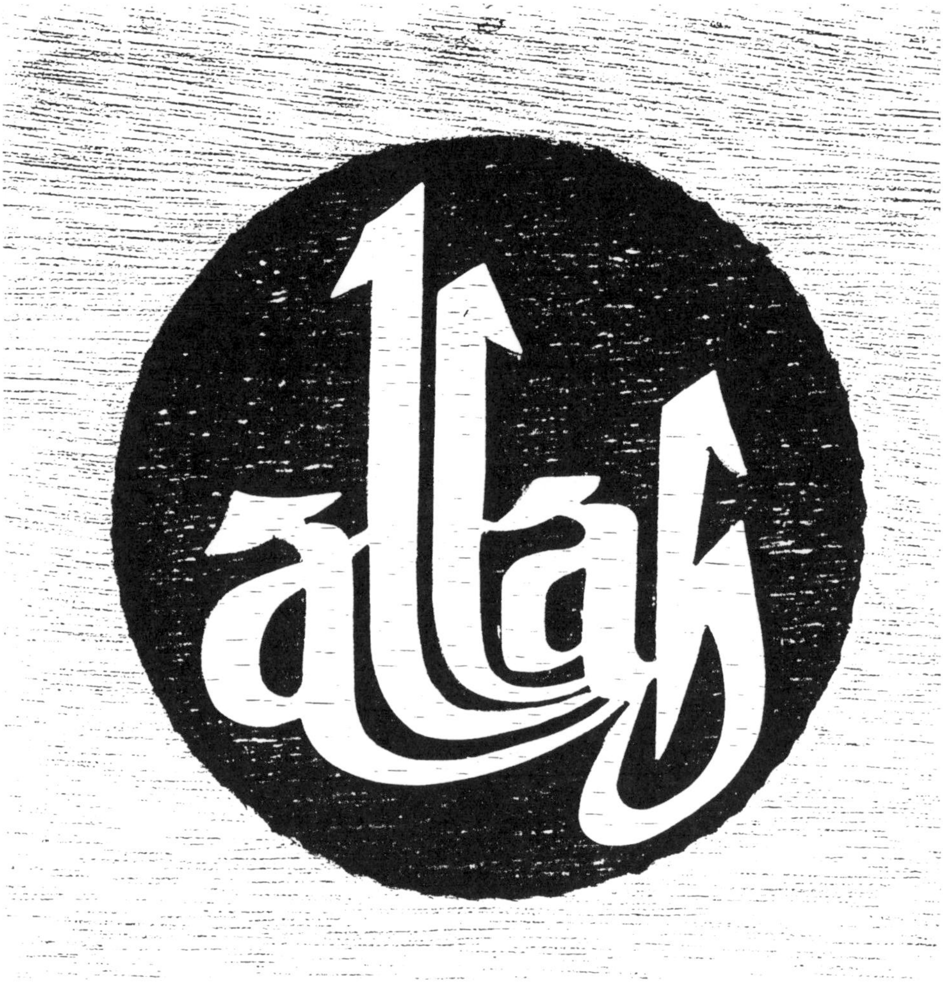

1. The name *Āllāh* in an openwork design in wood by Halil Acikgoz. Konya, Turkey, twentieth century.

2. Emblem of the city of Ilgin, Turkey. From a modern relief sculpted by Mehmet Buyukcanga, Konya, Turkey. The design is laid out so it can be read in Latin characters, but it still represents the correct Arabic spelling of the name.

3. The name *Āllāh* repeated four times in a calligraphy by Emin Barin (1913–1996) of Bolu, Turkey.

4. Wood-engraved frontispiece of the short story "Oasis of Roses" by Gabriele Mandel, published in Kabul, Afghanistan, in 1946.

5. "French-Arab" calligraphic anagram designed by Khalil Abu Arafa in 1957 in Jerusalem for an edition of the celebrated *Sons et lumières* festival of Paris.

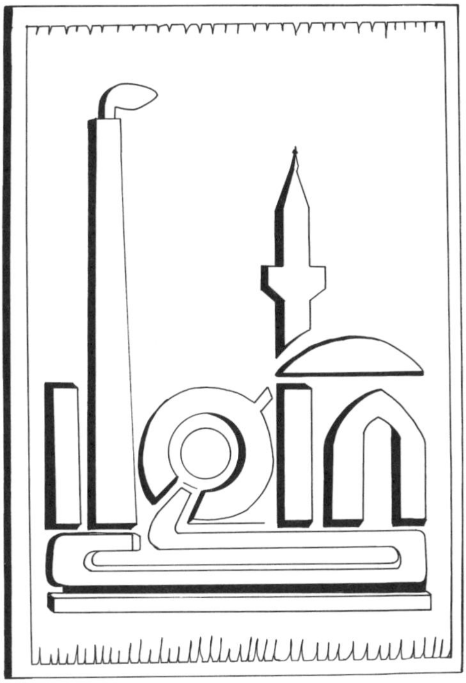

2

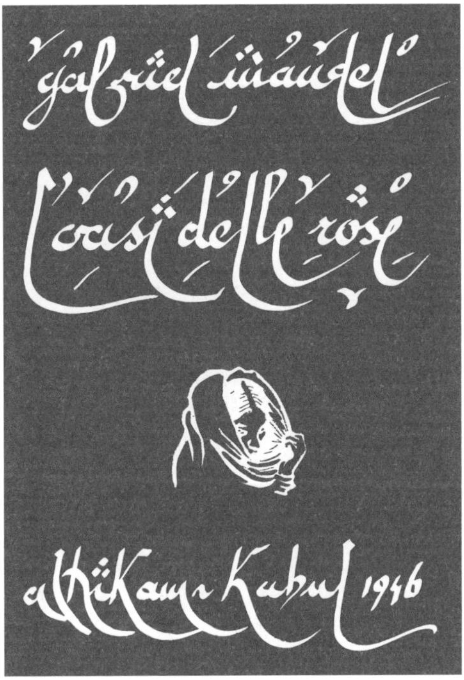

4

3

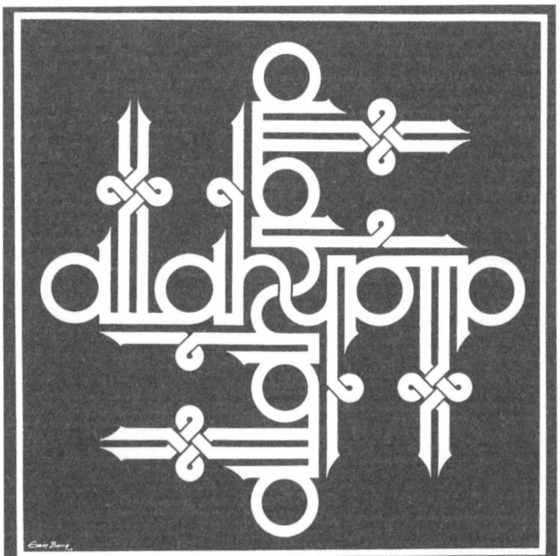

5

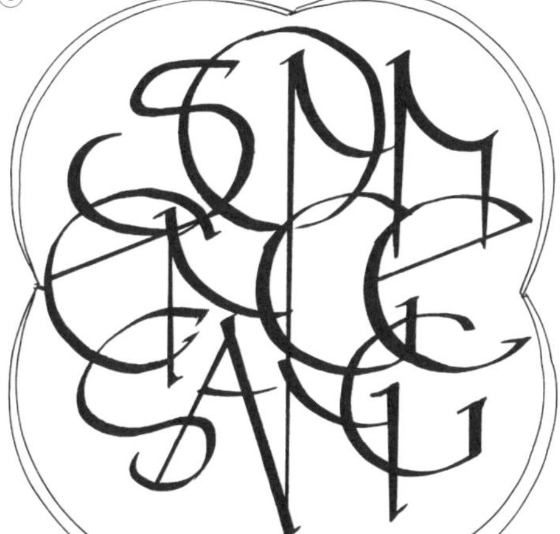

NARRATION THROUGH IMAGES

1

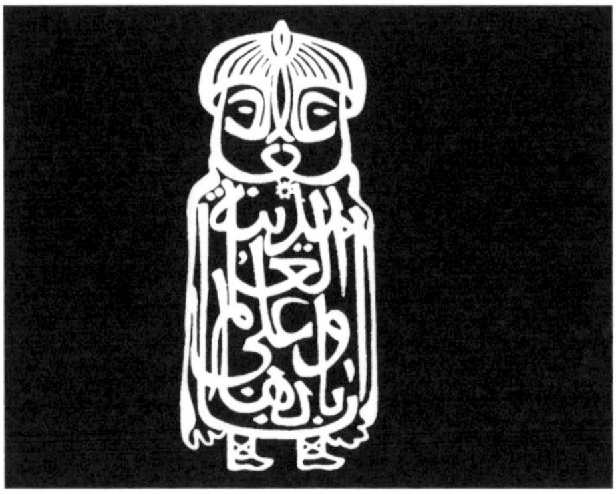

2

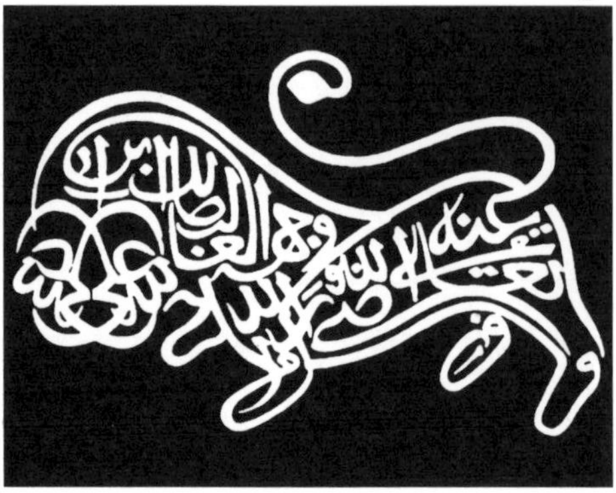

A Sufi short story.
1, 2, 3. He who is enamored (of God), passion symbolized by a lion, and the bow of spiritual strength.

4, 5, 6. The lover of God grasps the bow, stretches it, and throws an arrow against the lion-passion.

7, 8, 9. The lion bends down, avoiding the arrow, which strikes the eye of the beloved (God).

4

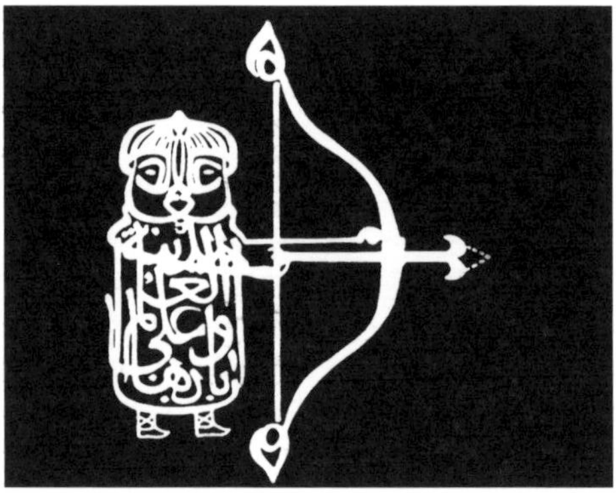

7

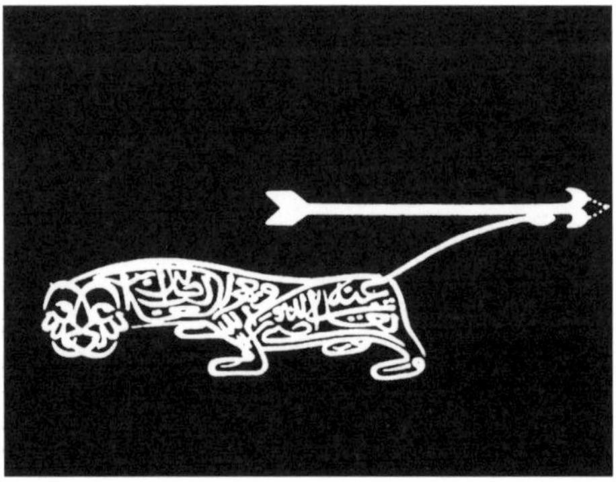

8

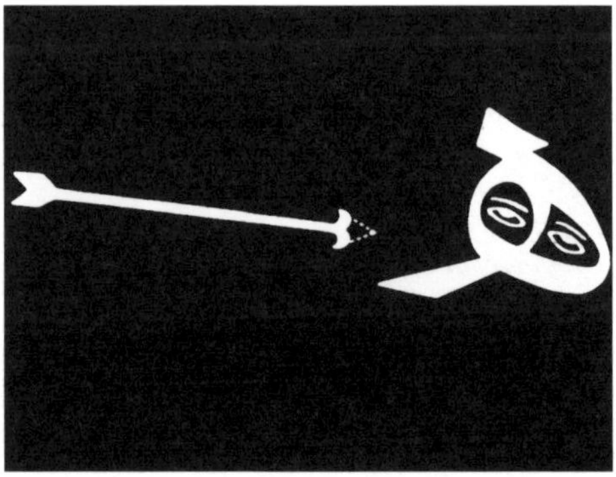

3

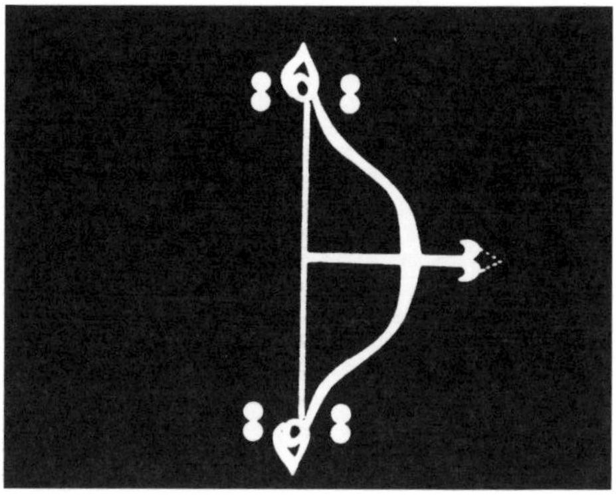

5

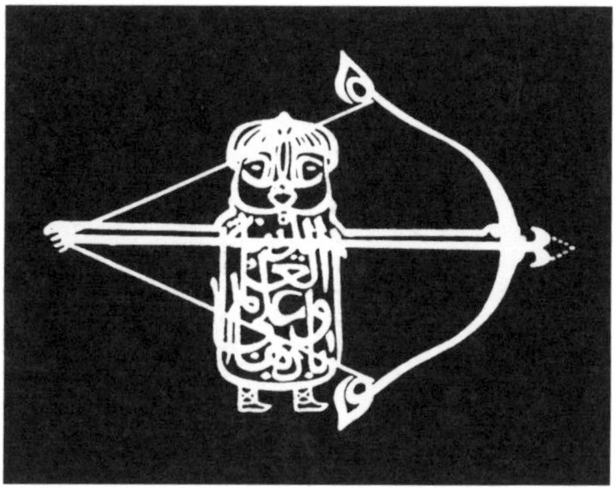

6

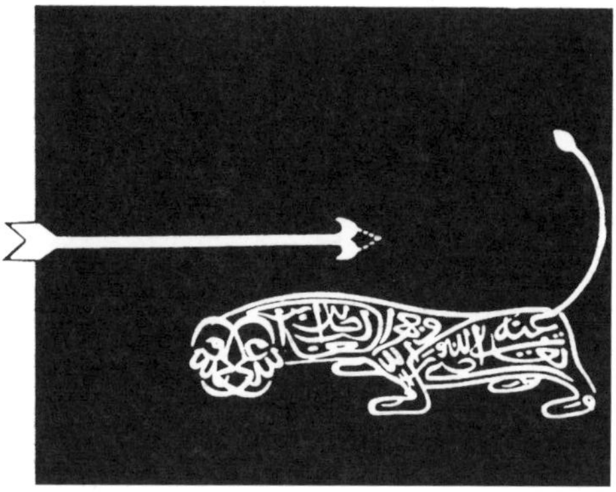

9

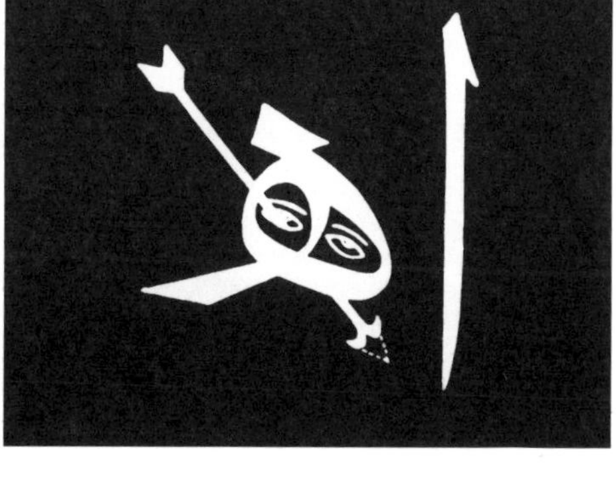

Calligraphic images from a Turkish film in which the mystical love story is narrated through figured drawings by Amentii Gemisi.

GLOSSARY

ābjad: The system of equivalence among the letters of the Arab alphabet and numbers. Because each letter corresponds to a number, and vice versa, names also yield significant numbers, and these numbers, in turn, yield other terms on which the art of esoteric interpretation is based. *See also* **'ilm āl-Ḥurūf.**

āqlām-i sitta: A term meaning "the six classic styles." They are: **muḥaqqaq**, **rīḥān**, **thuluth**, **naskhī**, **tawqī'**, and **riqā'**. A good calligrapher was expected to study, recognize, and write all of them.

āl-Āsma' āl-Ḥusna: The loveliest Names (of God). They are the ninety-nine name-attributes of God quoted in the Qur'ān that calligraphers often draw individually or in different combinations.

antonymy: *See* **recitation of the Qur'ān.**

basmala: The formula *Bismi Āllāhi āl-Raḥmani āl-Raḥymi* (In the name of God, the Mercy-giving, the Merciful) with which all of the Qur'ān's suras begin (except for the ninth), as well as each act of a pious Muslim.

budūḥ: An artificial talismanic name, usually inscribed within a magic square (*jadwal*). To some authors this word means "fat," referring to a woman; for others it is the name of a spirit (*jinn*) or an ancient magician-king; actually, it has no meaning at all in Arabic.

characteristics of the alphabet letters: *See* **recitation of the Qur'ān.**

Fertile Crescent (or Fertile Half-Moon): The geographic area extending from Egypt to Mesopotamia. Starting with the Romantic period, the Europeans gave it this name because this strip of tillable land running along the African coast with the sea to the north and the desert to the south is shaped like a moon sickle.

ḍamma: A diacritical mark, similar to a lower-case *waw*, placed above a letter; it indicates the short *u* vowel.

dīwānī: A strongly balanced, slanted cursive style, written from top to bottom and right to left; it is a combination of **thuluth**, **naskhī**, and **rīḥān**. It was probably created by the fifteenth-century Turkish calligrapher Ibrahim Munif; its preeminent exponent was the seventeenth-century calligrapher Shahla Pasha. The style takes its name from the Turkish term *Divan-i humayun*, which means Council of Ministers.

fatḥa: A diacritical mark consisting of an oblique hyphen placed above the letter; it indicates a short *a* vowel.

fawātiḥ ḥurūf muqatta'a: Letters found at the beginning of the twenty-nine suras of the Qur'ān. They are fourteen in all, half of the Arab alphabet: a, ḥ, r, s, ṣ, t, ', q, k, l, m, n, h, y. They are used in amulets and talismans.

ghubār or **ghubārī:** A term meaning "dust" or "dusty." Any kind of microscopic writing, especially using **naskh.**

hamza (*āl-Qaṭ'i* when disjunctive; *āl-Waṣli* when conjunctive): A diacritical mark consisting of a sort of small initial *'ayn* placed above the letter. Some grammarians consider it a consonant and position it in place of *alif* in the alphabetical sequence. It may be accompanied by short vowels (**ḍamma, fatḥa,** and **kasra**) and then it is read respectively *ū, ā, ī.* When this letter is at the beginning of a word and above the *alif*, it represents a sound immediately blocked by the movement of the glottis (the glottal stop); when it occurs in the middle of a word, supported orthographically by an *alif* or a *waw*— or even a *ya* without the two dots and pronounced *ā*—it signifies a clear detachment from the preceding syllable, or a pause in the voice. When it occurs at the end of a word, it is written without the supporting letter and therefore on the line, and it reads *a'*.

ḥarf (plural, *ḥurūf*): A letter of the alphabet (*see* **ḥurūf āl-Hijā'**).

hat: *See* **kḥaṭṭ.**

ḥurūf āl-Hijā': Letters of the alphabet; singular, *ḥarf*. The Islamic science that includes the subdivision of words into single letters, the study of their articulation, and the type of sound or pronunciation with the relative points of the phonetic system (*makhārji*). Thus, distinctions are made between the guttural (or laryngeal) letters *āl-Ḥalqiyya*; the prepalatal letters *āl-Nit'iyya*; the lingual letters *āl-ḍhawlaqiyya*; and the labial letters *āl-Shajiriyya*. According to the rules of articulation the letters are separated into "striking" or voiced (*majihūra*) and "stifled" or unvoiced (*mahmūsa*); velar (*muṭbaqa*) or "open" and non-velar (*munfatiḥa*); raised (*musta'liya*) and lowered (*munkḥafida*). According to the degree of openness, they are separated into occlusive (*shadida*), constrictive (*rikhwa*), and intermediate (*bayniyya*).

Ḥurūf, 'ilm āl: *See* **'ilm āl-Ḥurūf.**

ijāza: *See* **riqā'.**

'ilm āl-Ḥurūf: In Islam, the science of letters is a branch of *Jafr*, a philosophical term indicating a vision of the world on a supernatural, cosmic scale. From this, the word came to indicate the science of prophesying, or more generally, the science of foretelling and predicting the future by applying various techniques such as numerology and letter decoding. With time, a literary form of *Jafr* was born, apocalyptic and oracular at the same time, that based itself on the letters of the alphabet and in turn created the Cabala in the Jewish world. Handled by magicians, at first *Jafr* was only used to study onomatomancy proper (that is, the science of divination by interpreting the sound and pronunciation of words), but because of the esoteric meanings found in the apocalyptic texts, it later became a true, independent *sīmīya'* (σημεια in white magic). Each of the twenty-eight letters of the Arabic alphabet was assigned a numerical value that, instead of following the regular alphabetic order (**ḥurūf āl-Hijā'**), followed an order that was probably derived or adapted from similar Canaanite practices applied to the first eighteen letters of the alphabet (*ā, b, j, d,* etc.). For the last ten letters, the numerical value is chiefly Arabic (in the section relating to each letter we also give its numerical value). This system was also called **Ābjad,** from the first letters arranged in this manner.

jalī (jalīl): A term indicating any large writing style, especially the **thuluth.**

kasra: A diacritical mark consisting of an oblique stroke below the letter; it indicates the short *i* vowel.

kḥaṭṭ (in Turkish, *hat*): A term indicating both writing and calligraphy.

kīrāmīz (in antiquity, *pīrāmūz*): The first hand of Muslim Iran, of which no example has survived except for the facsimile of a page created by Badri Atabay in 1972.

Kufic (or Cufic): This term derives from Kufa, an Iraqi city founded in the year 638. Kufic writing styles were created not only in that area, but also in the region of Hijaz, for example, in Mecca and Medina. The term refers to a set of hands, usually angular and imposing, that are the first classical examples of Arabic writing. At first, Kufic did not have diacritical signs. According to Ibn al-Nadim, a tenth-century scholar, this script is derived from *āl-Hirī*, one of the four types of pre-Islamic scripts. These are *āl-Hirī*, meaning from the city of Hira; *āl-Ānbārī* (from the city of Anbar); *āl-Makkī* (from the city of

Mecca); and *āl-Madanī* (from the city of Medina). Until the ninth century, it was the most widely used hand for writing the Qur'ān; later, it lost its first place to the strong and fast imposition of cursive styles. Among the many forms of Kufic, especially those with foliate or plaited decorations, we note *āl-Kūfī āl-Muraqqa'*. A very elegant, aesthetically well-composed type is Qarmatian Kufic, also called Eastern Kufic.

madda: A term meaning "extension," also known as *alif madda*. When two beginning *alifs* are written one next to the other, or when a final *alif* is followed by a **hamza,** only one *alif* is written; a sign, the *madda* (a tiny *alif* written horizontally) is placed above it. It signifies an extension of the vowel *a*.

maghribī: An elaborate style from North Africa and Muslim Spain, derived from **Kufic** but more rounded. Some letters, such as *fa* and *qaf,* have their diacritical marks below instead of above.

maqsūra: A term meaning "restricted," also known as *alif maqsūra*; it is the letter *ya* without the two diacritical dots, placed at the end of a word and pronounced *ā*. It is equivalent to an *alif madda*.

muḥaqqaq: A term meaning "strong expression," or "tight"; a style with a narrow right angle in many letters. Its use began in the early fifteenth century; starting at the end of the seventeenth century, it was gradually replaced by the **thuluth** style.

musalsal: A term meaning "joined together"; used to express highly skilled calligraphy in which all the letters—preferably in the **thuluth** hand—are connected together with unusual, elegant rhythmic inventions.

muthannā: Also known as *mutannāzar*, or *müsenna*; a term meaning "self-facing." It is not so much a hand as a type of mirror, or specular, writing, when a sentence written from right to left is repeated identically from left to right. Developed by Turkish calligraphers, it was used especially with **thuluth** and Kufic hands.

naskh: A term meaning "suppression, cancellation"; an italic, or cursive, hand that originated in the earliest centuries of Arabic writing, and was already well structured by the eleventh century. It was the preferred hand in the Timurid age and again beginning in the eighteenth century, when it was revised by the Iranian Ahmad Nayrizi, who made it closer to the **nasta'līq.**

nasta'līq *(naskh-i ta'līq)*: A hand derived from combining the **naskh** and **ta'līq** hands, possibly the work of Mir Ali Tabrizi (d. 1446). Soon two currents developed: in Khurasan, by Mirza Ja'far-i Tabrizi and Azhar-i Tabrizi in the fifteenth century, and in Iran, by Abd al-Rahman-i Khwarazmi, though the latter soon disappeared. The preeminent calligrapher of the Khurasan hand was Mir Imad-i Hasani-yi Sayfi (d. 1616).

nunnation: *See* **tanwīn.**

recitation of the Qur'ān: The various rules for reciting the Qur'ān form a true discipline (*tajwīd*) based on correct psalmody (*tartīl*) of the various letters, both consonants (*ṣāmita*) and vowels (*muṣawwita*), with rhythms, accents, and pauses that take into account characteristics such as sonority, elevation, occlusion, softening, tonicity, moderation, whistling, vibration, softness, deflection, repetition, diffusion, extension, concealment, nasalization, and antonymies such as whispering, lowering, opening, volubility, atony. For each letter of the alphabet, we have given its intrinsic value according to the recitation of the Qur'ān.

rīḥān (or *rīḥanī, rayḥān, rayḥānī*): A word for the herb basil; a reduced version of **muḥaqqaq**, when used in the **naskh** format. It was replaced in the seventeenth century by *naskh*.

riqā' (in Turkish, *ijāza* or *khatt-i ijāza*): A reduced version of **tawqī'.**

sauāqiṭ āl-Fātiḥa: The seven letters of the Arab alphabet (*f, j, sh, th, z, kh, ẓ*) that are not included in the text of the first Qur'ān sura (*āl-Fātiḥa*) and are considered important in the preparation of talismans.

shahāda (or *tashahhud*, a testimonial of faith): The formula "[āshhadu anna] lā īlāh īlla Āllāh, [āshhadu anna] Muḥammad rasūl Āllāh": "[I witness that] there is no other God but God, [I witness that] Muhammad is God's prophet."

shikasta ta'līq: From *shikasta*, meaning "fractional": an Iranian variant of **ta'līq** but written more rapidly, developed in the fourteenth century by Khwaja Taj Salmani-i Isfahani (d. 1491). Difficult to read, it lost ground in favor of **nasta'līq** at the beginning of the sixteenth century.

shikasta nasta'līq (*khatt-i shikasta*): A type of **nasta'līq** with influences from **shikasta ta'līq,** which originated in Iran under Safavid rule at the beginning of the eighteenth century. It was used especially for correspondence, and became widespread in Ottoman Turkey for official correspondence, but not much else.

siyāqat (*siyāq*): A writing that was already in use under the Omayyads for accounting registers and everyday bureaucratic records, and still used today.

sukūn: A term meaning "quiet," also known as *jazm* (truncated); a small circle on top of the letter meaning the absence of a brief vowel.

taḥrīrī: A term meaning "epistular"; a simplified form of **shikasta nasta'līq** used for everyday correspondence.

ta'līq: A term meaning "suspension"; probably a combination of **tawqī', riqā'**, and **naskhī**. It is attributed to Khwaja Abu al-Al (tenth century) or Hassan ibn Husayn ibn Ali Farisi Katib (tenth century), who were probably inspired by the sinuous shapes of the Pehlevi and Avestic alphabets. Beginning in the eleventh century, it was especially used for official bureaucratic documents. It was already fully developed by the thirteenth century, though it became fashionable only a century later, especially thanks to Ahmad ibn Ahmas-i Shirazi. It began to decline at the end of the same century, being replaced by a more calligraphic version, the **shikasta ta'līq.**

tanwīn: Nunnation; it is the doubling of **ḍamma, fatḥa,** and **kasra** (the short vowels *u, a,* and *i*) at the end of a word (twice *u*, or a special sign; twice *a*, twice *i*). As a result, these vowels are read respectively *un, an,* and *in,* and indicate the indeterminate article respectively for the nominative, accusative, and indirect cases.

tarassul: A term meaning "correspondence"; the scribes of the Council of Ministers gave this name to a simplified form of **shikasta ta'līq.**

tashdīd: Reinforcement, also known as *shaddah*: a mark that signifies a double consonant, marked as a small initial *sin* above the letter. The term is derived from the verb *ishtadda* (to be strong, robust, intense, to intensify, to be accented).

tawqī': A variant of **thuluth** with more compressed and rounded letters. In this hand, the letters *ā, d, dh, r, z, zh, l,* and *w* are connected to the following letter by a thin, sinuous upward stroke. It is used especially in colophons.

thuluth: A term meaning "one-third," because the third part of each letter is slanted; in Turkish, *sülüs*. This hand is still used today, especially in book titles. Specialists in this hand were Baysonghor (d. 1433), Asad Allah-i Kirmani (d. 1486), Abd al-Baqi-i Tabrizi (sixteenth century), Kamal al-Din Hafiz Harawi (d. 1566), Ali Quli-i Shirazi (sixteenth century), and Ali Ridha Abbasi (seventeenth century).

waṣla: A term meaning "connection," also known as *alif wasla*. A diacritical mark linking the pronunciation of the last short vowel declination of the previous word to the first syllable of the following word; the corresponding *alif* is mute.

INDEX